NOTE

Oxford Historical Monographs will consist of books which would formerly have been published in the Oxford Historical Series. As with the previous series, they will be carefully selected studies which have been submitted, or are based upon theses submitted, for higher degrees in this University. The works listed below are those still in print in the Oxford Historical Series.

DUCAL BRITTANY
1364–1399

Relations with England
and France during the reign of
Duke John IV

BY

MICHAEL JONES
M.A., D.Phil.
Lecturer in European History
University of Nottingham

OXFORD UNIVERSITY PRESS
1970

Oxford University Press, Ely House, London W.1

GLASGOW NEW YORK TORONTO MELBOURNE WELLINGTON
CAPE TOWN SALISBURY IBADAN NAIROBI DAR ES SALAAM LUSAKA ADDIS ABABA
BOMBAY CALCUTTA MADRAS KARACHI LAHORE DACCA
KUALA LUMPUR SINGAPORE HONG KONG TOKYO

PRINTED IN GREAT BRITAIN
AT THE UNIVERSITY PRESS, OXFORD
BY VIVIAN RIDLER
PRINTER TO THE UNIVERSITY

PREFACE

THE research for the thesis on which this book is based could not have been undertaken but for a generous grant from the President and Fellows of Trinity College, Oxford. Their encouragement was invaluable. I also received substantial financial aid from the Sir Richard Stapeley Trust, and smaller grants from the Trustees of the Arnold Fund, from the Committee for Advanced Studies, Oxford, and from the Committee of Deans, University of Exeter. The French Government kindly financed some of my research on Brittany by a travel award. I wish to thank all these bodies for their support. I am grateful to the Trustees of the British Museum, l'Administrateur Général de la Bibliothèque Nationale, and M. X. du Boisrouvray, Directeur des Services d'Archives de la Loire-Atlantique, for permission to print documents in their care.

It is a pleasure to acknowledge the guidance and helpful criticism of my former supervisor, Professor John Le Patourel, at all stages of the production of this work. Dr. Pierre Chaplais, who gave me instruction in the sources and advice on particular documents, later examined my thesis and has been very generous with his time in helping me. Mr. James Campbell, to whom I owe my interest in the fourteenth century, has been a source of inspiration by his encouragement and searching criticisms. Dr. Alan Rogers has offered me some constructive suggestions, and I have had many valuable conversations with Dr. Malcolm Vale. Mr. Keith Bowler has kindly drawn the maps. My thanks are due to all of them for their friendship. I would also like to thank the staff of the Clarendon Press for their aid with the preparation of the manuscript.

My wife, despite numerous other commitments, has been of inestimable help in assisting me and it is to her that I gratefully dedicate this book.

M. C. E. J.

University of Nottingham

CONTENTS

LIST OF ILLUSTRATIONS

ABBREVIATIONS

THE following abbreviations will be used throughout this work; full reference will be found in the Bibliography. Documents cited in footnotes by a class number only are to be found in the Public Record Office, London.

I. GENERAL

A.I.V.	Archives départementales d'Ille-et-Vilaine, Rennes.
A.L.A.	Archives départementales de la Loire-Atlantique, Nantes.
A.N.	Archives Nationales, Paris.
Anglo-Norman Letters, ed. Legge	*Anglo-Norman Letters and Petitions from All Souls MS. 182,* ed. M. D. Legge, Oxford 1941.
Anselme	Père Anselme, *Histoire généalogique et chronologique de la maison royale de France,* 3rd edn., Paris 1726–33.
Arch. dép.	Archives départementales.
Arch. hist. Poitou	*Archives historiques du Poitou.*
Assoc. Bret.	*Association bretonne, Comptes rendus.*
B.E.C.	*Bibliothèque de l'École des Chartes.*
Bib. mun.	Bibliothèque municipale.
B.I.H.R.	*Bulletin of the Institute of Historical Research.*
B.M.	British Museum, London.
B.N.	Bibliothèque Nationale, Paris.
Borderie	A. de la Borderie, *Histoire de Bretagne,* 6 vols., Rennes 1896–1914.
Cartulaire du Morbihan	'Cartulaire du Morbihan', ed. P. Lacroix-Thomas, *Bulletin de la Société polymathique du Morbihan,* 1934–8.
C.Ch.R.	*Calendar of charter rolls.*
C.C.R.	*Calendar of close rolls.*
C.D.I.	*Collection de documents inédits sur l'histoire de France.*
C.F.R.	*Calendar of fine rolls.*
C.Inq.M.	*Calendar of inquisitions, miscellaneous.*
C.I.P.M.	*Calendar of inquisitions, Post mortem.*
Complete Peerage	*The complete peerage,* ed. G. E. C[okayne], new edn., ed. V. Gibbs, H. A. Doubleday, G. H.

	White, and Lord Howard de Walden, 13 vols., London 1910–59.
C.P.M.R.	*Calendar of plea and memoranda rolls of the City of London*, ed. A. H. Thomas.
C.P.R.	*Calendar of patent rolls.*
Delachenal	R. Delachenal, *Histoire de Charles V*, 5 vols., Paris 1909–31.
E.H.R.	*English Historical Review.*
Foedera	*Foedera, conventiones, litterae, etc.*, ed. T. Rymer *et al.*, 20 vols., London, 1704–35; ed. A. Clarke *et al.* for the Record Commission, 4 vols., London 1816–69. This latter edition will be used for the period to 1383 and the original edition, vols. vii–viii, from 1383.
Froissart	Cited in two main editions: (i) *Chroniques de Jean Froissart*, ed. S. Luce *et al.*, 14 vols., Société de l'histoire de France, 1869–1966 continuing; (ii) *Œuvres de Jean Froissart*, ed. Kervyn de Lettenhove, 25 vols., Brussels 1867–77.
Gale	*Registrum honoris de Richmond*, ed. R. Gale, London 1722.
Gaunt's Register 1372–6	'John of Gaunt's register 1372–6', ed. S. Armitage-Smith, Royal Hist. Society, Camden, 3rd ser., xx, xxi (1911).
Gaunt's Register 1379–83	'John of Gaunt's register 1379–83', ed. E. C. Lodge and R. Somerville, Royal Hist. Society, Camden, 3rd ser., lvi, lvii (1937).
Hist. MSS. Comm.	Historical Manuscripts Commission.
Invt. Somm. Arch. Dép.	*Inventaire sommaire des Archives départementales.*
Knighton	*Chronicon Henrici Knighton*, ed. J. R. Lumby, 2 vols., R.S., 1889–95.
Lobineau	Dom Gui-Alexis Lobineau, *Histoire de Bretagne*, 2 vols., Paris 1707.
Lot et Fawtier	*Histoire des institutions françaises au Moyen Âge*, ed. F. Lot and R. Fawtier, 3 vols., Paris 1957–62.
M.H.B.	*Mémoires de la Société d'histoire et d'archéologie de Bretagne.*
Nicolas	N. Harris Nicolas, *Proceedings and ordinances of the Privy Council of England*, i. 1386–1410, London 1834.
Palgrave	Sir Francis Palgrave, *Antient kalendars and inventories of the Treasury of His Majesty's Exchequer*, 3 vols., London 1836.

Plaine, *Procès*	Dom F. Plaine, *Monuments du procès de canonisation du bienheureux Charles de Blois, duc de Bretagne, 1320–64,* Saint-Brieuc 1921.
Pocquet, *Les Papes*	B.-A. Pocquet du Haut-Jussé, *Les Papes et les ducs de Bretagne,* 2 vols., Paris 1928.
Preuves	Dom P. H. Morice, *Mémoires pour servir de preuves à l'histoire ecclésiastique et civile de Bretagne,* 3 vols., Paris 1742–6.
Rev. Hist.	*Revue historique.*
R.H.D.F.E.	*Revue historique de droit français et étranger.*
Rot. Parl.	*Rotuli parliamentorum,* vols. ii, iii (1783).
R.S.	Rolls Series.
S.H.F.	Société de l'histoire de France.
Tout, *Chapters*	T. F. Tout, *Chapters in the administrative history of medieval England,* 6 vols., Manchester 1920–33.
T.R.H.S.	*Transactions of the Royal Historical Society.*
V.C.H.	*Victoria County History.*

II. GEOGRAPHICAL

ar.	arrondissement	cme.	commune
c.	canton	dép.	département
ch.-l.	chef-lieu		

III. PUBLIC RECORD OFFICE REFERENCES

Documents have been cited by class names rather than by call numbers; full reference will be found in the Bibliography, where classes are listed numerically. The following classes are most frequently abbreviated:

Accts. For.	Exchequer, Lord Treasurer's Remembrancer, Enrolled Accounts, Foreign (E. 364).
Accts. Var.	Exchequer, King's Remembrancer, Accounts, Various (E. 101).
Anc. Pet.	Special Collections, Ancient Petitions (S.C. 8).
Exch. Dip. Doc.	Exchequer, Treasury of the Receipt, Diplomatic Documents (E. 30).
Exch. T.R. Misc. Books	Exchequer, Treasury of the Receipt, Miscellaneous Books (E. 36).
Min. Accts.	Special Collections, Ministers' Accounts (S.C. 6).

Note. Throughout this work the year may be assumed to begin on 1 January. Where possible sterling or *livres tournois* (*l.t.*) equivalents have been given for amounts stated in documents, which were reckoned in money current in Brittany. But where such equivalences are impossible to calculate, the amount is expressed in *livres bretonnes* (*l.br.*). For difficulties in determining the fluctuating value of money in Brittany in this period see H. Touchard, *Le Commerce maritime breton,* pp. 97–100. As a rough guide it may be stated that the money current in Brittany and the *livre tournois* reached parity in 1374.

INTRODUCTION

THE diplomatic and military relations of Brittany with England and France between 1364 and 1399 were influenced largely by the actions and aspirations of one man. Duke John IV of Brittany was, on the one hand, under various legal obligations to France because of the ducal throne to which he had ascended, while, on the other, his youth and upbringing had made him beholden to England. In 1345 John de Montfort, the father of the future John IV, did homage to Edward III of England for the duchy of Brittany, which he was disputing with Charles de Blois, a nephew of Philip VI of France. Later that year Montfort died, and Edward III, who had been appointed guardian of his infant son, assumed full responsibility for the Montfortist cause in the duchy where his troops already held a considerable number of forts. Young John de Montfort was brought up at Edward's court and was in every way dependent on English support until he gained his duchy in 1364. During the reign of the Duke (1364–99), England and France were in conflict. This presented John with problems regarding his allegiance as Duke and his natural sympathies. But it also provided him with the opportunity to exploit his position as Duke by diplomacy and to satisfy a growing Breton desire for independence from Valois France. This work examines some of the effects of John IV's intrigues with the two great powers.

The historiography of John IV's reign begins with the account written by his secretary and apologist Guillaume de Saint-André shortly after John had done homage to Charles VI of France in September 1381.[1] With its unashamed partisanship, this first work has, for better or worse, set a norm which has influenced all those writing about the Duke. Not that all have been pro-Montfortist. Indeed a strong reaction to Saint-André's views has characterized most of the work done since A. de la Borderie's first important paper,

---

[1] *Le Libvre du bon Jehan, duc de Bretaigne*, ed. Charrière, *C.D.I.*, 1839.

'La politique de Jean IV, 1364–73' (1855).[1] John IV
appeared to La Borderie in the guise of a Breton traitor,
responsible for prolonging the strife of the Breton Civil War
(1341–64) by provoking Charles V of France through his
political ineptitude and misplaced allegiance to England,
and thus causing a further period of anarchy in the duchy
from 1373 to 1381. John's actions stand in direct contrast
to those of Blois, whom he defeated at the battle of Auray
(1364). This contrast is intensified by an adulation of Blois
which has reached hagiographical levels. It is true that contemporaries were impressed by Blois's piety and asceticism
and that his own family pressed for his canonization soon
after his death on the battlefield, but his claims to sanctity
were not finally recognized until this present century.[2]
Nevertheless, much of John IV's history has been written
under the shadow of Blois.

La Borderie emphasized the extent to which John IV was
dependent on England and English advisers from 1364 to
1373, and later historians have echoed his words. Particularly is this the case in shorter histories of the duchy which
are so often a précis of La Borderie's imposing *Histoire de
Bretagne* (6 vols., Rennes 1896–1914). Unfortunately, La
Borderie's final account of John's reign in volume iv of his
Histoire was seen through the press after La Borderie's
death, and there is reason to believe that it was not the fruit
of his most mature consideration of John. In the *Histoire* the
chapters on John begin with an almost word-for-word repeat
of the 1855 paper, but the later parts of the reign are not
treated in so much detail. Further, there are amongst the La
Borderie papers at Rennes a considerable quantity of notes
on the post-1381 period which were never incorporated in
the *Histoire*.[3]

A result of La Borderie's work has been the division of
John's reign into two periods—before and after 1381—
since it was necessary to find an origin for the quasi-
independent outlook which characterized the government
of fifteenth-century dukes of Brittany in their relations with
France. The rough outline of La Borderie's pattern emerges

---

[1] *Revue de l'Ouest*, ii (1855), 545–68.   [2] Plaine, *Procès*, introduction.
[3] A.I.V., sér. 1 F, La Borderie papers.

by explaining away John's earlier ineffectiveness as Duke as being due to his morbid concern with the wishes of his English guardian, father-in-law, and ally, and by accounting for his constructive ambitions in the 1380s and 1390s in terms of release from his English preoccupations. In the early work of B.-A. Pocquet du Haut-Jussé this division is explicitly stated,[1] although his later papers make it quite clear that certain developments during the Civil War and before 1373 are of a piece with what came later. We are indebted to M. Pocquet du Haut-Jussé for several very important and illuminating essays on fourteenth-century Brittany, and especially for his concern with the constitutional and theoretical developments of ducal power; nor has his study of legal forms been divorced from an attempt to see how the Duke's powers in action differed from his theoretical claims. In this he has been an eminent successor to Marcel Planiol, whose *Histoire des institutions de la Bretagne* (3 vols., Rennes 1953–5), although only recently published, was written in the 1890s.[2] M. Pocquet du Haut-Jussé's doctoral thesis *Les Papes et les ducs de Bretagne* (2 vols., Paris 1928) deals with a much longer period than John IV's reign, but is still the most detailed narrative, not merely on ecclesiastical matters, but on the general political history of the fourteenth-century duchy. The debt owed to M. Pocquet du Haut-Jussé's work, with its concern for ducal relations with France, for example, will be obvious throughout this book. Where amplifications or modifications are suggested, it is because the matters under consideration here have not been his main concern or because they throw into relief some aspects of the period which have been of greater interest for Breton and French historians.

Military and political affairs in Brittany have attracted a larger number of historians than have the legal and constitutional problems of the period. A pioneer study by Siméon Luce, *Histoire de Bertrand du Guesclin; la jeunesse de Bertrand* (Paris 1876), set a high standard of scholarship.

---

[1] For example, 'François II, duc de Bretagne, et l'Angleterre', *M.H.B.* ix (1928), 171.

[2] See the *Avant-propos* by M. Durtelle de Saint-Sauveur (i. 9–18) for the circumstances.

Most regrettably, Luce did not live to complete his life of the Constable. Some forty years ago problems of the Civil War in Brittany were reviewed in an interesting paper by E. Déprez.[1] Although the thesis of English exploitation of a defenceless duchy, which Déprez accepted from Luce and La Borderie, now requires modification, most general histories of the period still echo Déprez's views.

The most important recent contribution to Breton four-teenth-century history has been the publication of M. Henri Touchard's *Le Commerce maritime breton* (Paris 1967), which deals very comprehensively with many problems of medieval Breton economic history. I was aware of M. Touchard's forthcoming thesis when preparing my own; consequently in the present work I have only touched upon the subject of economic history in the most general terms.

R. Delachenal's *Histoire de Charles V* (5 vols., Paris 1909–31) sets Breton ducal affairs (up to 1380) in a wider context of French history and offers some criticism of minor points in La Borderie's work, while accepting most of his general conclusions. The most important attempt to rewrite the political history of Anglo-French relations at the end of the fourteenth century, and the part taken by Brittany in them, may be found in the work of J. Calmette and E. Déprez, *La France et l'Angleterre en conflit* (Paris 1937). All that need be said here is that serious qualifications must be entered about their plausible account of Anglo-Breton relations. Professor Perroy's *The Hundred Years War* (Eng. tr. 1951) is generally much more valuable.

Particular episodes of Breton history have interested English historians concerned with the effects of the war with France on domestic policies in England; for example, C. C. Bayley in his well-argued paper 'The Campaign of 1375 and the Good Parliament'.[2] And, since many interesting papers have been devoted to the study of army size and to the financing and organization of expeditionary forces and campaigns, it was a natural corollary that some recent work should have been done on the organization of forces occupying castles and towns in France for Edward III

---

[1] 'La querelle de Bretagne', *M.H.B.* vii (1926), 25–60.
[2] *E.H.R.* lv (1940), 370–83.

between the great *chevauchées*. It is now clear that there were
innovations in Brittany which had important effects on the
way in which occupying troops acted towards those subject
to them, who were sometimes inhabitants of a friendly
territory. This side of warfare and the general strategy of
the English kings in their war with France have been
emphasized here, rather than the actual campaigns, many
of which have received attention elsewhere.

The main aim of this book is to examine the relations of
the duchy of Brittany with England and France. By investi-
gating John's career it is hoped to find out how far his
upbringing in England and his dependence on English aid
to win his duchy were reflected in his policies once he
became Duke, and how far, in the course of his long reign,
he was able to emerge from his early tutelage to become a
ruler with distinctive policies. The extent to which he was
able to use his position as Duke of Brittany to play a decisive
role in the Anglo-French war is examined in detail.

It is necessary, therefore, to discuss John's relations with
his own people and with his sovereign, the King of France.
It seems best to begin by examining John's domestic administration to see whether precedents set in the previous
twenty years of English control in half the duchy, with all
that this implied for the infiltration of Englishmen into ducal
service and Breton society, left their mark on Brittany after
1364. An attempt is made to establish the nature of Edward
III's holds over the Duke by a discussion of the methods of
administration and personnel used by John IV, as well as by
describing the legal commitments which John agreed to in
1362. As his reign unfolds, it is necessary to see how the
Kings of England and France manipulated the various
strings which tied John and his duchy to them.

It will be shown that a strict division of John's problems
after 1364 into the categories of domestic and foreign
policies cannot do justice to the complexity of his position
as a former client of England and a legal subject of the King
of France. The interaction of John's attempt to reduce the
powers of his seigneurs in Brittany and their opposition to
his pro-English policy led to a renewed exile in 1373. John's
return in 1379 and his apparently successful rule thereafter

raise the problem of whether his policies after 1381 differed from those he used before 1373. This problem can be answered from two points of view, John's relations with his subjects and his relations with the great powers. This entails extended discussion of his political role in the 1380s and 1390s in a period during which England and France were at first still at war and then reconciled to a succession of truces.

A study of ducal relations with the great powers leads naturally to an investigation of English military intervention in the duchy. The nature of this intervention is of interest and importance; it is characterized by the holding of Brest castle. Brest was valuable as a military stronghold and as a link in a chain of English-held fortresses around the coast of France. The difficulties of maintaining it and its political value to the English, in their relations with both Brittany and France, are germane to this discussion. Likewise, the connection between Brittany and the earldom of Richmond, although as old as the Norman conquest of England, deserves attention because of its potential value to the Duke, not merely in terms of prestige, but as a possible source of patronage for gaining English supporters to his cause. These two inquiries into conditions at Brest and the holding of Richmond, together with the discussion of John's domestic administration, are the main digressions from a story which centres upon John's relations with England and France in a period of war which has been described as 'more dangerous and burdensome to England than any she was to fight until the Anglo-Spanish war of 1585–1604'.[1]

The main sources for this work are the great collections of documents especially accessible in Rymer's *Foedera* and Dom Morice's *Preuves*.[2] Publication of Chancery rolls has lightened the task of research. Extensive use has been made of the financial records of the Public Record Office, while an important source of diplomatic evidence has been British

---

[1] J. Campbell, 'England, Scotland and the Hundred Years War in the Fourteenth Century', *Europe in the Late Middle Ages*, ed. J. Hale *et al.* (1965), p. 211.

[2] See list of Abbreviations: *Foedera* and *Preuves*. A. de la Borderie, *Correspondance historique des bénédictins bretons 1688–1730* (1880), is an interesting commentary on the researches of the Breton Maurists of an earlier generation whose work Morice largely plagiarized. B.N. MSS. fr. 22319–62, for the notes of Dom Lobineau, Dom Morice, and their co-researchers.

Museum MS. Cott. Julius B. vi. Among French sources, the ducal archives at Nantes, despite pillaging by the seventeenth- and eighteenth-century Benedictines and later Breton and foreign antiquaries, still contain important records. At Paris the notes made by the Benedictines in their travels, other scattered documents at the Bibliothèque Nationale, and the remains of the royal archives at the Archives Nationales constitute valuable caches of documents. For this particular study the loss of almost all the ducal financial records leaves a disastrous gap in the evidence. Administrative sources have been used wherever possible. Chronicles have provided some interesting supplementary material.

By setting out some of the problems of Breton history at the end of the fourteenth century in detail, by surveying the existing literature, by subjecting known documents to criticism, and by using newly discovered evidence, it may be possible to show that John IV's career can be interpreted (as far as diplomatic and military matters are concerned) in much more rational terms than those frequently used to describe the 'murderer' of Blois, and that John realized quite as clearly as his Penthièvre opponents what the needs of the duchy were.

I

THE FIRST TREATY OF GUÉRANDE
AND ITS ANTECEDENTS

ON Easter Sunday 1365 Jean de Craon, Archbishop of Reims, published a treaty in the church of Saint-Aubin at Guérande.[1] This treaty settled the succession to the duchy of Brittany which had been disputed on the death of Duke John III in 1341 by two claimants—the late Duke's younger half-brother, John de Montfort, and Joan de Penthièvre, niece of the late Duke and of his half-brother. This dispute, which had led to a state of civil war in the duchy and active intervention by the Kings of England and France, was soon caught up in the greater struggle between the two Kings. It had divided Brittany for almost a quarter of a century; now, at last, peace was being declared. The victorious party to the succession dispute was that led by John de Montfort, son of the claimant of 1341, who had defeated and killed Charles de Blois, the husband of Joan de Penthièvre, in battle outside the walls of Auray on 29 September 1364. Despite his acknowledged ties with Edward III, it was his claim to the duchy which was being admitted by the Archbishop on behalf of his master, Charles V of France. The recognition of claims, which John had made good by his sword, was the prelude to a period of reconstruction in the duchy. For the first time since 1341 the duchy was under one ruler. The provisions of the treaty were intended to bring peaceful conditions back to Brittany by regulating the new Duke's relations with his rivals in the Penthièvre party. The compromise achieved in settling the claims of supporters of the former contestants created the framework in which the new Duke would work to re-establish his authority. The mediation of French representatives and John's acknowledgement of his subordination to the King of France likewise outlined

[1] *Preuves*, i. 1588–98.

the future legal relationship of the Duke to his sovereign, although the final word on this subject had not yet been spoken, since John's performance of homage to Charles V was still to be done. The treaty closed one episode, the Civil War, and opened a new phase in Breton history, the reign of Duke John IV. Underlying the politics of the moment, however, was the peculiar position in which the duchy of Brittany was placed. A partly independent duchy, in French law a parcel of the kingdom of France, it still had important connections with England. The ruler of the duchy had thus to take at least three major interests into consideration—the King of France, the King of England, and his own people.

The prime factor governing the Duke of Brittany's relations with the King of France in the fourteenth century was his creation as a peer of France in 1297.[1] This entailed doing liege homage and fealty for the duchy, and encumbered the Duke with a number of obligations, both of a personal and private nature and of a public character, towards his sovereign, the King. Amongst these were his obligations to give counsel to his sovereign, to appear on ceremonial and judicial occasions, and to do armed service with the royal host, when required. These services had been exacted from John III by the last Capetian kings.[2] In theory the Duke of Brittany, like a Count of Flanders or a Duke of Burgundy or even a Duke of Guyenne, acknowledged the King's sovereignty in his duchy with all that this recognition occasioned.[3] Ducal courts depended, in the final analysis, on the *Parlement* of Paris. The validity of royal *ordonnances* in the duchy was acknowledged. The King's right to impose taxation, to make ecclesiastical appointments, and so on was admitted, and examples of ducal compliance with royal wishes and demands can be found in the period around the

---

[1] B.-A. Pocquet du Haut-Jussé, 'Le grand fief breton', Lot et Fawtier, i. 276.

[2] C. H. Taylor, 'The Composition of Baronial Assemblies in France, 1315–20', *Speculum*, xxix (1954), 438; B. C. Keeney, *Judgement by Peers*, pp. 114–15; M. Sautel-Boulet, 'Le rôle juridictionnel de la cour des pairs aux XIIIᵉ et XIVᵉ siècles', *Recueil de travaux offert à M. Clovis Brunel*, ii. 507–20.

[3] P. Chaplais, 'La souveraineté du roi de France et le pouvoir législatif en Guyenne au début du XIVᵉ siècle', *Le Moyen Âge*, lxix (1963), 449–67; C. M. Martin, 'The Enforcement of the Rights of the Kings of France in the Duchy and County of Burgundy, 1285–1363', Oxford B.Litt. thesis (1965).

turn of the century and in the early years of John III's reign.[1]

But alongside the royal interpretation of sovereign rights can be set the notion of ducal regalities, a notion most comprehensively expressed in the legal arguments maintained by John de Montfort's lawyers in 1341, but which can be paralleled in examples drawn from the reign of Duke John I onwards. Based, it must be admitted, on frequently false and anachronistic arguments and examples, on the idea that Brittany had once been a realm in its own right, the ducal theory was set in opposition to royal claims.[2] More seriously, since practical difficulties hampered the kings of France from enforcing their will, ducal exercise of regal and sovereign rights occurred. These precedents soon hardened into custom. Philip IV had been able to interfere in such matters as taxation in the duchy, but his successors did so less frequently, and by the reign of John III these matters were considered within the sphere of ducal prerogatives. Effective royal control of the Duke's mint was similarly weakened, whilst interference by Royal representatives in judicial matters became more scarce. The cases of defendants who appealed directly to the King, thereby infringing ducal rights, were returned to ducal courts.[3] John III's performance of his military service, as on the Cassel campaign of 1328, was only done after the King had issued letters confirming that the occasion would not be taken as a precedent.[4] In this way a *modus vivendi* had been established between the Dukes and their sovereigns, where the respective spheres of their influence had been mapped out. The same watchfulness exercised by the kings of England with regard to their rights as Dukes of Guyenne is paralleled in the case of Breton relations with Capet and Valois France. The French kings found it politic to temporize and to accept some of the practical limitations thus

[1] Pocquet, loc. cit.
[2] *Preuves*, i. 1415–19, for an abbreviated summary of Montfort's case taken from a roll at Nantes (A.L.A. E 6); J. Le Patourel, 'The King and the Princes in Fourteenth-Century France', *Europe in the Late Middle Ages*, ed. J. Hale *et al.*, p. 167.
[3] Pocquet, Lot et Fawtier, i. 276–7, and Fawtier, ibid. ii. 154–6.
[4] *Preuves*, i. 1351.

imposed on the exercise of their sovereign rights in Brittany before 1341. We should, however, avoid dramatizing the antagonism between the interests of the Kings and Dukes. Unlike the King-Duke in Guyenne, the Duke of Brittany could rarely oppose the King of France by force, and, in general, breaches in the accepted code of behaviour were smoothed over by diplomatic means.

The Duke of Brittany's relations with England before 1341 can be dealt with a little more summarily. Once again there were personal, feudal ties linking the Duke and the kings of England. These stemmed from William I's grant of Richmond to Count Alan, a cadet of the reigning comital house, who had accompanied him in 1066.[1] Count Alan's right to Richmond had eventually descended to the counts of Brittany, and in the later thirteenth century the kings of England had confirmed them in their possession of the earldom in return for liege homage. This tenure was often dependent on the political needs of the King. He could bring pressure to bear on the Count by giving or withholding, confiscating or returning, the honour of Richmond.[2] Consequently succession to the earldom was a little unsure, and it was this fact which allowed Edward I to establish the second son of Duke John II of Brittany as Earl in 1306.[3] But the threat that Richmond and Brittany would henceforward descend in different branches of the same family was averted in 1334 on the death, without heirs, of John de Bretagne; and John III of Brittany, his nephew, was allowed to hold the earldom. Whatever the political motives which dictated the English kings' actions with regard to Richmond, John III expressed the ducal attitude plainly enough. Richmond was 'come nostre propre heritage a nous deu et appartenant naturelment come au duc de Bretaigne pour raison du droit de nos devancierz et par raison de nostre duchie et non a autre . . .'.[4] This personal interest of the Dukes must be taken into account in discussing their relations with England

---

[1] *Complete Peerage*, x. 779 ff.

[2] Ibid. 802 (confiscation in 1235), 810 (restoration in 1268), and 812 (confiscation in 1296), etc.

[3] Ibid. 815, and I. Lubimenko, *Jean de Bretagne, comte de Richmond*, passim.

[4] Exch. Dip. Doc. 61 (Letters of John III, Senlis, 8 May 1334).

in the course of this survey. From the point of view of the duchy as a whole, the main concern of the Breton people with England stemmed from the growing commercial and economic links across the Channel, salt and canvas, in particular, being exported from the duchy in large quantities.[1] Brittany's position astride the main Anglo-Gascon trade route was likewise of economic and strategic importance to England. The economic history of the duchy has been treated very fully in the recent work of M. Henri Touchard,[2] and it is not proposed to deal further with it here, although economic considerations should be borne in mind in assessing the importance of the political and military policies of the Dukes and Kings in the later fourteenth century.

In matters of domestic administration the reign of John III had been one of relative stability and consolidation. The efforts of the thirteenth-century Dukes to gather into their hands an adequate demesne and resources, which would enable them to control their greater subjects, had been largely successful.[3] The discontent which such measures had aroused at the time was now largely forgotten, and the Dukes enjoyed revenues brought in by ducal monopolies such as the right to issue *brefs de mer* (safe-conducts of various types for ships coasting round Brittany), by licences for castle-building, by customs and admiralty dues, from *sécheries* (fish-drying factories), ducal mills, ovens, and sluices, and from the *rachat* (a fee for seigneurs to enter on their inheritances).[4] As the greatest landowner, sole authority for the issue of coin, and possessor of regalian rights over the Church, with his judicial eminence in the duchy and with his right to demand the usual feudal aids from his vassals,[5] the Duke was financially in an impressive position

---

[1] A. Bridbury, *England and the Salt Trade*, pp. 56–75; F. Mace, 'Devonshire Ports in the Fourteenth and Fifteenth Centuries', *T.R.H.S.*, 4th ser., viii (1925), 124–6.

[2] *Le Commerce maritime breton* and various papers; see Bibliography.

[3] Y. Renaudin, 'Les domaines des ducs de Bretagne. Leur administration du XIIIᵉ au XVᵉ siècle', summarized in *Positions des thèses de l'École des Chartes* (1957), pp. 123–5. I have consulted the copy kept at the Arch. dép., Nantes.

[4] Pocquet, Lot et Fawtier, i. 274–5; H. Touchard, 'Les brefs de Bretagne', *Rev. d'hist. économique et sociale*, xxxiv (1956), 116–40; and Renaudin, op. cit., pp. 46–51.

[5] *La Très Ancienne Coutume de Bretagne*, ed. M. Planiol, § 260.

despite the lack of any over-all form of taxation. To help realize these assets, quite sophisticated administrative machinery had been created by recent Dukes.[1] Although the administration was directed closely from the household of the Duke, experts could be deputed to deal with financial, administrative, and judicial matters whenever necessary.[2] The abuses dealt with in the 'Constitutions' of John III, a document compiled between 1334 and 1341, were those associated with the spread of corrupt practices in an increasingly bureaucratic administration.[3] This was already well staffed by officials seeking to fill their pockets at the expense of the Duke in whose name they acted, whose authority was obviously recognized, and whose writings and seals could be profitably forged. Again the competence of the ducal courts, organized in a hierarchy of ascending authority from the local level, through the courts of the eight *sénéchaussées* of the duchy, to the seneschal's court of Rennes, the *curia* and the *Parlement* of the Duke, was fully recognized.[4] It was only after all these courts had been exhausted that appeals were allowed to the *Parlement* of Paris, and then only in two cases: false judgement or denial of justice.[5] It is an index of respect for the law and the growth of peaceful litigation in the duchy that it was necessary for practising lawyers to compile a compendium of local laws and customs known as *la très ancienne coutume* for use in ducal and seigneurial courts sometime in the first half of John III's reign.[6]

Although it must be admitted that progress, in the shape of increasing ducal centralization and power, was not made equally in all fields of ducal endeavour, the seigneurs, who had previously opposed such an extension of control, were now willing to admit ducal leadership. The more so, it would seem, because the Duke was prepared to grant con-

[1] B.-A. Pocquet du Haut-Jussé, 'Le plus ancien rôle des comptes du Duché, 1262', *M.H.B.* xxvi (1946), 49–68.

[2] For ducal administration, see Chapter II.

[3] *La Très Ancienne Coutume*, ed. Planiol, pp. 345–54.

[4] A. Oheix, *Étude sur les sénéchaux de Bretagne*, pp. 53–6, 78–82.

[5] Cf. the quotation from Beaumanoir in J. Strayer, 'The Laicization of French and English Society in the Thirteenth Century', *Speculum*, xv (1940), 82 n. 3.

[6] Dated by Planiol to 1312–25, op. cit., p. 7; his remarks on its nature, ibid., pp. 15–16.

cessions to them to exercise within their own demesnes a strict control over their tenants.[1] Individual complaints about ducal rule could be settled, at the highest level, in the *Parlement* of the Duke, which was essentially the ducal *curia* expanded to admit all the Duke's major vassals. Laws were made as a result of consultation between the Duke and these vassals, both lay and ecclesiastical, although John III issued *ordonnances* which had a general application to all his demesne tenants without the help of *Parlement*.[2]

Limitations to the exercise of ducal power existed within the duchy, therefore, in the recognition of seigneurial rights (and also of certain corporate ones); but, as in the case of the Breton church by John III's time,[3] the seigneurs saw that their privileges were dependent on the temporal protection of the Duke against the King (or Pope). They opposed any proposal which threatened to leave them exposed to more direct control by the King.[4] So, as in the case of the Duke's relations with the two sovereigns, a neat balance of interests had been achieved between the Duke and his subjects before 1341.

With the declaration of war between England and France in 1337 John III's position became more difficult. Vassal of both contending kings by right of his holdings in France and England, John was faced with a problem of dual allegiance, not uncommon in feudal society, which had faced his predecessors and was to be a major feature of John IV's reign. His duties as a peer of France were quite explicit, and he did indeed serve with the French royal army in the Flemish campaigns of 1339–40.[5] Unlike a number of other nobles who held lands in both countries, John did not lose either set of his lands by his services.[6] Edward III was

---

[1] B.-A. Pocquet du Haut-Jussé, 'La genèse du législatif dans le duché de Bretagne', *R.H.D.F.E.*, 4th ser., xl (1962), 351–72.

[2] Pocquet, loc. cit., and P. S. Lewis, 'The Failure of the French Medieval Estates', *Past and Present*, 23 (1962), 7.

[3] B.-A. Pocquet du Haut-Jussé, *Les Papes*, i, *passim*.

[4] Borderie, iii. 403, and R. Cazelles, *La Société politique et la crise de la royauté sous Philippe de Valois*, pp. 140–3, for seigneurial opposition to John III's plans to make Philip VI his heir.

[5] E. Déprez, *Les Préliminaires de la guerre de Cent Ans*, pp. 259, n. 7, 329, n. 2; Borderie, iii. 397, has exaggerated John's contribution.

[6] Cf. Cazelles, op. cit., pp. 133–50.

prepared to see John serving against him and yet maintain friendly relations with the Duke. The Duke and his servants remained *personae gratae* at Westminster and Paris. Neither the interests of the Duke nor those of his people were well served by the outbreak of war; whilst English concern for the vital Anglo-Gascon sea-route perhaps explains Edward's refusal to confiscate Richmond. But the death of John III and the emergence of two candidates for his title upset the delicate balance which the former Duke had maintained by his strict adherence to the accepted chivalric code of his time.

The submissions of both candidates, acknowledging the unquestioned sovereignty of the King of France over Brittany, were long and fully argued.[1] But the request to Philip VI to judge which candidate ought to be allowed to do homage for the duchy merely postponed the outbreak of civil disorder, since he was almost certain to decide for the right of his nephew as husband of Joan de Penthièvre. Philip's support of Charles and Joan was implicit in certain agreements made with his approval in May 1341;[2] whilst Edward III appears to have taken the initiative in offering help, an alliance, and compensation to John de Montfort.[3] Both sovereigns had thus taken up their respective positions when appeal to the *Parlement* of Paris, garnished with peers, was made in August 1341.[4]

The opportunity to bind the duchy closer to the crown; the personal involvement of the King; the need to ensure that Brittany did not present another bridgehead into France for Edward III, as Flanders had done in the previous four years; the military support and resources of men and shipping to be obtained in the duchy; the opportunity to consolidate royal control of the coasts from the Channel round to La Rochelle—all these reasons guaranteed that

---

[1] Above, p. 3, n. 2.

[2] A. Du Chesne, *Histoire de la maison de Chastillon-sur-Marne*, pt. ii, *Preuves*, p. 120; Borderie, iii. 415, 423–4.

[3] J. Le Patourel, 'Edward III and the Kingdom of France', *History*, xliii (1958), 186.

[4] Arch. dép. du Nord, Lille, B 818, no. 7401 (letters patent of Philip VI containing protest of Joan, Lady of Cassel, against the claims of Montfort and Blois, letters dated 'in parliamento nostro' 24 Aug. 1341). The *Arrêt de Conflans* allowing the claim of Blois to do homage for Brittany was dated 7 Sept. 1341 (*Preuves*, i. 1421–4).

Philip VI would intervene in the duchy. He was probably also encouraged to this end by the nature of the territories already possessed by Joan and her husband in the duchy. These were, at once, both extensive and compact in the north-eastern part of the duchy, affording easy lines of communication with Normandy.[1] Events in the duchy after John III's death also quickly revealed that a large number of the most important seigneurs and a majority of the nine bishops supported Joan.[2] The import of such evidence was not lost on Philip VI.

As a short-term explanation of Edward's intervention in Brittany in 1341, Froissart's account, that he did so to distract Philip VI,[3] cannot be dismissed lightly. The opportunity was not to be missed to bring new pressure to bear on the French after the relative failure of the Flemish campaigns to endanger the stability of the French monarchy. But more important from Edward's point of view was the opportunity to ensure the safety of the sea-route around the Breton coast, and in particular around the Finistère peninsula. This interpretation would seem to be justified by the preliminary campaigns of the war, which were waged not so much to accomplish the succession of John de Montfort to the ducal throne as to occupy a number of strategically important coastal districts.[4] Such a consideration has to be borne in mind throughout the Hundred Years War in discussing Breton relations with England and France in the light of the cardinal role Guyenne played in English policies. From Bordeaux all shipping had to round the dangerous headlands of Finistère on its way to England or to points further up the Channel and into the North Sea. Once safely into the Channel a choice of routes presented itself. A direct route led to the ports of Cornwall, and an indirect, more lengthy one led along the north Breton littoral, passing the Channel Isles and the Cotentin peninsula, until a short sea-crossing could be made to Southampton or more easterly

---

[1] A. de la Borderie, *Essai sur la géographie féodale de la Bretagne*, pp. 60-1 (and important map); Borderie, iii. 401-4.

[2] Ibid. 425, for poor seigneurial response to Montfort's call; ibid. 414, seven out of nine bishops pronounced for Blois.

[3] Ed. Luce, ii. 139-41.

[4] J. Le Patourel, *E.H.R.* lxxi (1956), 329-30.

ports.[1] Control of this latter route was difficult because of the inability of medieval ships to stay at sea for long periods; whilst, although Edward held, and had reinforced, the Channel Isles, they had not proved defensible against a sustained French attack.[2] As isolated outposts of English control, as watering spots and safe harbours, they had their value; but the worth of the islands in the war with France was not substantially increased until they formed part of a chain of defences ringing Valois France in the last quarter of the century.[3] For Edward's strategy, control of the Finistère peninsula seemed to offer a far better guarantee for the safety of English shipping. Although Brittany might have presented another bridgehead for his attacks on France,[4] the physical isolation of the duchy from the rest of Valois territories was a disadvantage when, as Edward was to prove, landings could be made more easily on the Norman shoreline. How far Edward's reasoning took into consideration the fact that it was in the coastal regions of the west and the north that ducal control was perhaps at its height, we cannot tell. But it is true that it was in these regions that ducal power, as opposed to that of the greatest seigneurs, had achieved some of its triumphs. Ducal demesne in the Finistère peninsula had been augmented by disinheriting some seigneurial families and by curtailing the rights of others.[5] Likewise in the present day *département* of Morbihan, the former *sénéchaussées* of Cornouaille and Broërec, ducal demesnes were extensive, especially around Vannes; whilst John de Montfort's own patrimony (the seigneury of Guérande) was becoming increasingly important as a centre of the salt industry.[6] Such territories and the resources they

---

[1] T. Williams, 'The Importance of the Channel Isles in British Relation [*sic*] with the Continent during the Thirteenth and Fourteenth Centuries', *Bull. de la Soc. Jersiaise*, xi (1928), *passim*, for sea-routes.

[2] In 1338, for example; Déprez, op. cit., p. 188.

[3] See below, chapter III.

[4] Cf. É. Perroy, *The Hundred Years War*, p. 115.

[5] Borderie, iii. 353 ff.; Touchard, *Rev. d'hist. économique et sociale*, xxxiv (1956), 123–4.

[6] L. Maître, 'Domaines de Bretagne dépendants de la couronne ducale', *Annales de Bretagne*, xxxviii (1928), 188–207; for Vannes, see below, Chapter II; F. Bock, 'Some New Documents Illustrating the Early Years of the Hundred Years War, 1353–6', *Bull. John Rylands Library*, xv (1931), 88, and Bridbury, *Salt Trade*, p. 41, for Guérande.

offered, together with the fact that communications with England were relatively easy by sea, indicate why Edward III was interested in the fate of Montfort's claim to the duchy.

Broadly speaking, Breton society was split in two, both socially and physically, by the events of 1341. To summarize the alignments briefly indicated above, the eastern parts of the duchy tended to favour the claims of Joan de Penthièvre, whilst the western and northern littoral regions tended to support John de Montfort. The concomitant of this division was that the greater seigneurs supported Joan and the lesser supported Montfort, but these alignments also emphasized a far earlier division of the duchy. A map of the Celtic-speaking regions of Brittany in the ninth century shows that the language was spoken west of a line running approximately from Pontorson south to Rennes and Saint-Nazaire.[1] But by the twelfth century the Celtic-speaking area had contracted and had been pushed west approximately to the line of the Vilaine river. Rennes had become the city 'qui reste, en face de l'Armorique bretonnisée, le rempart franc'; the Île-de-Guérande was an isolated Celtic-speaking region, as it is to this day; whilst Nantes and its surrounding district already tended to live apart from the rest of the duchy.[2] The more fertile eastern and southern parts of the duchy had fallen to an 'alien' Gallo-Norman nobility, who, much as their companions across the Channel after 1066, were subduing a foreign land and introducing the exotic plant 'feudalism'.[3] These were the forbears of the great seigneurs of John III's time, and indeed of the Duke himself. The Penthièvre apanage created for Guy, younger brother of John III, in 1317 was in many ways the re-creation of the county of Penthièvre held by Count Eudo in the eleventh century. As a result of the attack on the remnants of a former powerful Celtic society, the new nobility assimilated something of the independence which had characterized their predecessors and subjects in the

---

[1] M. Le Lannou, *Géographie de la Bretagne*, i. 177.
[2] Ibid. 178–83.
[3] Sir Frank Stenton, *The First Century of English Feudalism, 1066–1166* (2nd edn., 1961), pp. 27–8.

east. But more specifically Celtic elements had been driven underground, or survived only in the western parts of the duchy. In broad terms, the Civil War of 1341–64 reopened and sharpened the division between Bretagne-Gallo or Haute-Bretagne, the area under Penthièvre influence, the region of the great seigneuries, and Bretagne-Bretonnante or Basse-Bretagne, the area which was prepared to acknowledge Montfort's claim, the region of the lesser *noblesse*.[1] It was a division which was recognized by the ducal administration even after the war.

The actual course of the Civil War need not concern us greatly. The territorial dispositions and composition of the parties to the struggle were quickly established. Even the intervention of the respective sovereigns, in the form of armed expeditions to the duchy or of attempts to settle the dispute by way of treaty, did little to alter the positions adopted.[2] Once Edward III had ensured that by means of his armed help vital ports would be occupied and that the Montfortist party (even without its leader) would not be driven out of the duchy, except by a very considerable effort on France's part, he was content to allow a series of royal lieutenants acting on his behalf and on that of his infant ward, John de Montfort, son of the original claimant (who had died in 1345), to administer the English-occupied areas of the duchy much as they chose.[3] The accompanying map indicates the extent of Anglo-Breton control, and emphasizes its coastal nature. Even when Charles de Blois fell into Edward's hands in 1347, little attempt was made to bring the war to a conclusion. The occasional alarm of a more substantial Franco-Breton attack seldom materialized and was beaten off when it did.[4] The story of the war is mainly that of siege and counter-siege by small forces, usually under the command of the King's lieutenant, but quite often led by individual captains whose relationship to the main Anglo-Breton administration was at first ill-defined and, latterly,

[1] Borderie, iii. 534, composition of the Penthièvre party.
[2] E. Déprez, 'La querelle de Bretagne', *M.H.B.* vii (1926), 25–60.
[3] J. Le Patourel, 'L'administration ducale dans la Bretagne montfortiste, 1345–62', *R.H.D.F.E.*, 4th ser., xxxii (1954), 144–7; id., *History*, xliii (1958), 186–9.
[4] Borderie, iii. 530–2, and T. F. Tout, 'Some Neglected Fights between Crécy and Poitiers', *E.H.R.* xx (1905), 726–30, for the battle of Mauron, 1352.

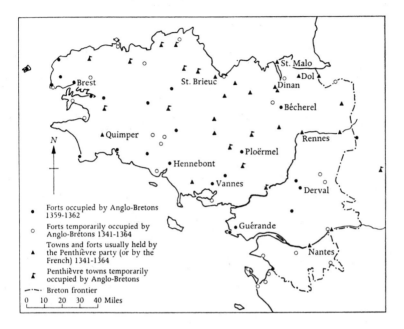

Brest
St. Brieuc
St. Malo
Dinan
Dol
Bécherel
Quimper
Rennes
Ploërmel
Hennebont
Vannes
Derval
Guérande
Nantes

• Forts occupied by Anglo-Bretons 1359-1362
○ Forts temporarily occupied by Anglo-Bretons 1341-1364
▲ Towns and forts usually held by the Penthièvre party (or by the French) 1341-1364
ᴦ Penthièvre towns temporarily occupied by Anglo-Bretons
—·—· Breton frontier

0 10 20 30 40 Miles

N

frequently insubordinate. These captains used their positions to establish personal control over regions whose inhabitants found it expedient to comply with their every demand.[1] Yet, as will be seen in a later chapter, the Anglo-Breton administration, struggling against difficult conditions, fighting a war with inadequate financial resources, acknowledged its responsibility towards the subject Breton people.[2] Men who were acutely aware of the deficiencies in this administration attempted to regulate relations between the King's officers and the freebooting captains; and in the last few years of the English occupation the relative stability of the opposing forces and frontiers, between the Anglo-Breton and Franco-Breton castles and towns, allowed the functioning of rudimentary administrations, which even on the English side attempted to incorporate features of the former ducal administration.[3]

[1] S. Luce, *Histoire de Bertrand du Guesclin*, pp. 87 ff.; Borderie, iii. 511.
[2] Below, Chapter VI.
[3] Le Patourel, loc. cit., and below, Chapter II.

The condition of the duchy after nearly twenty years of civil strife and disorder presents quite a complex picture. Two administrations—the Anglo-Breton and the Penthièvre—vied with each other to control regions which were disputed between them, and to eke out the ducal resources which each found in the areas it already possessed. Often the administrations were in conflict with their own servants, the captains who controlled the armed garrisons in the field and who saw the war as an opportunity to make their fortunes. The captains' acknowledgement of a particular allegiance might often depend on considerations which bore little relation to the justice, or otherwise, of the respective claimant's cause.[1] Thus on the Anglo-Breton side a number of Englishmen infiltrated Breton society by their acquisition of lands, titles, and wives;[2] whilst 'loyalist' Breton seigneurs, supporters of Blois and Penthièvre, were not averse to using the misfortunes of the unhappy couple to enrich their own estates. They exacted donations of ducal demesne from them and, by timely demands, gained other rewards for their services.[3] Such derogations of ducal power would demand attention from whichever candidate finally triumphed.

The military stalemate in the duchy had further emphasized that a solution to the succession problem might depend, in the final analysis, rather on the political fortunes of the contending sovereign powers than on the unaided efforts of the candidates. Certainly the fate of the duchy in the 1350s seemed to lie in the hands of Edward III, whose capture of Blois followed by the French disaster at Poitiers left him with all the political advantages.[4] Whatever Edward's intentions had been in his negotiations with Blois in 1353 (when he seems momentarily to have deserted the cause of John de Montfort for the prospect of peace and alliance with Blois),[5] the apogee of his power, in regard to the duchy, was the first treaty of London, 1358. By this date he

---

[1] For the career of Raoul de Caours, one of the most notorious turncoats, see *Arch. hist. Poitou*, xvii (1886), 27 ff., and Luce, op. cit., pp. 88–90.

[2] See below, Chapter II.

[3] *Preuves*, i. 1590.

[4] J. Le Patourel, 'The Treaty of Brétigny', *T.R.H.S.*, 5th ser., x (1960), 19–39, and Delachenal, ii. 410–11.

[5] Bock, *Bull. J. Rylands Library*, xv (1931), 84–91.

had released Blois on almost impossible conditions of ransom, holding his two eldest sons as hostages in the meantime, and he had forced the captive French King into agreeing to transfer the sovereignty of Brittany to England, no matter what the final outcome of the succession dispute might be.[1] Edward, apparently, could not lose. Yet two years later he modified his demands. Sovereignty over the duchy was returned to France, whilst the complexity of the succession dispute led the two Kings to agree to the appointment of a special commission to settle this problem, so that disagreement might not jeopardize the more general terms of peace agreed upon at Brétigny-Calais in 1360.[2] Attempts were made to fulfil these terms, and up to the summer of 1362 there was little chance for either candidate to play a serious role in the Anglo-French war.[3]

The breakdown of the Anglo-French *entente*, with the failure to implement the clause '*Cest assavoir*', the unavailing efforts of the two sovereigns and of those appointed to the commission to settle the succession, and the expiration of the truces which had been concluded for the duchy brought a turning-point in the Civil War. Although the English King attempted to adhere to the terms of Brétigny-Calais by abstaining from direct intervention in the duchy and by refraining from using Breton problems as a reason for reopening the Anglo-French war, his handing over of the Anglo-Breton administration to young John de Montfort, recently come of age, and the intransigence of Joan de Penthièvre led to renewed war. For the first time since 1345 the two candidates for the succession met face to face.[4]

---

[1] *Foedera*, iii. 336–7; Le Patourel, art. cit., p. 26.

[2] Ibid., p. 31, and *Foedera*, iii. 487–94, 516.

[3] Negotiations were held at Saint-Omer in April 1361; see Guillaume de Saint-André, *Le Libvre du bon Jehan, duc de Bretaigne*, ed. E. Charrière, ll. 544–54. Montfort's account for his journey there is contained in Accts. Var. 314/16, and his appointment of proctors in B.M. Add. MS. 24062, fols. 163ʳ–164ʳ. Messengers were dispatched to Paris in July 1361 'pro negociis tangentibus comitem de Montfort', Issue Roll 408 m. 32 (3 July). Both the Dauphin (instructions to envoys coming to England, printed in *Chron. des règnes de Jean II et de Charles V*, ed. R. Delachenal, iii. 100) and John II (letter to Edward III, B.M. Add. MS. 24062, fol. 171ʳ) were very concerned in 1362 to prolong the truces in Brittany.

[4] Borderie, iii. 574 ff.; *Chron. de Bertrand du Guesclin*, ed. Charrière, i. 207, ll. 5568–79.

John de Montfort was the only son of John de Montfort, younger half-brother of John III, and of Joan de Flandres, daughter of Louis de Flandres, Count of Nevers. The date of his birth is uncertain, although it appears to have been between 1339 and 1341.[1] He inherited his father's claims to the duchy of Brittany, by right of his descent from Arthur II of Brittany, and to the county of Montfort l'Amaury;[2] and from his mother came a number of claims on lands and rents in Rethel and Nevers.[3] But the misfortunes of the Montfort family in the early part of the Civil War had led to the exile of Joan de Flandres and her children, John and Joan, in England under the protection of Edward III, after her husband had been captured by the French. John's father, after escaping from France, did homage to Edward III in 1345 and committed his infant son into his care.[4] It seems likely, too, that the privations Joan de Flandres had undergone in her heroic defence of the duchy in 1342 and 1343 were responsible for the breakdown of her health, and for the fact that soon after going into exile she lost her reason and was handed over to the care of keepers.[5] John spent his childhood either in the household of Queen Philippa or in that of a great noble such as Henry, Duke of Lancaster, whom he accompanied on a campaign in the duchy in 1356–7.[6]

Although John had some personal servants, he does not appear to have possessed his own household; he depended largely on gifts from the King for an income, since the traditional Brittany–Richmond link had been allowed to lapse.[7] Indeed in 1361 Edward III got John to renounce all his

---

[1] *Complete Peerage*, x. 822, *contra* Borderie, iii. 572–3.

[2] Dép. Seine-et-Oise; A. Rhein, *La Seigneurie de Montfort-en-Iveline*, pp. 89–91.

[3] Cazelles, op. cit., p. 87.

[4] *Foedera*, iii. 39; Borderie, iii. 492–5.

[5] Pipe Roll 203 m. 41^r, accts. of William Frank for keeping the Duchess, 3 Oct. 1343 to 19 Nov. 1346; Déprez, *M.H.B.* vii (1926), 48.

[6] Exch. T.R. Misc. Book 205, p. 14 (1349–50), payment to Perota de Britannie of £5, her yearly fee as 'domicelle librorum Ducis Brittannie' in Philippa's household; *Anonimalle Chronicle*, ed. V. H. Galbraith, p. 48 (with Lancaster).

[7] The earldom of Richmond had been bestowed on John of Gaunt, Edward III's fourth son, in 1342 (*Complete Peerage*, x. 821). For the delivery of horses and saddles for the 1356 expedition from Edward III to young John, see B.M. Add. MS. 24512, fol. 21^r.

rights to Richmond, once John II of France had agreed to admit him to homage for the county of Montfort, which had been confiscated from John's father in 1341.[1] Edward's tutelage of John was, therefore, strict, but, apart from the episode in 1353, his concern for John's interests in Brittany was usually fair. Although the King's lieutenants in the duchy from 1342 were free to do much as they liked, by 1358 Edward began to take a much closer interest in the duchy, linking its administration with that at Westminster, limiting the lieutenants' powers, and keeping a much closer supervision of financial matters.[2] John was allowed to assume the titular captaincy of his seigneury of Guérande,[3] and his relations with William Latimer, the King's last lieutenant in the duchy, were close.[4] Throughout the period 1342–62 these lieutenants had acted in the names of the King and the Duke jointly. But any legal justification for Edward's continued maintenance of an administration in Brittany ceased in 1362. The return of the young claimant, under the eye of Latimer and aided by a number of Anglo-Breton garrisons, was achieved in July and August, and fighting soon broke out.

But before leaving England John had agreed to a number of conditions which were intended to tie him to Edward's interests. These links were both tangible and intangible. In the first instance, there was the matter of Edward's protection of the claims of Montfort. There was no denying that it was by this aid that John still had part of a duchy to return to. Secondly, there was John's marriage to the King's daughter, Mary, which had lasted only a few months but was an indication of personal esteem and of the importance which Edward attached to their relations.[5] Such links could be expected to create a debt of gratitude which would make the young Duke responsive to English blandishments

---

[1] *Foedera*, iii. 532, 543; *C.C.R. 1360–4*, 250.   [2] *Foedera*, iii. 404.

[3] He appears as captain of Guérande in the accounts presented by the Anglo-Breton treasurer of the duchy from 1358; Accts. Var. 174/4, for example.

[4] Below, Chapter II.

[5] Bock, art. cit., p. 80 is erroneous, and Borderie, iv. 133 is not very explicit on John's first marriage. To references in *Complete Peerage*, x. 822 add Issue Roll 408 m. 32 (3 July 1361), payment to Montfort of £20 'in recompens' tante summe per ipsum mutuate et diversis ministrallis ad suum maritagium liberate', and ibid. m. 38 (13 Sept. 1361), payment to a clerk of the King's household of £200 'super expensis faciendis circa sepult' domine Marie filie Regis, ducisse Britannie'.

at a later date. Perhaps more realistically, however, there were a number of political, financial, and legal ties: a treaty of alliance (which conformed to the terms of Brétigny-Calais);[1] an acknowledged debt of 64,000 nobles to Edward, and the handing over of two castles as surety for this sum; and a renewed promise not to marry without Edward's consent.[2] Surveyed by his former English mentor, Latimer, surrounded by Englishmen in his immediate entourage and in strong points in the duchy, whose own financial claims on John were not inconsiderable,[3] John was in no position to forget Edward's 'generosity'. These features of John's connection with Edward III were bound to influence his actions in the years immediately following his return, especially since it was on the armed support of the Englishmen still in Brittany that he depended for his final success.

Although without official English support, the circumstances of John's return and the events of the next couple of years merely made him more dependent on the unofficial support of Latimer and the captains. Replacements for the English captains holding castles in 1362 were few and were made from the same class of career soldier, whose members had been establishing themselves in Brittany in the previous few years.[4] New debts to them were piled up.[5] The financing of the administration in John's hands continued on the lines established by the Anglo-Breton administration as a wartime expedient.[6] There was little chance to devise new methods of government when the Montfortists were busy defending or extending the territories under their control. Another feature of the period just before Auray was John's growing dependence on the Black Prince for advice, for

---

[1] *Foedera*, iii. 662, and B.M. MS. Cott. Julius B. VI, fol. 8ʳ⁻ᵛ (letters of Edward III confirming alliance, 7 July 1362).   [2] *Foedera*, iii. 658–64.

[3] See Appendix of Documents, no. 2.

[4] *Foedera*, iii. 658 (June 1362), order to English castellans to hand their charges over to John de Montfort. Collet castle, held by Walter Huet, was officially delivered on 16 July (Accts. Var. 28/3), but it was still in Huet's hands in 1368 (*Preuves*, i. 1622, and A.L.A. E 154). At Hennebont, John appointed Thomas Fog as captain in Dec. 1362 (ibid. E 136/5). Suscinio, captured from Blois in 1363, had an English captain in 1367 (Plaine, *Procès*, pp. 334–5, 345); Appendix of Documents, no. 2.   [5] Below, Chapter II and Appendix B.

[6] Below, p. 27. The *brefs de mer* from Mar. 1364 were farmed by Matthew Gournay (Appendix of Documents, no. 1).

encouragement, and for troops. The Prince's attempts to solve the disputed succession by a partition of the duchy in the winter of 1363–4 again foundered on Joan de Penthièvre's intractability.[1] The result of this defiance was the siege and battle of Auray, leading to John de Montfort's victory.[2]

John's immediate problem after Auray was to come to an agreement with Charles V. The Duke's desires were well paraphrased by a later chronicler who put into the mouths of John's envoys this speech:

> Sire, a vous nous envoie le conte Jan, qui de la duche de Bretaigne s'attend avoir l'honneur. Bien scait le conte et recognoist que [de] vous la duche doibt estre tenue o certaine redevance. Si est advenu que, par les guerres qui ont este entre Charles de Bloys et luy et les grandes batalles, est diminuee la Chevalerie et le peuple du Pais et le povair de France pareillement et par la bataille d'Auroy derroine avenue, qui est grand pitie et domage de toutes pars, Sire, sachez que de tout couer desire votre grace avoir et devers vous fere ce quil est tenu et pour ce faire est prest de venir vers vous quand il vous plaira a ce que le temps advenir, il tiengne son pays en paix, et qu'il le reliefue de ses advereittez que trop longuement ont dure . . .[3]

In practice John proved to be less eager to do homage to Charles V, because of the attendant obligations of service. He quickly entered upon the policy of procrastination and subtle obstinacy which was to mark his relations with France. The first date for the performance of homage was postponed and, when it was finally performed, the formula used allowed the Duke's advisers to argue that it was no longer liege but only simple homage.[4] The results of this

---

[1] Luce, op. cit., pp. 579 ff. (Nov. 1363), and *Preuves*, i. 1565–6 (Feb. 1364).

[2] John justified taking up arms in a letter to the Count of Flanders in April 1364 after the failure of peace talks (Delachenal, iii. 542). Dom F. Plaine, 'La journée d'Auray', *Assoc. Bret.* (1875), pp. 85–100; Borderie, iii. 581 ff.; and Delachenal, iii. 154–9, for the battle of Auray. Further minor details can be added from the *Chronica Johannis de Reading at Anonymi Cantuariensis*, ed. J. Tait, pp. 161, 218, 318; *Anonimalle Chronicle*, ed. Galbraith, p. 51, and certain unedited English chroniclers (Bodl. MS. Rawlinson B. 152, fol. 45ᵛ, for example), but all accounts confirm the numerical superiority of Blois's army and its substantial losses.

[3] Jean de Saint-Paul, *Chronique*, ed. La Borderie, p. 22; cf. John's letter to the Count of Flanders, written 'sur les champs', Auray, Oct. 1364, printed in Delachenal, iii. 549.

[4] *Foedera*, iii. 753; *Preuves*, i. 1599, 1607–13; and below, p. 47.

development on Franco-Breton relations must be traced in later chapters.

With regard to England, John's problems were relatively clear-cut. He knew the extent of his various obligations, and he knew what holds Edward could use to remind him to perform them. Englishmen in the duchy, whose influence on the treaty of Guérande can be seen in clauses confirming several of them in the positions they had already won;[1] castles still held for Edward by Latimer and his lieutenants; control over John's closest rivals for the ducal title, the hostages John and Guy de Bretagne, sons of Blois and Joan de Penthièvre;[2] the opportunity to offer Richmond as a bait for John's alliance—these are some of the main ways in which Edward could coerce, cajole, or bribe John; whilst the growth of the Black Prince's influence, despite quarrels with his father, was a further indication of John's apparent dependence on the English.[3]

But John's own interests and those of his duchy might diverge from those of the two sovereigns, especially if the course of developments in the years prior to 1341 were to be resumed. In the first place, a wholesale reconstruction of ducal administration was called for, with a welding together of the two parts of the duchy which had been governed by the Montfortist or by the Penthièvre party. In both areas a skeletal government based on the former ducal administration had existed; but in the Anglo-Breton district, how far had Westminster methods and personnel modified traditional Breton administration? Who, indeed, was the Duke to entrust with the reconstruction and day-to-day running of his government, and who were his new councillors to be? How far was the spirit of compromise apparent at Guérande to be carried in composing the quarrels, returning the confiscations, and settling the damages caused by the civil strife of the past twenty-five years? These and similar questions about John's relations with his own people

---

[1] *Preuves*, i. 1593, where the estates mentioned—Derval, Rougé, Plumoisan, Saint-Pol, Rays, Quimerch, Roche-Moisan, Roche-Periou, Guémené-Guingan, and Château-Blanc—were all in English hands; see below, pp. 48 ff.

[2] In England since 1353, and hostages since 1356. John IV had pledged himself to obtain their release and the marriage of his sister to John de Bretagne at Guérande.

[3] Below, p. 45.

might demand a different solution from that required by John's position as a subject of the King of France and as a former client of the King of England.

It was unlikely that John would be able to return immediately to that position of balance which characterized the last few years of John III's reign. But he was, after Guérande, for the first time in a position to chart his own course and that of his duchy through the troubled waters of the Anglo-French sea, overlain as the ocean was by an uneasy calm—the respite that broke with the storm of Gascon Appeals in 1368–9. A situation existed in which the Duke and his duchy could play an independent role in the greater Anglo-French conflict. But would his success lead only to a renewal of the rivalries engendered by John III's death? What strength was there in the notion of ducal regalities after the Civil War? John's first concern was the restoration of his position as Duke of Brittany.

II

DUCAL GOVERNMENT
1364–1373

WHEN the chronicler Jean de Venette sat down to write his account of events in the previous two years, some time in the late summer of 1365, he gave quite an objective description of affairs in the duchy of Brittany. However, throughout his account one can sense his apprehension that the peace so recently completed at Guérande might prove illusory and that the horrors of war might once more engulf the Armorican peninsula.[1] Later historians have echoed Venette's sentiments when they write that Brittany's greatest need in 1365 was peace, and have added to his commentary by suggesting a further requisite— independence.[2] The new Duke and his supporters were not popular. The task before them, the reconstruction of ducal government, was unlikely to increase their popularity with erstwhile opponents. In such circumstances the treaty of Guérande, with its engineered compromises, might be severely tested. Leaving aside the issue of 'independence' for the moment because it concerns Brittany's external relations with France and England, how did the Duke tackle his domestic problems?

A sketch of the relative strengths and weaknesses of the ducal position before 1341 has already been given. In many respects ducal administration on the eve of the succession war was still that of a complex seigneurial demesne, albeit the territorial extent of the demesne was considerable, and the Duke exercised authority over a large number of baronial vassals, with their own demesnes, all bonded together within a compact and well-defined geographical region. Perhaps the best indications of this seigneurial aspect of ducal govern-

---

[1] Jean de Venette, *Chronique*, ed. R. A. Newhall, pp. 18, 126–8.
[2] Particularly Borderie, iv. 5–26, repeating almost word for word a paper written in 1854: 'La politique de Jean IV, 1364–73', *Rev. de l'Ouest*, ii (1855), 545–68.

ment, and an index to developments which took place during and after the Civil War, are to be found in the financial administration of Brittany.

The ducal accounts which survive cover most of the 1260s and the early 1300s.[1] There is then a long gap before the inconclusive accounts presented by the Anglo-Montfortist treasurer in the 1340s and the more comprehensive ones of Giles de Wyngreworth, treasurer of the duchy from 1359 to 1362.[2] But these later accounts are for a divided duchy during a war. The earlier ones reveal that there was no permanent seat at which accounts were heard, no set term for accounting, and no organized *chambre des comptes*, although there obviously were clerks who specialized in financial matters. These clerks introduced order into the haphazard presentments of local receivers and officials when registering their accounts. The development of rudimentary bureaucratic procedures was also marked by the preparation of *brefs* for sale outside the limits of the duchy. Although the place of account was not fixed, the movements indicated by surviving accounts show that receipt was usually within the diocese of Vannes, and on most occasions close to the ducal manors of Muzillac and the Rhuys peninsula.[3] By John III's reign there were semi-regular sessions for accounting, one of which was at Easter.[4]

The early accounts were presented by seneschals of the ducal demesne,[5] or by the castellans who seem to have replaced them in the reign of John II,[6] by demesne farmers, foresters, custumers, and millers, by ducal chaplains and by

[1] Pocquet, *M.H.B.* xxvi (1946), 49–68, and Renaudin, 'Les domaines', pp. 278 f.

[2] Pipe Roll 198 m. 41, account of John Charnels, 1345: 'Idem non respondet de aliquibus exitibus, redditibus seu proficuis tam dicti ducatus et aliarum terrarum que sunt de hereditate predicti heredis [John de Montfort] quam custumarum et reddituum predictorum in Vasconia percipiendorum a predicto xv° die Novembris anno xix seu deinceps eo quod propter guerram tam fortem in partibus illis existentem nullos exitus inde percepit nec percipere potuit ut dicit per sacramentum suum'; 1359–62 accounts are in Accts. Var. 174/4 and 5, 175/4, and 176/9, and have been analysed by K. Fowler, 'Henry of Grosmont, First Duke of Lancaster, 1310–1361', Leeds Ph.D. thesis, 1961, appendix F.

[3] H. Fourmont, *Histoire de la Chambre des comptes de Bretagne*, p. 4.

[4] *Privilèges de la ville de Nantes*, ed. La Nicollière-Teijeiro, p. 5.

[5] Oheix, *Étude sur les sénéchaux*, p. 50.

[6] Renaudin, op. cit., pp. 63–83.

important officers, including the master-moneyer and the receivers of the *brefs* at La Rochelle and Bordeaux. All these officials, however, were only part-time financial officers. The seneschals of the eight *sénéchaussées* mentioned in the *Livre des Ostz* (1294),[1] for example, had judicial and military responsibilities as well as financial ones. Matters of dispute arose occasionally between the Duke and his demesne tenants, and these were either settled by the dispatch of *enquêteurs* to establish the rights of contending parties or by individual settlements with the Duke in his *Parlement*.[2] Bargains were struck and local taxes commuted by a guarantee to the Duke of equivalent income from other sources. The principal reason for this amateur organization lay in the Duke's inability to impose over-all taxation, which would necessarily require a much more elaborate collecting and accounting mechanism.

To eyes, medieval or modern, accustomed to the ordered Exchequer procedures of Westminster, particularly to the system of 'view and audit', to fixed sessions of account, the well-defined responsibilities of sheriffs, and the ritual 'course of the Exchequer' with its minute examination of particulars of account, this ducal seigneurial administration looks primitive. But a comparison of Breton developments with those in other provinces of France reveals a state of affairs in which Brittany is not particularly backward. In general, French financial institutions were much slower to develop than English ones. It was not until the beginning of the fourteenth century that the royal *chambre des comptes* at Paris obtained the accounting competence which the English Exchequer had enjoyed since the reign of Henry II, and it was from Paris that the majority of provincial administrations took their lead.[3]

Towards the end of the thirteenth century financial practices in Brittany and Burgundy had been similar.[4] In

[1] A.L.A. E 132.

[2] *Cartulaire de l'abbaye de Saint-Sulpice-la-Forêt*, no. vii (1335), for *enquêteurs*; *Privilèges de la ville de Nantes*, ed. La Nicollière-Teijeiro, pp. 1–3.

[3] Cf. Lot et Fawtier, ii. 240–2.

[4] H. Jassemin, 'Le contrôle financier en Bourgogne sous les derniers ducs capétiens, 1274–1353', *B.E.C.* lxxix (1918), 102–41; and J. Richard, 'Les institutions ducales dans le duché de Bourgogne', Lot et Fawtier, i. 209–47.

both provinces there was still confusion between the revenues collected for the Dukes' households, which came mainly from domanial revenues, and extraordinary revenues from the administration of justice or from feudal incidents. Actual accounting techniques were similar, and both rulers took a personal interest in holding days of account with their clerks about them, much as King John in England and Louis IX in France had taken an active interest in the dispensing of justice. From this point it was but a short step for the Duke[1] to delegate his authority when he was forced to be absent, and his clerks would quickly form the nucleus of a *chambre des comptes*.[2] Yet in the small official class that served the needs of the Dukes of Burgundy and Brittany, specialization was not the rule, and those holding account sessions might themselves be responsible for the presentation of individual accounts.

The simple feudal Burgundian system grew rapidly in the early fourteenth century. Accounts were held more regularly, at more or less set terms, and usually at the same place. Records were kept, and officers bearing the title *gens* or *maîtres des comptes* appeared, working in an office which became known as the *chambre*. The existence of a terminology is not in itself sufficient proof of the existence of a fully institutionalized body, but there was already a distinction between the private finances of the ducal household and the *chambre* dealing with public accounts. The promising developments of this Burgundian administration were accelerated after 1350, with increased royal control during the minority of Philip de Rouvres and after the accession of Philip the Bold in 1363.[3]

Royal influence, as we have seen already, was not so apparent in fourteenth-century Brittany, nor had royal precedents been followed with the exuberant precocity that marked, for example, the establishment of a *chambre des comptes* in the county of Forez in 1317.[4] John III still

---

[1] To avoid confusion I have referred to the ruler of Brittany in this paragraph as 'Duke', although strictly speaking he was usually referred to as 'Count' until 1297.

[2] Jassemin, *B.E.C.* lxxix (1918), p. 113.

[3] Richard, Lot et Fawtier, i. 233; R. Vaughan, *Philip the Bold*, pp. 115 ff.

[4] É. Perroy, 'L'État bourbonnais', Lot et Fawtier, i. 298, and id., 'Feudalism o Principalities in Fifteenth-Century France', *B.I.H.R.* xx (1943-5), 182.

depended on local officials using the castellany as the basic
unit in the accounting system. It was the stimulus of ducal
needs in the crisis of the Civil War that provided the incentive
for developing a more sophisticated financial machine and
supplied the place of royal example to the rulers of the
divided duchy. Domanial revenues continued to be important to Charles de Blois and his wife,[1] but their expenses
soon drained this source. They were forced to run the risk of
unpopularity by impressing on their subjects the need for
some more general form of taxation. The lack of sympathy
for their point of view, even in times of extreme urgency, is
remarkable, and a gradual hardening of attitudes can be
detected. An instance that provides an insight into ducal
practice may be found in 1345. The burgesses of Nantes,
jealous of their privileges, were also anxious to see some
return for their contributions to the war-effort. They wanted
the local customs dues on merchandise sold in the town, the
'rentes, rachaptz et revenuz de la recepte de nostre dite
ville' (i.e. the traditional revenues), and an extraordinary five
sous levy on each hearth in parishes up to five leagues
around the town to be applied to local defence measures,
the nature of which the town's captain would stipulate.
Promises were sworn that neither the present contribution
of the town nor that of the church would be taken as precedents. But although it was further agreed that the rich
would aid the poor, a medieval commonplace, the Blois
government recognized that the threat of force was still
necessary. Villagers were obliged to render watch- and
guard-duties (quar ce nous apartient de nostre noblesse), and
'if they default we wish and order that their goods be taken
to offset the expenses of our said town'. The captain and
inhabitants of Nantes were to judge the adequate performance of these services.[2] Three years later Blois was in cap-
tivity, but Joan de Penthièvre was still concerned for the
safety of Nantes and made reference to 'les imposicions et
gabelles imposees a cause de guerres', mentioning that any
surplus was to go to her. She also decreed that any dispute
should be referred to 'our beloved and faithful councillors,

---

[1] A.L.A. E 211, accounts for the castellany of Touffou, 1348–51.
[2] Privilèges de la ville de Nantes, ed. La Nicollière-Teijeiro, pp. 8 f.

the men who hold our accounts', so that they might 'ordonner et les dictes choses esclarcir et declairer'.[1] Another stage in this development was reached with efforts to raise Blois's ransom in 1356–8 by means of a general *fouage* (hearth tax) on seigneuries and a levy on towns under Penthièvre control. It is at this moment that a receiver general for the duchy appears alongside the Duke's personal treasurer,[2] whilst the existence of specialized financial officers, together with their records, is further implied by mandates such as one sent in 1360 by Blois which ordered 'the men presently holding our accounts and their successors to make allowance in future accounts for whatever the receiver of Suscinio pays at this present time'.[3]

As far as can be told, the Anglo-Breton administration did not attempt to impose general taxation. Its revenue was mainly extradomanial, derived from individual castellanies by sums, known as 'ransoms', raised at twice-yearly intervals on parishes within the castellany. The ransoms were usually calculated in money, but could be exacted in kind or in services as well.[4] Accounts for some of the castellanies and their ransom districts survive after 1358. Certain traditional revenues, such as *brefs*, were let out at farm.[5] But it is extremely difficult to trace pre-war domanial income in these accounts and ransoms; war-time expedients, devised by the Anglo-Breton government and their agents, did not finally cease functioning until Michaelmas 1365.[6] Perhaps the most important Anglo-Montfortist precedent was the use of Vannes as an administrative centre, though even before 1341 it seems that some ducal archives were being kept there.[7]

---

[1] Ibid., pp. 10 f.

[2] *Preuves*, i. 1522, 1532, 1454–5 (redated by Borderie, iii. 561 n.).

[3] *Cartulaire du Morbihan*, no. 543.

[4] Accts. Var. 174/4 and 5, 175/4, 176/9. For these ransoms see K. Fowler, 'Les finances et la discipline dans les armées anglaises en France au xivᵉ siècle', *Les Cahiers vernonnais*, iv (1964), 63–4, and below, pp. 163 ff.

[5] A.L.A. E 201 (1364), printed below, Appendix of Documents, no. 1.

[6] *Preuves*, i. 1594.

[7] The Anglo-Breton treasurer of the duchy was also receiver of Vannes although he usually exercised his office by deputy (Accts. Var. 175/1, nos. 11, 20–3, 27–9, etc.); cf. *Privilèges de la ville de Nantes*, ed. La Nicollière-Teijeiro, p. 6.

The reign of John IV saw a major change in the organization and sources of ducal revenue. It has been categorically stated that this change occurred almost immediately after Auray; but the only documents quoted in support of the argument come from the 1390s. By then a *chambre des comptes* was fully institutionalized with its own officers, records, procedures, and administrative competence.[1] M. Pocquet du Haut-Jussé, summarizing largely from the work of Planiol, has likewise described the *chambre* at Vannes with its president and auditors examining the accounts of the receiver-general of the duchy, domanial officers, and local receivers of *fouages*. He emphasized that members of the *chambre* were not mere collectors but had considerable powers of discretion, free from ducal interference, to examine complaints and take decisions on how revenue should be levied and collected. A limitation to their powers was ensured by right of appeal to the *Parlement* of Brittany.[2]

Naturally these summaries gloss over changes which took place during a number of years and give a rather false picture of the early completeness and unity of *chambre* practice under John IV. Yet it is clear that Fourmont's bald assertion is largely correct. A *chambre des comptes* can be found before 1373. It had its seat at Vannes in a building formerly owned by the Sires de Largoët, which had become in turn the *hôtel de monnaie* of John II and the *chambre des comptes* of John IV before a final transformation into Vannes town hall.[3] Sessions for account appear to have been usually at Easter and All Saints, although individual accounts were still allowed to run for an indeterminate length of time. In May 1367 William, Lord Latimer, referred to his 'derrain acompt fait a Vannes le xv^e jour de Novembre [1365]'.[4] In 1368 Colin de Tours, receiver of the castellany of Champtoceaux, petitioned the '*Chambre de Comptes*' for the payment of his wages for the last six years, and in October 1369, apparently after an examination of documents brought

---

[1] Fourmont, op. cit., pp. 4-8.

[2] Pocquet, Lot et Fawtier, i. 281-3, utilizing Planiol, *Histoire des institutions de la Bretagne*, iii. 231-301.

[3] *Congrès archéologique de France*, lxxxi, p. 433.

[4] Appendix of Documents, no. 2.

before them in the *chambre*, the clerks pronounced on his case.[1] In 1373, at a time when normal ducal governmental practices were being abandoned because of the Duke's desperate political situation,[2] a commission of *'gens de comptes'*, sitting in the seneschal's court at Nantes, audited Tours's accounts since 22 November 1369 and collated them in a register, just as they had done on a similar occasion three years before.[3] It is probably not coincidental that a number of important transactions between the Duke and his English mercenaries were sealed at Vannes in November 1365 and November 1366.[4] In 1367 a reference to 'the dean of Nantes, Mr. Guillaume Soude and Jean le Barbu holding the accounts' indicates the identity of some members of the *chambre*.[5]

Once again, therefore, Brittany is seen to be in the mainstream of administrative developments in provincial France. Louis II, Duke of Bourbon, established a *chambre* at Moulins in November 1374, probably inspired by royal practice and by the *chambre* in the county of Forez, which he had attached to his domain only two years previously.[6] John, Duke of Berry, founded his *chambre* at Bourges in 1379, and Philip, Duke of Burgundy, reformed the administration of his unwieldy apanage by dividing his territories and establishing *chambres* at Lille and Dijon in 1386.[7] These royal cadets

[1] A.L.A. E 232 (petition c. 1368); ibid. (1 Oct. 1369, recognition of Colin's claims from 9 May 1367 to 22 Nov. 1369).   [2] See below, pp. 72 ff.

[3] A.L.A. E 233 (26 Mar. 1373); cf. ibid. E 232 (6 Dec. 1369).

[4] Ibid. E 154 (8 Nov. 1365), agreement between John IV and Robert Knolles for the exchange of Fougeray and Château-Blanc castles for ones on the ducal demesne; B.N. MS. Nouv. acq. fr. 5216, no. 2 (1 Nov. 1365), agreement between John IV and Hugh Calveley on the extent of the Duke's debts to Calveley; A.L.A. E 154 (14 Nov. 1366), settlement of ducal debts to Walter Huet.

[5] B.N. MS. Nouv. acq. fr. 5216, no. 7 (21 May 1367). The Dean of Nantes was Guillaume Paris, an old Blois servant and possible chancellor of the divided duchy (Planiol, *Hist. des institutions*, iii. 163). Soude was John's personal treasurer. Jean le Barbu was a Breton clerk who had served John before 1364 (Accts. Var. 175/1, no. 65, 20 Sept. 1360, payment to him as councillor of the Duke).

[6] Perroy, Lot et Fawtier, i. 289 ff., and A. Leguai, 'Un aspect de la formation des États princiers en France à la fin du moyen âge: les réformes administratives de Louis II, duc de Bourbon', *Le Moyen Âge*, lxx (1964), 61–2.

[7] R. Lacour, *Le Gouvernement de l'apanage de Jean, duc de Berry, 1360–1416*, pp. 262–9; Vaughan, *Philip the Bold*, pp. 116 ff. The Duke of Anjou also had a *chambre des comptes* at Angers, which was being repaired in 1368 (A. Joubert, *Étude sur les comptes de Mace Darné, maître des œuvres de Louis Ier, duc d'Anjou*, p. 29).

and favourites, unlike John IV, had been able to call on royal expertise in a very practical manner by inviting or seconding royal officials to reform and staff their administrations.[1] For Brittany no firm date for the origin of the *chambre* can be given, but it obviously antedates some of those of John's princely equals.

Unfortunately there is not sufficient evidence to enable us to follow the history of the Breton *chambre des comptes* and its functions and officers with the precision that is possible elsewhere in France. But there is little doubt that it played a role in ducal administration equal in significance to that ascribed to the *chambre* in the Bourbonnais, for example.[2] Some illustrations of its consultative and executive operations have been given in relation to its dealings with Colin de Tours. The documentary evidence which survives for the period 1365–73 is small—Vannes was ransacked by the Vicomte de Rohan in 1373.[3] The evidence does suggest, however, that the period was fruitful in administrative advances, at least in the establishment of the *chambre*, whose practices had hardened into routine by the 1380s.

It has been necessary to stress the primary importance of aspects of financial administration in Brittany as an index of increasing ducal control and competence, and to set the institutions in their true French context for one other purpose. The developments traced above are seen as natural and indigenous ones. Despite the twenty years of English occupation and John IV's use of officers, both English and Breton, who had experience of Westminster methods,[4] the basic pattern of administration which emerges after Auray is the traditional Breton one. The English had not left John a model centralized government, since the Anglo-Breton treasurer was not solely responsible to Westminster for

---

[1] Vaughan, op. cit., p. 116.

[2] Leguai, *Le Moyen Âge*, lxx (1964), 64–5.

[3] 'Anglo-French Negotiations at Bruges 1374–77', ed. É. Perroy, *Camden Miscellany*, xix (1952), 34.

[4] Jean le Barbu (cf. above, p. 29, n. 5) was in London in 1361 (Issue Roll 408 m. 35), as was Soude in 1362 (Issue Roll 409 mm. 38 (22 Feb.), 44 (21 Mar.), and 45 (4 Apr.)). Jean de Lomene, Archdeacon of Vannes in 1360, had similar knowledge of English methods (Accts. Var. 175/1, nos. 59–61 and 65, payments to him in 1360). For Thomas Melbourne, see below, pp. 32, 38.

ducal revenues.[1] The Duke continued to use local receivers of the demesne, based on castellany units. They accounted for revenues in money and kind, as, for example, did the Duke of Berry's receivers.[2] And just as English Exchequer procedures and techniques do not seem to have penetrated into ducal administration, neither do English Chancery practices. The Duke, for example, continued to use a one-sided great seal, countersealed in the French manner by a small seal on the reverse.[3] The English indenture, a very characteristic document, was only used by the Duke when contracting with Englishmen, and even then only on very rare occasions, despite the administrative convenience of such an instrument not merely for military but also for civil purposes.[4] The use of notaries to publish or exemplify documents was a common feature of the ducal administration, just as it was in other parts of France. Their use in England was very much more restricted.[5] These small but significant details contribute to the picture of John reverting to traditional methods of administration. Like Charles de Blois, John had his private treasurer, whose accounts in the late 1370s were supervised and checked by a keeper of a counter-roll.[6] He also had his receiver-general, and it was

---

[1] Many of the castellans accounted directly with the King's chamber (Tout, *Chapters*, iv. 250).

[2] A.I.V. IF. 1111 (fragments of accounts for Auray castellany, 1366–9); A.L.A. E 232, E 233 (various financial documents, warrants, quittances, etc., for Champtoceaux; cf. the description of receipts at this castle in 1355–6, E. Bougouin, 'La navigation commerciale sur la Basse-Loire au milieu du xive siècle', *Rev. Hist.* clxxv (1935), 482–96); Lacour, op. cit., pp. 242 f.

[3] *Preuves*, ii, pl. 9, no. clxv; and Douët d'Arcq, *Collection des sceaux*, no. 546.

[4] I have found five indentures between the Duke and his servants in Brittany. See Appendix of Documents, no. 1; A.L.A. E 136, no. 5, an indenture between John IV and Thomas Fog for the keeping of Hennebont; ibid. E 142, an indenture between the Duke and Thomas Aldrewych to dwell with the Duke against all except the kings of England and France. These three examples date from the period 1362–4. The only other similar indentures found at Nantes are between Guillaume le Briz, ducal almoner, and Thomas Merdon, goldsmith, sealed on 12 May 1383 (A.L.A. E 209; cf. Borderie, iv. 131), and between John IV and Robert Elmet for the use of a ducal balinger kept at Brest by Elmet for 60 *écus* p.a. (ibid. E 162, 18 Dec. 1398).

[5] Cf. P. Chaplais, 'The Chancery of Guyenne, 1289–1453', *Studies Presented to Sir Hilary Jenkinson*, ed. J. Conway Davies, pp. 86–8.

[6] B.N. MS. Nouv. acq. fr. 5216, no. 5 (7 Sept. 1366), for Guillaume Soude acting as ducal treasurer; A.L.A. E 206 (counter-roll of Jankin Curteys for the expenses of the Duke's household, 1378–9).

this official, often confusingly referred to as treasurer or treasurer-general of Brittany, who was the most important officer in the ducal government apart from the chancellor. He was chiefly responsible for collecting and disbursing the *fouages* John was able to take.[1] His domination in financial matters, his control of the local receivers, and, in the case of Thomas Melbourne, receiver-general from 1365 to 1373, his close personal relationship with the Duke meant that he exercised a role comparable to that of Berry's treasurer-general or Bourbon's treasurer and receiver-general.[2] Indeed, Melbourne's importance in the ducal council makes it doubtful whether he was surveyed by that body in the way Bourbon's treasurer seems to have been. Although all financial mandates seem to have originated with the Duke himself, the receiver-general was competent to deal with problems arising from the interpretation and implementation of such mandates. He could on occasion exercise his office by deputy.[3] There is little evidence in this early period of his accounting at the *chambre des comptes*, though it is likely that he did so.

But if the organization of ducal financial affairs between 1365 and 1373 appears to stem directly from precedents of the Civil War period, the extension and increased incidence of the *fouage* as an extraordinary tax marks another significant stage of ducal progress from seigneurial to 'monarchical'[4] administration. Perhaps the best way to illustrate John's methods of imposing this tax is to take a specific example. On 7 March 1367 Jean, Vicomte de Rohan, recognized that he, together with the Sires de Laval and Châteaubriant and other nobles of the duchy, had consented to allow the

---

[1] Pocquet, Lot et Fawtier, i. 283.

[2] B.N. MS. Nouv. acq. fr. 5216, no. 5 (7 Sept. 1366), A.L.A. E 154 (Nov. 1366), and Appendix B, sections 3 and 4, below, pp. 216–17, for Melbourne acting as receiver-general. He may be the same man as Thomas Melbourne, rector of Howe, Norfolk, in 1351–2 (F. Blomefield, *An Essay towards a Topographical History of the County of Norfolk*, viii. 27). For his later ecclesiastical career in England see John le Neve, *Fasti Ecclesiae Anglicanae 1300–1541*, N.S., i, *Lincoln Diocese*, compiled by H. P. F. King (London 1962), p. 70; Pocquet, *Les Papes*, i. 392–3; Lacour, op. cit., pp. 168–71; and Leguai, *Le Moyen Âge*, lxx (1964), pp. 52 f.

[3] A.L.A. E 232 (10 Aug. 1372), Hochequin Thorp acting as Melbourne's deputy.

[4] A. de la Borderie, *Le Règne de Jean IV, 1364–99*, p. 5. La Borderie reserves 'monarchical' for changes after 1381.

Duke a *fouage* of one *écu d'or* on all their lands and men. The reason stated for this concession to John was his need of a loan (*pour cause des neccessitez que il a de chevance*). The levy was to be taken in two parts, half at the nativity of the Blessed Virgin (8 September) and half a year later. Rohan also sealed letters which allowed the Duke 'whenever he pleases, to commission his officers to inquire, at his own expense, into the number of hearths in each of our lands'. The *fouage* was to be raised on all Rohan's men 'without exception, apart from gentlemen, having men dwelling on their lands already contributing to the *fouage*, and poor people who because of their distress did not contribute to the ransoms of a former time'. From the sums raised Rohan was to take 1,000 *écus* for his compliance.[1]

The *fouage* was thus raised by general consent in *Parlement* or by individual agreement with important seigneurs.[2] Sometimes it was collected by ducal officers, sometimes by seigneurial ones. Some classes, including seigneurs, clerks, and paupers, escaped the levy, whilst the Duke, like the King of France, had usually to release to his seigneurs a proportion of the proceeds.[3] But although the *fouage* was in theory a gracious aid, the Duke's evident necessities, especially his military commitments, allowed him to demand, and take *fouages* with a regularity and intensity which ensured him an income more commensurate with his requirements than that furnished to himself and his predecessors by their demesnes. Despite later royal protests, the principle of *fouages*, taken when the Duke needed money, had been established by 1373.[4] It is little wonder

---

[1] *Cartulaire du Morbihan*, no. 556.

[2] Planiol, *Hist. des institutions*, iii. 273 ff.

[3] Cf. Bib. mun. Nantes, fonds Bizeul, MS. 1690, no. 5 (14 July 1384), letters patent of Charles VI guaranteeing Olivier de Clisson that the aids recently taken on his lands in Poitou would not be taken as a precedent, with similar letters from John IV exempting Clisson's Breton lands from a *fouage* in 1393 (B.N. MS. Nouv. acq. fr. 7621, p. 56).

[4] B.N. MS. fr. 22330, pp. 531–3, appointment of captain of Redon saving the rights of the abbey and 'ne voulons pas estre retarde un quart d'ecu qui nous est octroye par le dit Abbe sur chacun des dits feux a estre paye devant le saint Michel prochain pour ayder la deliverance du fort du Becherel au commun profit de tout le pais...', letters dated 7 May 1369; Pocquet, 'Les faux États de Bretagne de 1315 et les premiers États de Bretagne', *B.E.C.* lxxxvi (1925), 402–4, for royal criticisms of John's taxation.

that a recent writer discussing the ducal demesne during the period 1342–81 concluded: 'Durant cette période de quarante ans le duché de Bretagne cessa pratiquement d'être administré.'[1] This may well be true for the demesne now that new resources were available to the Duke, although dissent from this judgement may be registered with regard to other aspects of John's activities from 1365 to 1373.

Further, it may be noted that the period during which the *fouage* was established in Brittany corresponds to that described by Fawtier for Valois France as 'La période décisive pour l'histoire de l'établissement de l'impôt . . .'.[2] In many parts of France, on the royal domain, in Brittany, in Béarn and Gascony, to mention but a few, the 1360s witnessed a general response to a financial crisis facing all governments.[3] Fawtier's comments on Valois France have an equal validity for Breton history: 'Pendant ces années et longtemps après encore, nul n'a eu l'idée que les subsides accordés pour parer à une situation tragique, mais qu'on voulait croire passagère, s'enracineraient et deviendraient un jour ordinaires et permanents.'[4] Unlike the royal apanagists who had to use royal authority to raise taxes on their lands although they were allowed a percentage of the tax, John IV, like Gaston Fébus of Béarn, used his ducal authority. This was inevitable. Unlike the royal princes whose finances were now being underpinned to some extent by royal pensions and gifts,[5] the Duke of Brittany relied for his main extra-domanial income on the *fouage*, a tax which gave him a rough financial parity with his fellow princes.

But it should not be forgotten that John also took full advantage of rights which had been established before 1341. He charged towns dues on goods entering and leaving them, and did this solely by ducal authority.[6] The fiscal acquisitiveness of the Duke brought him into conflict with several Breton bishops whose episcopal towns looked to

[1] Renaudin, 'Les domaines', p. 160.

[2] Lot et Fawtier, ii. 256.

[3] P. Tucoo-Chala, *Gaston Fébus et la vicomté de Béarn, 1343–1391*, pp. 136–9; Perroy, *The Hundred Years War*, pp. 159, 162; cf. Lacour, op. cit., pp. 250–7.

[4] Lot et Fawtier, ii. 256.

[5] Lacour, op. cit., p. 235; Vaughan, op. cit., pp. 230 f.

[6] *Preuves*, i. 1603; cf. Planiol, *Hist. des institutions*, iii. 233.

them for protection.[1] It is unfortunate that the only accounts for John's exercise of *régale*—the enjoyment of episcopal temporal rights during a vacancy—come from the period after 1381. John, like his predecessors, had exercised this right before then, and a valuable one it could be, as the later accounts witness.[2] John also anxiously maintained seigneurial and ducal rights over the coasts and rivers of the duchy, a particularly lucrative source of revenue with the increase in trade that occurred in Brittany during his reign.[3]

Earlier Dukes had achieved a monopoly in minting coins in Brittany, although their currencies were controlled by the King.[4] Both sides during the Civil War had exploited this right, although one commentator has said: 'toutes ces monnaies sont d'une frappe détestable à peine lisible.'[5] Nevertheless, some gold coins bearing the legend 'Dei gratia' in the Duke's title were struck by Blois, and John IV seems to have followed this precedent.[6] In this the Dukes of Brittany paralleled the activities of the Dukes of Burgundy. In both provinces there was a steady and profitable emission

---

[1] Pocquet, *Les Papes*, i. 385–6, 394.

[2] A. de la Borderie, *Nouveau Recueil d'actes inédits des ducs et princes de Bretagne*, xxvi, nos. 62, 92 (1306–8); A.L.A. E 211, accounts for the temporalities of Rennes during a vacancy from 26 July 1383 until 22 Sept. 1384 show the receiver accounting for 10,072 *l.br.*; ibid., accounts for Nantes from 1 July 1392 until Mar. 1393, likewise show large sums of money passing through the receiver's hands, much of which was used by the Duke to pay his officers, etc., e.g. 12 *l.br.* 10s. to Jean Carnac 'nouvellement retenu pour la garde de lartillerie de mondit Seignour', and 133 *l.br.* 'A plusours personnes par mandement de Mons. le duc du derrain jour daoust lan mil iii^c iiii^xx et doze pour plusours enprises et reparacions artilleries et autres choses necessaires ou chastel de la tour neuve de Nantes par lavisement et ordenance de Gilequin de Lebiest cappitaine dudit lieu'.

[3] Bougouin, *Rev. Hist.* clxxv (1935); P. Jeulin, *L'Évolution du port de Nantes*, pp. 63, 66; Borderie, iv. 126.

[4] *Preuves*, i. 1258 (11 Nov. 1315), order from Louis X to John III not to mint more money for the moment because of complaints against his coinage which the King wished to investigate. As early as the thirteenth century the Duke had reserved the crime of striking false money in the duchy to his own judgement (Oheix, op. cit., p. 76).

[5] A. Blanchet and A. Dieudonné, *Manuel de numismatique française* (4 vols., Paris 1912–36), iv. 127; see also A. Bigot, *Essai sur les monnaies du royaume et duché de Bretagne* (Paris 1857), pp. 124 ff., closely followed by F. Poey d'Avant, *Monnaies féodales de France* (3 vols., Paris 1858–62), i. 89–136, and E. Caron, *Monnaies féodales françaises* (Paris 1882), pp. 35 ff., for descriptions of Breton coins during this period.

[6] Cf. Poey d'Avant, op. cit. i, nos. 464–74, 614, 657, etc.; Touchard, *Le Commerce maritime breton*, pp. 97–100.

of coinage controlled by the Dukes.[1] Guillaume de Saint-André, in his eulogy on John, wrote:

> Et fist faire monnoye nouvelle,
> A soult tres-bonne et tres-belle,
> Car de son droit le povoit faire,
> En son pays est Prince et maire.[2]

The exploitation of this and the other resources mentioned above produced a wealth that allowed John to sustain some of the pretensions claimed for him by his eulogist.

In yet another field, that of law, John showed himself aware of tradition whilst conscious of the need to streamline processes in order to exploit the considerable rewards accruing from judicial fees. Certainly, after 1365 the judicial hierarchy from the local ducal and seigneurial courts to the seneschals' courts, and from there to Rennes (or Nantes) or *Parlement*, was to be seen in the duchy.[3] The seneschals' courts were also important for the large amount of civil business in the form of contract-witnessing that was transacted in them. Between these courts and the Duke's council passed numerous letters and orders concerning inquiries into every kind of right.[4] Business in the few years after Auray was heavy, because there were many war claims to be adjudicated, particularly from religious foundations and others who had been unable to defend their rights in the civil commotions of the previous twenty years.[5] There is thus a very noticeable increase in governmental business transacted in these years, especially when we allow for the

---

[1] C. Martin, 'The Enforcement of the Rights of the Kings of France in the Duchy and County of Burgundy, 1285–1363', pp. 187 ff.; Poey d'Avant, op. cit. i. 135; Bigot, op. cit., p. 167, suggests that the use of the Breton arms and other heraldic devices on the coins of John IV is yet one more sign of Breton particularism, although Blanchet and Dieudonné, op. cit. iv. 128, show that there were inquiries into Breton imitations of royal coinage during the 1380s and 1390s. For a document of the reign of John III dealing with a similar situation, see A.N. J 240, no. 25.

[2] Ed. Charrière, ll. 1713–16.

[3] Texier, *Étude sur la cour ducale*, pp. 75–86. Renaudin, 'Les domaines', p. 82, questions whether this judicial hierarchy existed at the end of the thirteenth century.

[4] For example, *Preuves*, i. 1604, 1621–2, and *Cartulaire du Morbihan*, nos. 552, 561; B.M. Add. Ch. 8417 (14 June 1371) for a very fine impression of the seal of contracts at Nantes.

[5] *Cartulaire du Morbihan*, nos. 549, 551; *Cartulaire de . . . Saint-Sulpice-la-Forêt*, nos. v, xiv.

loss of whole series of records, such as those concerning ducal finances. Lawyers and notaries seldom feared unemployment.

In the *Parlement* of Brittany the Duke already possessed an appeal court, which a number of his contemporaries had to create for their own territories (for example, the *grands jours* established by Berry in 1370, the *jours généraux du Bourbonnais* created at about the same time, and the *jours généraux de Beaune* reorganized by Philip of Burgundy in 1372).[1] The main external pressure necessitating this response was princely fear of the *Parlement* of Paris, although there was also an element of convenience in this organization, even for the royal administration. Royal co-operation, for example, in setting up Berry's appeal court, is notable.[2] But in general these rulers, like the Duke of Guyenne (before 1337) and the Count of Flanders, sought to interpose another layer in the succession of courts leading to Paris, thereby attempting to cut out many appeals that had so frequently offered opportunities for royal interference in their territories.[3] Appeals, even when both sides recognized their legality, had been a most delicate barometer of royal and princely feelings, giving rise to endless friction. Thus in Brittany the sovereignty and ultimate *ressort* of the Paris *Parlement* were recognized in John IV's reign, as they had been in 1341, but in practice appeals were few.[4] This was partly because the balance of interests, as in the reign of John III, allowed the King to return appeals to ducal courts, and partly because the Duke actively discouraged such appeals.[5] Only the most powerful could hope to withstand ducal pressure against appealing. Besides its judicial business, which was being delegated to a commission of legal experts by the

[1] Cf. Leguai, *Le Moyen Âge*, lxx (1964), 60 f.
[2] Berry's *grands jours* were originally conducted by a commission sent from the *Parlement* of Paris (ibid.).
[3] For Guyenne, P. Chaplais in *Studies Presented to Sir Hilary Jenkinson*, pp. 64 ff.; for Flanders, R. van Caeneghem, 'Les appels flamands au parlement de Paris au moyen âge', *Études d'histoire du droit privé offertes à Pierre Petot*, pp. 61–8.
[4] *Preuves*, ii. 456–9.
[5] Ibid. i. 1244–5 (18 Sept. 1313); Texier, op. cit., p. 177 (5 Jan. 1367), Charles V returns case of *Bonabé de Rougé, Sire de Derval* v. *Guy, Sire de Laval and Robert Knolles* to ducal courts; for John's attack on the Count of Alençon when he appealed to Paris, see Pocquet, *B.E.C.* lxxxvi (1925), 402 ff.

end of John's reign,[1] the *Parlement* of Brittany met to
discuss financial and political matters. Its members were the
direct vassals of the Duke afforced by the members of his
council, and it was only after 1379 that any traces of consultation with representatives of the third estate occur.[2]
Nevertheless, the *Parlement* was called quite frequently in
the period before 1373 because of the Duke's extremely
heavy financial commitments. Such meetings were as
much political and propagandist as constitutional. But while
application of the *fouage*, for example, reveals that there were
theoretical limitations to ducal power and that seigneurial
jurisdictions were respected, the ducal council was concerning itself increasingly with every type of problem. Recourse
to it, rather than to *Parlement*, seems to have been encouraged by the establishment of *maîtres des requêtes* who
made preliminary inquiries before passing on the most
difficult cases to the council.[3] The *maîtres* came from the
inner circle of John's advisers.

The main executive instrument of government was thus
the Duke's council. It has been claimed that only the
Chancellor was indispensable for its meetings.[4] Some other
councillors may have held positions in it *ex officio*. The clerks,
who recorded council decisions in the form of mandatory
letters or grants, were usually from a small group in the
Duke's chancery. But membership was not fixed in size,
and all the evidence suggests that in Brittany, as elsewhere,
it was the Duke's pleasure and requirements that dictated
the composition of the council.[5] A specific councillor's oath
has not yet been discovered, but Thomas Melbourne's
fealty to John IV on 20 November 1368[6] covers the matter
of state secrets and may well indicate a typical declaration
by ducal councillors. In theory all the great seigneurs might
expect to be consulted at times other than during a *Parlement*, and some instances of them witnessing documents

---

[1] Lewis, *Past and Present*, 23 (1962), 7 n. 34.

[2] Pocquet, loc. cit.

[3] Planiol, *Hist. des institutions*, iii. 157, quoting Arch. dép. Morbihan, St. Guildas
4 (now *Cartulaire du Morbihan*, no. 551, 4 Nov. 1365).

[4] Planiol, op. cit. iii. 155.

[5] Cf. Bourbon's council, Leguai, op. cit., p. 50.

[6] Appendix of Documents, no. 3.

because they were present with the Duke can be cited; but in practice it was usual for the same councillors and officials to witness document after document.[1] It must thus be assumed that those whose names recur frequently formed the 'working' council which followed the Duke in his itinerations.

From the scrappy information available, it is clear that John consulted a wide cross-section of his subjects in council.[2] Naturally some of the great seigneurs who had served Blois and yet survived the *épuration* of the Civil War were not prominent in John's service. But some were,[3] and from the lower strata of Breton society John drew almost without distinction from those who had served him before Auray and those who had served Blois. The new allegiance of John's Chancellor, the born-trimmer Hugh Montrelais, Bishop of Saint-Brieuc since 1357, probably explains the presence of a number of Blois clerks in John's chancery.[4] Likewise in the council John drew indiscriminately on former friends and enemies. It is certainly not true, as MM. Planiol and Pocquet du Haut-Jussé suggest, that John's council was dominated by Englishmen.[5] From a pool of about thirty to forty possible members of the small inner council, only about five to eight men were English, and of

---

[1] Taking the documents in the *Cartulaire du Morbihan* as a sample, for the period 1365–73, the Dean of Nantes (Guillaume Paris) witnessed four times (nos. 549, 567, 574, 575), the Dean of Clisson twice (nos. 560, 567), Jean le Barbu twice (nos. 549, 567), Alain Raoulin twice (nos. 567, 574), Thomas Melbourne thrice (nos. 557, 567, 575), whilst the Vicomte de Rohan and Guy, Sire d'Assérac, did so only once each (nos. 567, 572).

[2] See Table of Allegiances, col. 2, below, pp. 57–9.

[3] Pocquet, op. cit. i. 350, for Guy, Sire de Laval, and Charles de Dinan, Sire de Montafiliant. Laval's father was killed at La Roche Derrien whilst fighting for Blois, and his brother was captured there (Anselme, iii. 628). Dinan's father was killed at Auray (ibid. viii. 578).

[4] Pocquet, op. cit. i. 335, 350, 371, 401, for Montrelais. Guillaume Paris, Jean Talliandier, Guillaume and Geofrey le Voyer were Blois's clerks (cf. *Foedera*, iii. 360); whilst Guy Cleder was important in Joan de Penthièvre's service (Pocquet, op. cit. i. 380).

[5] Planiol, op. cit. iii. 155, and Pocquet, op. cit. i. 370. M. Pocquet du Haut-Jussé speaks of Guy, Sire d'Assérac, as 'l'un des rares conseillers bretons de Jean IV' (p. 370); yet there are references to at least twenty Breton councillors of the Duke in the period 1365–73 mentioned pp. 350–92. Typical of attendances in council is the list of those present on 13 May 1370 (B.N. MS. fr. 22339 fol. 50ᵛ); it consisted of the Abbot of Prières, the Deans of Nantes and Clisson, Mᵉ Alain Raoulin, Jean le Barbu, Jean Kermolay, and Mace Raguenel, all Bretons.

these only Latimer (before 1368) and Melbourne held positions of real authority.[1] The same proportions of Bretons to Englishmen can be discovered by examining lists of office-holders or the names of those entrusted with such important strategic items as the castles.

Yet there was one place where the Duke was surrounded by Englishmen, and that was his household. Despite the departmentalization and specialization that have been discerned in other aspects of government from 1365, it is necessary to remember that much still depended on the active participation of the Duke. In such an organization the household retained considerable importance. Charles V was worried by John's reliance on Englishmen, and the Duke sought to excuse himself by pointing out that he had been brought up in England and that automatically some Englishmen had become household officers. He had married an English wife and she also had a small retinue of her countrymen as servants.[2] But what was the size and influence of this household?

The only occasion on which John had a large entourage before 1362 was for his journey to Saint-Omer in 1361. On this diplomatic embassy Edward III footed a considerable bill in order that his protégé might not be overshadowed by the Penthièvre representatives. Over seventy people accompanied John.[3] But after 1362 it is more difficult to find evidence for the size of John's household. Such evidence as there is suggests that there had been little increase in size over that of John II's household, which in 1305 comprised about eighty members.[4] A reorganization

---

[1] Planiol, op. cit. iii. 154, and A. de la Borderie, *Les Neuf Barons de Bretagne*, pp. lii–lvii, for ducal council numbers. See Table of Allegiances for further details, below, pp. 57–9.

[2] *Preuves*, ii. 34.

[3] Accts. Var. 314/16, accounts for the journey undertaken between 24 Mar. and 19 Apr. 1361. Over £579. 14s. 10d. was spent.

[4] Pocquet, Lot et Fawtier, i. 273. In 1305 there were 31 esquires forming a ducal bodyguard. A similar number was said to accomplish the same service in 1368 (D. Secousse, *Mémoire pour servir à l'histoire de Charles II, roi de Navarre*, pp. 380 f.). There were 7 household clerks in 1305. 2 papal chaplains and 6 clerks were the subject of a petition to the Pope in 1378 (*Cal. Papal Petitions, 1342–1419*, 547); they were William Wells, confessor, Jean Moysan and Thomas Melbourne, papal chaplains, and Jean Cosiere, Guillaume Tellet, Jean Choisan, Guillaume

of the household in 1405 for John V similarly suggests that John IV, although not miserly, had not spent extravagantly on surrounding himself with court officers and flunkeys. Even in the 1420s, when many household duties were shared in rotation, only about 250 people seem to have been attached to the court.[1] In John IV's time there was less duplication, but the Duke had his special officers, his minstrels, his manors and gardens.[2] The organization of the household into a number of domestic departments (six can be found in 1370) was otherwise similar to that found in other noble households in France and England at this period.[3]

The only slightly remarkable feature thus remains the number of Englishmen in John's household: two masters of the household, John Basset and Adam Hoke; John Curteys, the ducal butler; Norman Basset, John Wodeward, Adam Blakemore, and John FitzNicol—all these held positions during the period 1365–73.[4] It cannot be

Morice, and Jean Huguet, clerks of Nantes and Saint-Malo dioceses (Arch. Vat., *Segreto, Registri delle Supliche, Clement VII antipapa*, xlviii, fol. 208ᵛ. I owe this reference to Miss Lesley Steer). In 1402 there were 6 chaplains and 2 clerks in the household (Planiol, op. cit. iii. 58).

[1] Pocquet, Lot et Fawtier, i. 279, and Planiol, op. cit. iii. 54.

[2] Pocquet, *Les Papes*, i. 368, for ducal almoner; for the ducal confessor, p. 40, n. 4 above; for ducal avener, A.L.A. E 232 (23 July 1367), a quittance issued by Guillaume Hurtaut for 140 loads of hay; for Henri le Parisi, master of the Duke's hunting, see F. Bruel, 'Inventaire de meubles . . .', *B.E.C.* lxvi (1905), 203 n.; for ducal minstrels, see E. Izarn, *Le Compte des recettes et dépenses du roi de Navarre en France*, p. 150. In a moment of crisis the Duke solaced himself by ordering them to play louder (Planiol, op. cit. iii. 124). For manors and gardens, see Borderie, iv. 133, and Planiol, op. cit. iii. 66–7.

[3] A.I.V. IF. IIII (1366–72), a fragment of household accounts showing a division of the household into the Pantry, Buttery, Kitchen, Poulterer's department, Scullery, and Spicery. The Richmond accounts (ibid. E 117) show a similar division. For Berry's household, Lacour, op. cit., pp. 148–53. For a sumptuous English household of the same period, see M. Aston, *Thomas Arundel*, pp. 234, 410 ff.

[4] A.L.A. E 204, and *Preuves*, i. 1611, both 1366, for Basset. An old *routier* who had served with the Anglo-Navarrese companies (Cherest, *L'Archiprêtre*, p. 393) and with Chandos in 1361–2 (Froissart, ed. Lettenhove, xviii. 441, and *Foedera*, iii. 656), Basset received protections to stay abroad in the Black Prince's service in 1364 and 1365 (*Foedera*, iii. 719, and Gascon Roll 77 m. 1), and so probably came into ducal service with Chandos just before Auray. Hoke had come to Brittany in the company of Roger David (see below, p. 49) and by 1367 was captain of Suscinio, remaining in ducal service until 1374 at least (Treaty Roll 32 m. 6; Plaine, *Procès*, p. 345; and *Foedera*, iii. 1009). For Curteys, see *C.P.R.* *1367–70*, 133, and ibid. *1381–5*, 491. In Joan Holland's will he is referred to as her

denied, either, that some of these men, fifth columnists according to Charles V's calculations, were involved in very important secret negotiations which John held after 1369, although it seems that their loyalties lay with the Duke rather than with England.[1] However, it will almost certainly remain impossible to weigh the true significance of this English complexion of the Duke's immediate entourage. Some household officers did hold strategically important posts—FitzNicol, Admiral of Brittany in 1370, is a case in point.[2] But evidence of grants and rewards to them does not suggest undue partiality by the Duke, and the more important governmental tasks were carried out only after advice had been obtained from the council. The making of foreign policy involved many of the most influential of John's Breton advisers, and it is, indeed, possible to trace the replacement of some Englishmen by Bretons. Robert Neville, Marshal of Brittany in 1365–6, for example, had been succeeded by the old Blois supporter Sylvestre de la Feuillée, and it was not English captains deserting the Duke in 1373 who made his position hopeless but Bretons who turned *en masse* to Charles V.[3]

The role of the household in the formation of policy as well as its position in Brittany remain therefore somewhat obscure. This obscurity illustrates the difficulties surrounding a correct assessment of John's attitudes in the years after Auray. On the one hand he was trying to balance his respect for the past, his obligations to Edward III and his English servants; whilst on the other he was trying to come to terms with the present, with the need for efficient government and for selecting trustworthy servants without antagonizing his former opponents. The employment of men from both sides of the scale, in both public and private capacities, was a realistic if misunderstood policy.

servant (A.L.A. E 24). *C.P.R. 1367–70*, 130 (Norman Basset); ibid. *1370–4*, 91 (Curteys, Wodeward, and Blakemore); Izarn, op. cit., pp. 152, 382 (Hoke), and 136 (FitzNicol).

[1] See below, pp. 65ff.

[2] *C.P.M.R. 1364–81*, 123. He graduated from Chandos's service to that of the Duke (*Foedera*, iii. 444) and had been attached to the embassy of 1361 as a valet (Accts. Var. 314/16 m. 2).

[3] *Preuves*, i. 1602, 1605, for Neville. Pocquet, *Les Papes*, i. 389, for La Feuillée. For the desertions, see below, pp. 72ff.

It was misunderstood not only by Charles V but by Edward III; and this focuses attention on some aspects of the problem of Breton 'independence'. To La Borderie, John, was for the first twenty years of his reign, a convinced Anglophile.[1] He orientated his policies to suit the whims of Edward III. He generously rewarded Englishmen in his service. He relied on their advice. He married into the English royal circle, and he fled to England when his people turned against him in 1373. No service he could do for England did he fail to perform. Much of this summary cannot be gainsaid. John's reliance on Englishmen had steadily increased between 1362 and 1364. It was with some justification that instructions issued by Edward III to an envoy in 1366 were highlighted by La Borderie as giving an insight into English dominance in ducal affairs.[2] Edward was continuing to treat John as a minor unfit to manage his own government. This intrusion, so La Borderie argued, was a slight on the sovereign powers of the Duke and a continuation of unwarranted and unwanted interference. It was also a flagrant breach of the Anglo-French treaty of 1360. But after quoting the instructions and a few of the most notable examples of English rewards in the duchy, La Borderie passed on to the politics of the war period, when John's clash of allegiance became acute.

Looked at more carefully, Lambert's instructions reveal a sight which was disturbing to English eyes, and one which scarcely justifies the picture given of John's anglophilia. Edward III feared, and his fears had some justification in fact, that John was placing fortresses in the hands of Bretons

[1] Borderie, iv. 5 ff.

[2] Ibid. 13, where the instructions are printed from a Bréquigny transcript. Two exemplars survive (B.M. MS. Cott. Claudius D. III, fol. 111, old foliation fol. 86, printed in Froissart, ed. Lettenhove, xviii. 480, and Cott. Julius B. VI, fol. 5). The dating of this document has caused some confusion, because only Edward's thirty-ninth regnal year is specified. But the clerk Lambert can be identified with Lambert de Trekingham, who, as John's messenger, was in England in Feb. 1366 (B.N. MS. Nouv. acq. fr. 5216, no. 3). Trekingham was yet one more Chandos follower in ducal service (*Foedera*, iii. 444). John IV petitioned the Pope for him in 1363 (*Cal. Papal Petitions 1342–1419*, 420). On his later career see John le Neve, *Fasti Ecclesiae Anglicanae, 1300–1541*, N.S., vii, *Chichester Diocese*, compiled by Joyce M. Horn (London 1964), p. 8, and ibid., N.S., iii, *Salisbury Diocese*, compiled by Joyce M. Horn (London 1962), p. 48.

whom Edward automatically assumed to be disloyal. The
implication of Edward's peremptory request that neither
Brest, Saint-Mathieu, nor any other port should be delivered
to Breton guardians was that the position obtained by the
Anglo-Montfortists before 1362 should not be sacrificed.[1]
This emphasized Edward's economic and military interest
in the control of Brittany's western coastline. Further
concern was also expressed about John's conduct of his
government. Edward urged him not to rely too much on
Bretons but on Englishmen who had not failed him in the
past. The Duke, it was hoped, would treat them better in
the future: 'Item, que pour les causes susdictes le duc
monstre meillour amour, et face meilloure chere en temps
avenir a les Engleys, qu'il n'ad fait par avant; car le roi ad
entendu par tout plein des entrevenants que le duc, quant a
ce n'ad pas tout au point fait.' The inference is again clear.
John was not solely relying on their advice, but wisely, from
his standpoint, he was taking Bretons into his confidence.
This feature of John's government has already been demonstrated with regard to the council and those whom he
placed in charge of his castles. The evidence of Guillaume
de Saint-André, ducal secretary, chronicler, and apologist,
must always be used with caution because of its obvious
bias, but he thought it worthy of comment that immediately
after Auray John retained many Bretons and 'moult les
ama et les tient chiers'.[2] Evidence of later household appointments and the granting of *fief-rentes* also supports this view,
as does John's help to former enemies to discharge their
ransoms after Auray.[3]

It seems apparent that Edward wished to halt this reconciliation. Lambert was to offer the prospect of a summer in

[1] Matthew Gournay seems to have given up the captaincy of Brest sometime
between 1362 and 1364, possibly in exchange for the farm of the *brefs* at Bordeaux
and La Rochelle (Appendix of Documents, no. 1).   [2] Ed. Charrière, l. 1608.

[3] B. D. Lyon, *From Fief to Indenture, passim*, for general description of the *fief-
rente*. Homage was a key point of the agreement. Evan Charruel was granted a
certain unspecified rent and *bouche de cour* for household services in Feb. 1371
(A.L.A. E 142); ibid., 15 May 1371, the Duke granted Pierre de Lesnerac 200*l.br.*
p.a. as a *fief-rente*, and ibid., 1368 and 1370, a similar *fief-rente* for Sylvestre de la
Feuillée where no specific rent is mentioned. *Preuves*, i. 1581, obligation of Guy,
Vicomte de Fou, for 1,000 francs to John IV, who had paid Chandos to secure
Fou's release after Auray.

England with the thrills of the chase. Recognizing the harder realities of political life, Edward advised John on the construction of a council of regency during his absence. Two governors, both English of course, were to be appointed. John was aware of his obligations; some of the financial ones he was discharging at this very time.[1] But he was not prepared to leave Brittany for England, and in several other ways he manifested an independence of spirit that must have come as something of a surprise to Edward. Two aspects in particular reveal the trend of John's policy. His friendship and dependence on the Black Prince had begun soon after his return to Brittany in 1362. John had accompanied the Prince on a tour of Aquitaine and Poitou in the winter of 1363-4, and Edward had attempted to solve problems by bringing the contestants together at Poitiers on two occasions.[2] Thereafter more positive and partisan aid was given to John by Chandos's troops.[3] It was thus a natural step when, shortly after Guérande, a treaty of alliance between John IV and the Black Prince was arranged. It was sealed in the autumn of 1365; and probably sometime early in 1366, John married the Prince's stepdaughter, Joan Holland.[4] In the meantime the treaty, with the usual prolix protestations of aid and sustenance, did promise solid advantages in trading rights. The Prince also promised not to maintain any of John's enemies. Almost as common form, papal censure was invoked against any breaking of its terms. But the strongest guarantee lay in the interests of those

---

[1] See Appendix B, section 1, 6 Apr. 1366.

[2] J. Delpit, *Collection générale des documents français qui se trouvent en Angleterre*, p. 117, for John with the Black Prince at Agen on 12 Jan. 1364. He was with Edward at Poitiers in Nov. 1363 and in Feb. 1364, see p. 19, n. 1, above.

[3] Cf. Froissart, ed. Luce, vi, pp. lxviii, 150.

[4] A.L.A. E 119, no. 5 (20 June 1365), preliminary agreement which recited the terms of Brétigny-Calais with regard to the settlement of the Breton succession and confirmed that both parties (Black Prince and John IV) would adhere to it, saving their ligeance to France, except that the Prince would aid John 'a conquerir, garder et deffendre la dicte duche de Bretaingne et les droiz et choses a icelle appartenanz vers et contre touz nez et a naistre'. Ibid., no. 6 (7 Sept. 1365), of final version alliance. It is not clear whether John's ratification (Exch. Dip. Doc. 213) is for the first or the second agreement, because it is badly damaged. Borderie, iv. 13, says John and Joan Holland had been married in London by May 1366. But the marriage must have taken place by 26 Mar. 1366 (*Cal. Papal Letters*, iv. 54), and probably at Nantes (cf. Froissart, ed. Luce, vi. 182).

witnessing the agreement. The presence of a number of former Blois servants on this occasion indicates how correct were Edward III's fears of John's policy of appeasement.[1] The treaty was of considerable prestige value to John (without being too ambitious a start to his foreign policy), and it should have been acceptable to Edward III. But its corollary, John's marriage, seems to have taken place without the consultation rendered legally necessary by John's earlier agreements with Edward III, and, like the Prince's own marriage, may have been distasteful to the King.[2] Certainly his hold over the Duke was weakening.

The other notable feature of John's foreign policy was his relationship with France. After French mediation at Guérande, homage to Charles V was unavoidable. Some prevarication in this matter, as well as in the fulfilment of some of the terms agreed at Guérande, was only to be expected. But in the early autumn of 1366 John went to Paris to do homage.[3] The ceremony, conducted with full pomp, was not without incident. The homage owed for lands held by the Duke in France was undeniably liege. After accepting the Duke's excuses for earlier non-appearance, the royal advisers also accepted John's offer to do homage in the form in which his predecessors had done it. When he came forward, bare-headed, to kneel before the King, the Bishop of Saint-Brieuc read out a statement in French in which John acknowledged that he was doing homage 'modo et forma quibus illud prestare et facere consueverunt sui antecessores duces Britannie . . . offerens vobis os et manus'. The King took the Duke's hands between his own, kissed him, and thus completed the formal symbolism of liege homage.[4] But the formula used on this occasion,

[1] A.L.A. E 119, no. 6. Those present included Hugh Montrelais, Jean, Sire de Beaumanoir, Baldo Doria (cf. L. H. Labande, *Les Doria de France*, p. 42), Thomas de Fontenay, and Geoffrey le Fevre, who were Bretons or former Blois servants.

[2] J. Moisant, *Le Prince Noir en Aquitaine*, p. 73. The English King seems to have been completely ignorant of John's marriage—there is no reference to it in Lambert's instructions, as there surely would have been if Edward had wanted to remind the Duke of his obligations.

[3] *Preuves*, i. 1607–13; Planiol, *Hist. des institutions*, iii. 82; P. Jeulin, 'L'hommage de la Bretagne', *Annales de Bretagne*, xli (1934), 435–7.

[4] Cf. M. Bloch, *Feudal Society* (tr. L. A. Manyon, London 1961), pp. 145 ff., 216 ff.

despite the recitation of two former homages obviously liege, was ambiguous. The royal legal advisers recognized this and attempted to force the Bretons to define their position. Hugh Montrelais retorted that they had got what they asked for. The Breton version of the homage, transcribed in a late fourteenth-century hand at the back of the *Livre des Ostz*, is marginally glossed as simple homage.[1] The ceremonial had definitely been that of liege homage. Thus there is much to be said for the suggestion that John thought that he could give verbal satisfaction to Charles V and yet interpret his obligations merely as those of simple homage.[2] The evidence for events in December 1366, open to partisan interpretation, is equivocal. It is tempting to think that John's actions on this occasion owed much to a scene he had witnessed at Agen nearly three years before.

On 12 January 1364 Gaston Fébus of Béarn had acted in a rather similar way when doing liege homage for Gavardan and Marsan to the Black Prince, both as representative of Edward III and in his own right as Prince of Aquitaine, and in refusing to do liege homage for Béarn.[3] At Agen the Black Prince seems to have been taken by surprise and, rather than provoke a nasty incident by constraining Gaston to redefine his position, he allowed him to depart after it had been agreed to search records for precedents. Thereafter in practice, however, Gaston acted as a sovereign lord in Béarn, and the bond of vassalage was broken. In John's case the royal clerks were more tenacious. But the ambiguity introduced in December 1366 symbolized Brittany's struggle to escape from the residual sovereignty of France. It was to colour the rest of John's reign, and was the basis for a further submission to France in 1381.[4] For the moment Charles V was unable to give all his attention to Brittany, and in some respects Franco-Breton relations slipped back to the balance achieved before 1341. The Duke was left to make his peace with his subjects.

Signs of ducal initiative in re-establishing a more broadly

[1] Planiol, op. cit. iii. 82.

[2] Jeulin, *Annales de Bretagne*, xli (1934), 436.

[3] Tucoo-Chala, *Gaston Fébus*, pp. 94–6. For John's presence at Agen on this occasion see p. 45, n. 2, above.

[4] *Preuves*, ii. 376; Jeulin, *Annales de Bretagne*, xli (1934), 440.

based government and in establishing a foreign policy
which attempted to steer between the lines that Edward III
and Charles V sought to circumscribe are interesting features
of the period after Auray. In domestic affairs, however, a
number of difficulties were not easily solved. There were, for
example, the problems of English settlement in Brittany and
John's debt both to his mercenaries and to Edward III. John's
fulfilment of his obligations was further delayed after 1368 by
the appearance of companies of *routiers* in the Breton Marches.

There were several spectacular cases of Englishmen
carving out seigneuries for themselves in the duchy during
the Civil War. After Auray, Robert Knolles and Walter
Huet were chief amongst those who had their possessions
confirmed. Chandos, it was said, also received large territorial rewards, although the authority for this is an inquiry
made in 1500.[1] It is difficult to tell what advantages the
owners of these estates drew from them. For many the
acquisition of a title was in itself a matter of great concern.
Titles complemented a prestige and nobility won by the
sword, and on some occasions made respectable those whose
gains had been made by the most unorthodox and illegal
methods.[2] The way in which Knolles juggled with his
estates in Brittany suggests that to him, at least, it was
worth the effort to establish legitimate titles to land. Thus he
exchanged lands illegally occupied for those donated from
ducal demesne, while outlying parts of his seigneury were
sold for more compact estates.[3] Certain provisos in these
agreements suggest that Knolles was realistic and that he did

---

[1] Borderie, iv. 14; Lobineau, ii. 536–7.

[2] Cf. M. Keen, *The Laws of War*, pp. 254–7.

[3] Already in the early 1350s Knolles held Fougeray and Gravelle castles (Treaty
Roll 30 m. 12). He was confirmed in his possession of them by Edward III and
John IV (*Foedera*, iii. 498, 622; A.L.A. E 154). In 1365 he sold his interest at
Gravelle to Amaury de Craon for 10,000*l.t.* (B. de Broussillon, *La Maison de Craon*,
1050–1480, i. 375). In an agreement with John IV sealed on 8 Nov. 1365 (A.L.A.
E 154, no. 1) reference was made to a 5,000*l.br.* rent which Knolles was taking from
the Duke and which was partly coming from the revenues of Fougeray and
Château-Blanc castles. But under the terms of the treaty of Guérande these were
to be given back to their former owners. The Duke thus made arrangements for
Knolles's pension to be taken on the castellanies of Conq, Rosporden, and Fouesnant.
Knolles and his assigns were to hold Conq 'sa vie durant', and 'apres le deceps
doudit Mons. Robert nous . . . ranvons, reprendrons et retrouvons a nous les diz
chastel, ville et chastellenie de Quonq . . .'.

not foresee a long occupation of these lands by his successors. But, apart from the occasional sortie under the Black Prince or his own *chevauchée* of 1370–1, Knolles and his Amazonian wife, Constance, made the duchy their home until 1373. His respectability in Breton society was further insured by papal favours as early as 1363.[1]

Huet, like Knolles, owed his fortunes to war, and there is evidence to suggest that some profit was brought back to England. But it cannot now be decided whether this came from his Breton estates or from several lucrative pensions.[2] For a period Huet was firmly settled in Brittany, living the life of a full feudal seigneur, married to a Breton heiress, employing a Breton confessor, receiving a pension from the Duke, and negotiating settlements with the former owners of the lands he occupied and enjoyed. He was killed on Gaunt's expedition (1373–4), but as late as 1390 John IV was willing to pay his heir in the duchy 1,300 francs for various letters and titles appertaining to Huet's estates.[3]

The landed wealth of another English adventurer, Roger David, whose career mirrors that of Huet and Knolles, was finally acquired by the Duke in 1371 when he bought the rights of David's widow, Jeanne de Rostrenen, to the seigneury of Guémené-Guingan. He paid 1,000*l.br.*, and 1,000*l.br.* were promised as an annual pension.[4] It is unlikely

---

[1] *Cal. Papal Letters*, iv. 54. In the 1365 transaction (above, p. 48, n. 3) Knolles styled himself 'Seignour de Derval et de Rouge'. In 1368 he had a safe conduct to come to England with his wife and 60 followers (*C.P.R. 1367–70*, 98). On 2 Feb. 1368 he was with John IV at Dinan (Plaine, *Procès*, p. 283). By the summer he was rumoured to be near Millau in Rouergue ('Documents sur la ville de Millau', ed. J. Artières, *Arch. Hist. de Rouergue*, vii (1930), 153, no. 313). For later events see, *inter alia*, Froissart, ed. Luce, viii, pp. lxx ff.

[2] *C.P.R. 1364–7*, 295; Chancery Warrants, file 511, no. 5880 (16 Jan. 1390), note of manors once owned by Huet in Salop. For his pensions see *C.P.R. 1364–7*, 222 and 305, for 500 marks p.a. from Edward III, and A.L.A. E 154, 400*l.br.* in perpetuity and 400*l.br.* for life granted to him by John IV.

[3] *Preuves*, i. 1622; Plaine, *Procès*, p. 284; A.L.A. E 162 (18 Nov. 1390), for a document listing letters and title-deeds as well as ransom agreements connected with Huet's Breton estates. Borderie, iii. 511 n., for parishes ransomed from Collet castle. In Sept. 1365 the Sire de Château-Fromont, Lieutenant-General for the Duke of Anjou in Anjou, wrote to Colin de Tours, receiver of Champtoceaux, then belonging to Anjou, warning him to pay 300 francs promptly to Walter Huet 'afin de eschever plusours maulx griefs et inconvenians que ledit Monssour Gautier entendoit et avoit desir et volunte de faire par luy et ses complices' (A.L.A. E 232). Deprived of ransom districts in Brittany, Huet was recouping himself by ransoming Champtoceaux.   [4] *Preuves*, i. 1665; *Foedera*, iii. 276, 278, 387, 699.

that such sums were paid for worthless deeds. If other important English captains at Auray did not put down roots in Brittany, they did so elsewhere in Normandy, Poitou, and Guyenne, where they acquired wives, lands, and titles with an aptitude similar to that of Knolles and Huet.[1] These career soldiers may have been amongst the first in the Hundred Years War to attempt to settle in their former stamping-grounds; they were certainly not the last.[2]

At a lower level still, there was an infiltration into Breton society by a number of lesser captains who found their champion in William, Lord Latimer, whose main task after 1364 was to see that John IV fulfilled his financial obligations to Edward III. The size of these meant some delay in payment; in May 1367 a detailed summary of debts owed to Latimer and to other English soldiers under him was compiled.[3] Services rendered as long ago as 1360–1 or at the siege of Bécherel (1363) were remembered. In October several important payments were made, including a composite one to Latimer in part settlement of the debts agreed upon in May.[4] In the meantime, however, some of the lesser captains had invested in lands in the duchy, as, apparently, had some of the minor officials of the Anglo-Montfortist administration before 1362.[5] Others continued to find employment in ducal service as castellans, household servants, retainers, and bodyguards.[6] The extent of this settlement of an English *noblesse* can only be traced piecemeal. Englishmen

[1] For Burley in Poitou see *Arch. hist. Poitou*, xxviii (1898), 149, xix (1888), 42, 129. *Foedera*, iii. 543, for confirmation of Saint-Sauveur-le-Vicomte to Chandos. Gournay later became seneschal of the Landes in Guyenne (Carte, *Catalogue des rolles gascons, normans et françois*, i. 165).

[2] Cf. A. Bossuat, *Perrinet Gressart et François de Surienne*, pp. 35 ff.

[3] Appendix of Documents, no. 2.

[4] Appendix B, sections 2 and 4.

[5] For example, Jack Ros, captain of Quimperlé in 1360–2 (Accts. Var. 175/5, 176/9), had his lands confiscated in 1373, when, together with lands of Hochequin Thorp (above, p. 32, n. 3), they could support a pension of 200*l.t.* (A.N. JJ 104, p. 89, no. 208). Huchon Peyntour, lieutenant of the receiver of Vannes in 1360 (Accts. Var. 175/1, no. 2, 22–3, 45, etc.), likewise had his lands confiscated during the Duke's exile when, together with Jack Pich's, they carried a 240*l.t.* pension (A.N. JJ 104, p. 86, no. 200).

[6] Appendix B, section 2 (Fog and Beauchamp); John Francis, who came over with Montfort in 1362 (Treaty Roll 45 m. 5), was found attesting Blois's miracles after a chastening experience (Plaine, *Procès*, pp. 343, 437). For other Englishmen in ducal service see above, p. 41.

did occupy positions of importance and power and hold
lucrative offices and lands, and were often to the forefront of
Breton affairs; but it is easy to see that their role has frequently been exaggerated.

Similarly John's payments to Edward III and Englishmen
in general, considerable as they were, have been used to
indicate another aspect of John's anglophilia.[1] It is necessary to distinguish certain characteristics of the payments.
In the first instance John's acknowledged debt to Edward
III was 64,000 nobles. Of this, instalments totalling over
£13,000, or almost two-thirds of the debt, were paid between
1366 and 1369.[2] Unpopular though the debt was, John was
in no position to refuse payment. He could only drag his
feet, a policy which was ultimately successful when the
course of events allowed him to persuade Edward III to
pardon the rest of the debt in 1372.

Likewise, payment of wages and pensions to those who
had helped him to his dukedom was not only forced upon a
grateful Duke by an overwhelming sense of gratitude but
dictated by more practical reasons. He required men like
Knolles, Huet, and Burley and their retinues to provide
him with an adequate force of troops to subdue possible
opposition. On the other hand, ejection of these captains
from their strongholds might be a dangerous business in the
uncertain days after Auray, and he would still be left with
the problem of Latimer and his lieutenants at Bécherel and
Plumoisan.[3] Once more, heavy but unavoidable demands
left John no alternative but to pay his former English
servants.[4]

If the payments to Edward III and the captains can be
termed, if only loosely, voluntary payments, those that John
paid to the companies were involuntary. They could not have

[1] Borderie, iv. 114.

[2] *Foedera*, iii. 661 (9, not 6, July 1362), recognition by John of debt of 64,000
nobles. Appendix B, section 1.

[3] Appendix B, section 2, for these payments. For loss of Plumoisan by alleged
treason, see Parl. and Council Proceedings, file 8, no. 17, a petition from Thomas
Kildestre to the King, c. 50 Edward III (1376). The crimes of Latimer's lieutenants
are notorious; see most recently J. G. Bellamy, 'Appeal and Impeachment in the
Good Parliament', *B.I.H.R.* xxxix (1966), 35–46. For payments to the lieutenants,
Appendix B, section 4.

[4] Appendix B, sections 2 and 4; Appendix of Documents, no. 4.

been foreseen; yet these payments made by the hands of the receiver-general, Thomas Melbourne, 'prestre de la nation dangleterre',[1] to companies largely composed of Englishmen were bound to cause resentment at the time, and have unfortunately caused some confusion in the minds of historians of a later generation, who have seen, once more, indications here of John's anglophilia.[2] John was well aware of the dangers which the companies posed to lawful government, and his policy of paying them to go away was perhaps the best he could adopt in the circumstances. It meant that he had to extort greater and greater sums by *fouages*, but it brought protection for his subjects, and he does seem to have co-operated with Charles V when a determined drive was made against the *routiers* in 1369. Similar co-operation with Charles II of Navarre will be noted in the next chapter.

The most important fact to note about John's payments to the *routiers* is that raising the money for these as well as for the payments to Edward III and the captains delayed the restoration of peaceful conditions in the duchy. These financial requirements led to the creation of a more comprehensive administrative machine to serve ducal needs. But the attempts to forbid seigneurial taxation of tenants were more than pinpricks to seigneurial *amour-propre*. The imposition of taxation solely for ducal purposes that were inimical to seigneurial interests accentuated the difficulties that hindered John's re-establishment of peaceful government.

Finally, we may shortly treat of John's relations with his subjects after Auray. For the first four years John was feeling his way. His appeasement of former opponents is noticeable, particularly amongst those who became his intimate advisers. From a Breton point of view the estrangement of John from Latimer, once the latter had accomplished an important service in obtaining a postponement of John's homage to Charles V, was welcome. This estrangement can probably be attributed to Latimer's presence as a persistent creditor at John's court. It is noticeable that, once

---

[1] Appendix of Documents, no. 3. All the payments in Appendix B, section 3, were made by Melbourne.
[2] Borderie, iv. 114.

John had discharged a considerable proportion of his debts to Edward III, Latimer left the duchy, where the guarding of his interests devolved upon lieutenants over whom he had little control.[1] But ducal policy in general was open to misconstruction as John sought to re-establish ducal control over seigneurs unaccustomed to such discipline since 1341. The application of ducal-seigneurial rights in many forms was unpopular and hit hard at the pockets of the seigneurs. John did not improve matters by condoning some irresponsible activities of his predominantly English household. At Dinan in February 1368, at the centre of the Penthièvre holdings, certain household knights had insulted a statue of Blois.[2] It is not necessary to believe the miraculous events which followed this incident, and it must be admitted that it was imperative for John to stamp out the cult growing up around the martyred figure of Blois; but the incident, one of several, does suggest the friction caused by John's unruly following. More importantly, the interference by ducal officials in the domestic affairs of important seigneurs caused much bad will. John threatened the temporal possessions of several Breton bishops by building towers and fortresses close to their episcopal towns—Solidor at Saint-Malo, Cesson at Saint-Brieuc, Odet at Quimper—and their ecclesiastical liberties by protesting his rights against the interference of the Archbishop of Tours, the metropolitan superior of the Breton bishops.[3] Amongst the lay aristocracy of the duchy a number of seigneurs were left with grievances after Guérande, notably Girard, Sire de Rays, Pierre de Craon, Sire de la Suze et Benasté, and Bonabé, Sire de Derval, who had all been dispossessed by English adventurers.[4]

It is thus not surprising that Charles V took advantage of seigneurial ill-feeling in the duchy when he wanted to embarrass and constrain the Duke. Girard de Rays, Pierre de Craon, and Bonabé de Rougé are to be found serving in

---

[1] Above, p. 51, n. 3. Latimer seems to have returned to England at the end of 1367 (*C.P.R. 1367–70*, 63); he was summoned to Parliament on 24 Feb. 1368 (*Reports on the Dignity of a Peer*, viii. 643). For his journey to Paris in 1366 see Appendix of Documents, no. 2, and *Preuves*, i. 1599, redated by Borderie, iv. 9.

[2] Plaine, *Procès*, pp. 283, 406–7; Pocquet, *Les Papes*, i. 358.

[3] Ibid. i. 385–6; *Preuves*, i. 1614.

[4] Ibid. i. 1593.

the armies of Bertrand du Guesclin (Constable of France
from October 1370) or receiving pensions from Charles V.[1]
The feud that was to dominate Breton internal politics to
the end of John's reign, that of the Duke and his former
friend Olivier, Sire de Clisson (created Constable of France
in 1380), originated in quarrels over the increase of ducal
power in relation to that of the greater seigneurs. It was
only gradually that Clisson moved towards France. As late
as 1369 he could be described as John's chief adviser and
found accomplishing delicate diplomatic tasks for the Duke.[2]
But in 1370, with the compliance of Charles V, he practised
an elaborate deception upon John IV. By exchanging some
of his Norman lands for Château Josselin,[3] formerly held
by Peter, Count of Alençon, and his son, and by substituting
the King for the Duke as superior lord of Josselin, Clisson
incurred ducal wrath.[4] Already prohibitions by the Duke on
Clisson's taxing of his tenants at Champtoceaux (possibly
part of a latent dispute with Thomas Melbourne) had
provided fuel for the flames which were fanned into life by
the exchange.[5] By 1370, therefore, divisions are once more
apparent in the duchy; in the next few years these widened
until the Duke was isolated, deserted by all but the most
faithful of his councillors. The story of these years, however,
is best told against the wider background of the Anglo-
French war.

[1] *Arch. hist. Poitou*, xxviii (1898), *passim* for career of Girard de Rays; *Preuves*, i.
1622, Anselme, viii. 573, and A.L.A. E 183 (10 May 1372) for Craon. In the last
document Pierre was forced to admit that a recent donation of his former lands,
returned to him by Charles V, was invalid and that 'le duchie de Bretaigne est si
noble qe le Roy ne autre ni ne nul ne puet avoir confiscacion en Bretaigne mais
seulement le duc de Bretaigne de ses nobleces et droiz Royaulx . . .'. He thus pledged
himself to pay whatever fine the Duke might impose upon him. The lands in question
were those held by Huet, above, p. 49. For Charles V's regrant of his lands to Rougé,
see A.N. JJ 105, p. 159, no. 293 (Nov. 1373).

[2] Secousse, *Mémoire pour servir à l'histoire de Charles II, roi de Navarre*, p. 428,
and *Preuves*, i. 1637.   [3] Dép. Morbihan, ar. Vannes, ch.-l. c.

[4] *Cartulaire du Morbihan*, nos. 563–5; *Preuves*, i. 1639–40.

[5] A. Lefranc, *Olivier de Clisson*, pp. 84 ff. Charles V was wooing Clisson as early
as 1368 when he granted him two years' remission of *fouages* on his Norman lands
in view of future services (B.N. Pièces originales, doss. 789, Clisson no. 2). He
became Joan de Penthièvre's lieutenant in 1369 (*Preuves*, i. 1631). The order
forbidding Clisson to tax his tenants is calendared in A.L.A. Répertoire des
Chartes de Bretagne, Mandements du duc Jean IV, Papers of Léon Maître, fol. 50
(14 Sept. 1368). Clisson obtained the seigneury of Guillac from Charles V in 1373

John had a difficult task before him in 1365. He tackled
the problem of reconstructing ducal power by reverting to
traditional forms of government. He consulted with a wide
cross-section of his subjects in *Parlement* and council. He
used officials whose roles were already partially defined.
Few innovations can be attributed to his English upbringing. Changes that were made—mainly in the realm of
finance—cannot often be attributed to any one source of
inspiration and are paralleled by contemporaneous developments elsewhere in France. They were stimulated by John's
obligations towards Edward III and the English captains.
But the *chambre des comptes* and the *fouage* were typically
French responses to extraordinary conditions, mainly in-
duced by war. Otherwise John's exploitation of his ducal
and seigneurial rights is fully in accord with the policies of
his predecessors. Yet his emphasis on ducal rights, on his
noblesses, in this period demonstrates John's concern for
his position.[1] The 'monarchical' approach, discerned by
some historians in John's attitude to government after
1381,[2] by which is meant his exploitation of the regalian
rights claimed but not usually exercised by his predecessors
for the benefit of Brittany, can be discerned much earlier.
The bases of ducal government before 1341, continued in
exiguous circumstances by Blois and Joan de Penthièvre,
and preserved beneath Westminster forms by Edward III,
were uncovered and strengthened by John from 1365 to
1373. This development of ducal authority, bound up as it
was with a corresponding weakening of seigneurial power,

(Lefranc, op. cit., *pièce justificative* no. 8); it had been formerly held by Melbourne
and FitzNicol (see A.L.A. E 236, fol. 91^r, printed in *Cartulaire du Morbihan*,
no. 573).

[1] This concern is particularly apparent in some of John's contracts, e.g. A.L.A.
E 140, no. 1 (10 Oct. 1367), Jean de Saint-Gilles undertakes the captaincy of Saint-
Aubin-du-Cormier for his 'tres redobte et souverain Seigneur lige Mons. Jehan duc
de Bretagne' for 500 francs p.a. He promised the Duke 'pourchacer, garder, pour-
suivre, maintenir et deffandre ses droiz, possessions et saisines envers touz et contre
toutes personnes qui vivre et puissent vivre et morir'. Jean de Keranlouet similarly
in 1371 (A.L.A. E 142) swears fealty against all who are opposed to John IV. The
hollowness of their promises in such agreements is made patent by their later
careers, see Table of Allegiances below, p. 57, s.v. Yet as late as 1394 Charles VI
considered this type of homage an infringement of his prerogatives by the Duke
(A.N. J 243, no. 76).

[2] Borderie, iv. 71 ff.

was a necessary step towards the assertion of Breton independence in foreign affairs. That the foundations laid by the Duke and his miscellaneous advisers were firm can be seen from some of the events of 1373–9. After the Duke's exile there was no large-scale importation of French royal methods. The privileges and practices of the duchy were respected in the main.[1] Olivier de Clisson recognized the importance of Vannes as an administrative centre, whilst in 1379 the Defence Leagues grounded their plans on finances raised by a *fouage*.[2] The speed with which this financial machinery was put into action in 1379 and the return to normal administrative practices within two years of the Duke's return from exile are further illustrations of the importance of the reconstruction of 1365–73.

[1] *Cartulaire de . . . Saint-Sulpice-la-Forêt*, no. ccxlviii, 30 Jan. 1377, order from Charles V to 'our receiver' of Quimper-Corentin to pay a certain rent which will be rebated in his accounts 'par noz amez et fealles gens de noz comptes a Paris', is one of the few indications of regal interference with the administration established before 1373. For Charles's careful orders concerning the minting of coins during the Duke's exile, see *Ordonnances des rois de France*, vi. 40 ff.; Delachenal, v. 236 ff.

[2] Lefranc, op. cit., p. 192; *Preuves*, ii. 216–17, 229–30.

TABLE OF ALLEGIANCES, 1364–1385

The following table is divided into three sections: columns 1 to 3, columns 4 to 7, and columns 8 to 12. These divisions correspond to a chronological division of careers: before 1373, from 1373 to 1379, and from 1379 to 1385. Pro-Montfortist characteristics are signified by an x, and pro-Penthièvre or pro-French characteristics by an o. The column numbers are explained below. The table is intended to give the broad outline of various careers from *c.* 1360 to 1385. It is not complete, nor does it show changes of allegiance over the course of a few months. The main sources for it are witness lists and musters found principally in *Preuves*. Pensions from Charles V and his son may be found in quittances, chancery registers, etc., in the Archives Nationales and Bibliothèque Nationale, Paris, or as published in *Comptes du Trésor*, ed. R. Fawtier.

Key to column numbers:

1. Those swearing fealty to John IV, 1364–73.
2. Ducal retainers, castellans, counsellors, servants, 1364–73.
3. In service of Joan de Penthièvre (1364–73), or witness at Blois inquiry (1371).
4. Serving in Du Guesclin's army in Normandy (1369–73), at siege of Bécherel (1371) or at siege of Brest (1373).
5. Men granted pensions, gifts, confiscated lands, or wages by Charles V, 1364–80.
6. Serving in Charles V's armies, 1373–9.
7. Serving Joan de Penthièvre, 1373–9.
8. Signatory of Defence Leagues of 1379.
9. Counsellor of John IV, 1379–85.
10. Serving in Clisson's army against John IV, 1379–81.
11. Agreed to second treaty of Guérande and fealty to John IV, 1381.
12. Men granted pensions by Charles VI (1380–5) or who were in the service of Louis, Duke of Anjou as counsellors, pensioners, or wage-earners (1365–82).

1. *Bretons serving Duke John before Auray* (1364)

	1	2	3	4	5	6	7	8	9	10	11	12
Barbu, Jean le	x	x			o				x		x	
Bazvalen, Jean	x	x							x			
Callac, Bonabé	x					o				o		
Clisson, Olivier, S. de		x	o	o	o	o	o			o		o
Kermavan, Tanguy de	x	x									x	
Saint-Gilles, Jean de	x	x			o							

2. *Bretons serving Charles de Blois before or at Auray*

	1	2	3	4	5	6	7	8	9	10	11	12
Beaumanoir, Jean, S. de		X	O	O	O	O		X	X			
Charruel, Évain	X			O	–	–	–	–	–	–	–	–[1]
Chauce, Alain		X					O	X				
Feuillée, Silvestre de la	X	X		O		O		X	X		X	
Guyon, Étienne							O	X	X		X	
Juch, Jean de	X			O	O	O	O					
Laval, Guy, S. de		X				O	O	X			X	O
Parc, Maurice de			O		O	O						
Paris, Guillaume		X									X	
Pledran, Henri		X		O		O	O	X	X		X	
Rochefort, Guy, S. d'Assérac		X	O	O		O		X	X			
Rohan, Jean, Vicomte de	X	X	O	O	O	O			X		X	O
Rougé, Bonabé, S. de				O	O	O				O		O
Saint-Brieuc, Hugh Montrelais, Bishop of	X	X	O									O

3. *Clerks in ducal service at some time*

	1	2	3	4	5	6	7	8	9	10	11	12
Cleder, Guy	X	O				O		X				O
Lesnen, Georges		O									X	
Prières, Henri le Barbu, Abbot of	X							X			X	O
Raguenel, Mace	X							X			X	
Saint-André, Guillaume de			?					X				

4. *Breton Seigneurs and Cadets*

	1	2	3	4	5	6	7	8	9	10	11	12
Chastel, Hervé, S. de				O	O	O					X	O
Clisson, Amaury de				O		O				O		
Coëtmen, Raoul, S. de	X						O	X			X	
Dinan, Charles, S. de Montafiliant	X	X	O	O		O	O	X	X		X	
Fontenay, Amaury de				O		O		X	X		X	
Fontenay, Thomas de		X			O	O		X	–	–	–	–[1]
Houssaie, Alain de la						O		X	X		X	
Houssaie, Eustace de la	X					O		X	X		X	
Hunaudie, Pierre, S. de Tournemine				O			O	X				
Kerimel, Geoffroi		X	O	O	O	O	O	X	X		X	O
Malestroit, Alain, S. de								X	X		X	
Malestroit, Jean de				O				X			X	
Montauban, Olivier, S. de				O		O		X	X		X	
Montfort, Raoul, S. de				O		O		X	X		X	
Penhouët, Guillaume, S. de				O	O	O					X	O
Tournemine, Pierre, S. de				O		O		X				

[1] Died.

5. *Breton Noblesse*

	1	2	3	4	5	6	7	8	9	10	11	12
Angoulevant, Berthelot d'	x	x		o		o		x	x		x	
Barillière, Jean, S. de	x	x				o				o		
Brochereul, Robert		x							x			
Guitté, Robert de	x	x		o		o		x	x		x	
Kaermartin, Guillaume		x		o	o	o						o
Keranlouet, Jean de	x		o	o	o	o						
Kersallion, Rollant								x	x		x	
Lannion, Briant	x	x		o	o	o					x	
Lanvalay, Robin	x			o		o		x			x	
Lévêque, Guillaume		x							x		x	
Maigne, Alain		x							x			
Mauny, Olivier de				o		o				o		
Moine, Olivier le					o	o					x	o
Parisi, Henri			o		o				x			o
Phelippes, Henri		x				o	o		x		x	
Poulglou, Geoffroi		x				o	o	x		o		
Trelever, Prigent						o			x		x	
Tresguidi, Maurice				o		o						o

III

WAR, EXILE, AND RETURN
1369–1381

(i) THE DEFECTION OF THE BRETON NOBILITY AND THE EXILE OF DUKE JOHN, 1369–1373

THE appeal of the Gascon seigneurs to the *Parlement* of Paris in 1368–9 resulted in renewed war between England and France. In June 1369 Edward III resumed the title 'King of France', troops were mobilized and alliances negotiated.[1] Edward may have informed John IV of some of his plans in the previous March.[2] Now the Duke's position became critical. It was less than five years since Auray, a victory won by English arms. To support Edward III openly would contradict the terms of John's homage to Charles V and provoke retaliation. John had to face this dilemma of allegiance, but his eventual alliance with England was not so inevitable as some historians have alleged. There is the problem of French provocation of John to set beside the righteous indignation of the long-suffering Charles V at the ducal *lèse-majesté*. In the light of John's domestic policies, it is inconceivable that he did not exercise the same sort of care for his rights and those of his duchy in planning his foreign policy. This would help to explain some of the devious political negotiations John entered into with England, France, and other interested parties at this time. Any analysis of these crowded events must take into account two apparent anomalies. First there is the three-year delay, once war had restarted, before the sealing and implementation of the Anglo-Breton alliance of 1372. Secondly, there is the Duke's failure to heed warning signs

---

[1] Delachenal, iv. 53–109; Perroy, *Hundred Years War*, pp. 160 ff.; *Rot. Parl.*, ii. 460; J. W. Sherborne, 'Indentured Retinues and English Expeditions to France, 1369–80', *E.H.R.* lxxix (1964), 720.

[2] Issue Roll 436 m. 30 (5 Mar. 1369), payment to 'Galfrido de Styvekele valleto hospicii Regis misso in negociis domini Regis versus partes Britannie'.

of the Breton nobility's defection, signs which are obvious to us and which can have been hardly less so to him when he saw his seigneurs serving in the royal armies. Perhaps the most we can hope to do here is to extract some few strands from the tangled skein of events in an attempt to resolve some of the paradoxes of ducal policy at this dangerous moment.

There is no denying that the war of 1369 was reopened by French initiative at a diplomatic and military level. Internal Gascon difficulties were exploited; whilst a bid was made for the loyalties of towns uncomfortably situated between zones of English and French influences. Military pressure, the presence of the king's lieutenant, and clerical propaganda tours all helped to influence the towns in question, although some legal opinions on the justice of the rival claims to the throne of France were also obtained.[1] Charles V gained some successes in southern France at the same time as his troops in northern and western France were tackling the *routier* nests of Normandy, Poitou, and Anjou and installing royal garrisons in their place. At a diplomatic level, Charles countered a possible Anglo-Flemish alliance by promoting the marriage of his brother Philip, Duke of Burgundy, to the Flemish heiress and forestalling English offers of marriage.[2] He also won over Charles II, King of Navarre. This king, nicknamed 'the Bad', was an unreliable ally, as his short-lived alliance with France proved. But he was a potentially dangerous enemy because of his large estates in Normandy.[3] In 1369, also, Henry de Trastamara, the French-supported candidate for the Castilian throne, overthrew his half-brother Peter I. He could thus discharge from his service a number of French captains, who returned, laden with grandiose titles, to fight in and lead the armies of Charles V.[4] Even when French forces made a rather ineffectual demonstration before Calais in the summer, the English counter-moves did little to assure potential allies

---

[1] *Anglo-Norman Letters*, ed. Legge, no. 138; cf. 'Some Documents regarding the Fulfilment . . . of the Treaty of Brétigny', ed. P. Chaplais, *Camden Miscellany*, xix (1952), 54–5.   [2] Vaughan, *Philip the Bold*, pp. 5 f.

[3] Delachenal, iv. 356–7.

[4] P. E. Russell, *English Intervention in Spain and Portugal in the Time of Edward III and Richard II*, pp. 49, 85, 150.

that England could still wage successful war.[1] Edward III
intended to lead his army in person on the Continent, but
the death of Queen Philippa seems to have drained his will-
power. The proposed expedition was transferred to Gaunt's
leadership, which was uninspired. The English war effort
was thus largely restricted to negotiations for allies.[2]

In northern France England possessed, in Calais, a foot-
hold for invasion, but her strategic position would be
strengthened by obtaining allies in Normandy and Brittany.
To nullify the advantages which Charles V possessed over
Charles II and Duke John by his sovereignty, Edward III
exerted his influence. This pressure resulted in an abortive
Anglo-Navarrese treaty in December 1370[3] and in an
Anglo-Breton treaty in 1372. Militarily it led to Robert
Knolles's expedition of 1370–1, which followed what was
becoming a traditional route for such *chevauchées*, through
Picardy and the Île-de-France. This expedition, whose
leadership was divided at the start, ended in disaster for the
rearguard at Pontvallain.[4] Stragglers who made their way to
'neutral' Breton territory were cut off by royal troops,
according to one chronicler, even in the act of boarding ships
for England.[5] The Anglo-Breton treaty led to a small
English expedition to the duchy in 1372, the arrival of
which was the signal for a train of events that was equally
disastrous from an English point of view. John IV was
forced to seek exile in England.[6] It is necessary to examine
a little more closely these unfortunate English attempts to
win allies.

Duke John and Charles II, as great vassals of France,
were faced with the same problems in 1369. In international
affairs both had ties which made it difficult for them to
remain neutral; whilst their domestic problems included one
which required common action. Their lands were subject to
depredation by the free companies infesting the Marches

---

[1] Vaughan, op. cit., pp. 8 f.
[2] Sherborne, *E.H.R.* lxxix (1964), 720–3.
[3] Delachenal, iv. 220–1, 356–7.
[4] Ibid. 301–41. For a joint indenture between Edward III and the expedition's
leaders, B.M. MS. Cott. Caligula D. III, fols. 114–15 (5 July 1370).
[5] *Chron. normande du quatorzième siècle*, ed. A. and E. Molinier, p. 198.
[6] Delachenal, iv. 464 ff.

between Brittany and Normandy.[1] Here both rulers had
ambiguous personal relationships with some of the *routier*
captains dating back to the time of Cocherel and Auray,
but at a meeting in July 1369 they agreed to help each other
against the companies.[2] Such joint action may have been
an attempt to restrict Charles V's interference—his troops
were already at work[3]—but the evidence for this is equivocal.

Edward III, for his part, recognized that the free companies could jeopardize his hopes of diplomatic success in
this quarter. In the winter of 1369–70 strenuous efforts
were made to come to terms with Charles II over English
garrisons in Normandy, especially at Saint-Sauveur-le-
Vicomte, and a sprat to catch the Navarrese King was a
suggestion that the fortress would be evacuated.[4] Difficulties
were smoothed over, and by the end of 1370 Charles agreed
to become an English ally. A tentative alliance with France
was thrown overboard in return for generous prospective
concessions, promised by an optimistic Edward from his
hoped-for realm of France.[5]

In Breton affairs Edward was less forthcoming. This was
a reflection of his view that the credit amassed before 1364
was still a valid currency. His investments were about to
be realized. John did give some passive aid, and troops,
destined for Guyenne, probably marched through the duchy
in April or May 1369. If it is true that some *routiers* joined
this force *en route*, thus vacating the Breton Marches, John's
domestic troubles were partially alleviated.[6] But Delachenal's speculations that John proposed an English alliance

---

[1] Ibid. 356 ff.; C. Samaran, 'Le "vuidement" de Château-Gontier', *Mélanges Louis Halphen*, pp. 641–4.

[2] Secousse, *Mémoire pour servir à l'histoire de Charles II*, i. 412; Izarn, *Le Compte des recettes . . . de Navarre*, pp. 136, 158.

[3] *Preuves*, i. 1623–4, 1632–4; H. Moranvillé, *Étude sur la vie de Jean le Mercier*, pp. 232 f.

[4] B.M. Add. Ch. 30–1, accounts of the Bishop of Avranches, Baudouin de Beaulo, and Sancho Lopez, for negotiations held in May 1370 with the captain of Saint-Sauveur; *Anglo-Norman Letters*, ed. Legge, no. 194.

[5] Delachenal, iv. 365–7; M. Masson d'Autume, *Cherbourg pendant la Guerre de Cent Ans*, pp. 13 f.

[6] Froissart, ed. Luce, vi. 116–18; Sherborne, *E.H.R.* lxxix (1964), 733; *Preuves*, ii. 34. Some of the *routiers* giving quittances to John in Dec. 1368 (Borderie, iv. 113; Appendix B, section 3) are to be found in Guyenne at a later date, e.g. John Nor-bury, captain of Libourne in 1377 (Accts. Var. 181/1, no. 18).

to Charles II during their meeting in July 1369,[1] based on preconceived ideas of the Duke's anglophile tendencies, are not supported by any evidence for John's compliance with Edward III's policy. Even in the autumn, when Edward confirmed his earlier alliances with the Duke, John's obligations were not specified.[2] Edward may have had the conditions of 1362 in mind. He still had several holds over the Duke, including the occupation of Bécherel and the power to threaten John by releasing John de Bretagne;[3] yet there is no record that John reciprocated Edward's advances. The indications are that John was being forced unwillingly into an open acknowledgement of Edward's claims.

John later complained, whether sincerely or not we cannot be sure, to Charles V about his difficulties in attempting to recover Bécherel and other castles held by Englishmen.[4] Early in 1369 he had contemplated, and may even have carried out, a siege of Bécherel.[5] The charges exacted by the garrison made ducal action imperative.[6] John could throw in his lot with Edward in an attempt to relieve the pressure of ransoming, a course adopted by Charles II with regard to Saint-Sauveur, or he could oppose English pretensions. This, indeed, appears to have been his answer. He was not prepared to go to any length to appease Edward. He welcomed the use of force against Bécherel. If such a course was repugnant to him personally, it was necessary for his duchy, and its interests came first. In 1371 there were several notable ducal supporters in the army laying siege to Bécherel.[7] For more than two years, John, studiously avoided committing himself to the English cause.

---

[1] Delachenal, iv. 356.

[2] A.L.A. E 119, no. 10, privy seal letters of Edward III, dated on the second day of a month, the name of which contains the letters 're', in the thirtieth regnal year of Edward's 'reign' in France (i.e. between June 1369 and Jan. 1370). An ultra-violet lamp failed to give further elucidation.

[3] *Anglo-Norman Letters*, ed. Legge, no. 265, an undated letter from John IV expressing concern at the possibility of the hostages' release; cf. Issue Roll 447 m. 30 (4 Mar. 1373), payment to Walter Leicester 'misso versus castrum de Devyses cum una littera de privato sigillo . . . de supervidendo statum et modum custodie filiorum Karoli de Bloys in custodia . . . existencium et ad informandum consilium Regis super eisdem'.   [4] *Preuves*, ii. 34.

[5] Ibid. i. 1632; B.N. MS. fr. 22330, pp. 531–3 quoted above, p. 33, n. 4.

[6] Appendix B, section 4.   [7] *Preuves*, i. 1657.

As the Anglo-Navarrese alliance of 1370 developed, John stood aside. He dissembled to Charles V, excusing himself from any scheme which the King could label treasonable. Some of these excuses may have been false. Others were well founded on a keen appreciation of Brittany's needs. Charles reciprocated by allowing the Duke to retain troops in the duchy rather than send them to the royal host, a response probably made in view of the potential danger to Brittany from the companies.[1] But the Duke was not easily won to the French cause either. Well informed of the Anglo-Navarrese *entente* by both principals, he sent his own envoys to London in the winter of 1370–1.[2] The stated business of these representatives was a private matter between the Duke and the contentious citizens of Saint-Malo. Yet the presence in England of Melbourne, FitzNicol, and Styvecle, who had been involved in John's conversations with Charles the Bad, is significant in view of the critical stage reached in the Anglo-Navarrese talks.[3] Considerable hopes had been placed in the success of Knolles's expedition by Charles II. Now its failure was just becoming known.[4] The English had suffered another set-back, and Edward's allies, real and potential, were exposed to the revenge of Charles V. The military fortunes of Valois France were in the ascendant. Finally, the Black Prince, once more out of sympathy with his father's ideas, scuttled the Anglo-Navarrese ship by refusing to agree to the alliance with Navarre. Charles the Bad, seeing his best escape-route in a new alliance with Charles V, abandoned England at the very moment that John IV rallied to Edward's call.[5]

The reasons for John's action are obscure. The reception of Knolles's scattered forces marked him out as an English sympathizer. Moreover the approach of royal forces under Du Guesclin, reinforced by many Bretons, threatened to

---

[1] Ibid. 1636. Refusal to join the royal host without letters o non-prejudice was a claim of some standing (cf. ibid. 1351).

[2] A.N. J 918, no. 29, a safe conduct for Melbourne 'qe attenduz le loialtee et bon port de nostre bien ame lige . . . avons retenuz pardevers nous et nostre service . . . come un de noz . . .', granted by Edward III on 30 Nov. 1370; *C.P.R. 1370–4*, 3; Izarn, *Le Compte des recettes . . . de Navarre*, pp. 169, 358, 369.

[3] *C.P.M.R. 1364–81*, 121, 123; Izarn, op. cit., p. 136.

[4] Delachenal, iv. 306–7; *C.P.R. 1370–4*, 18.   [5] Delachenal, iv. 364–8.

destroy John's work since 1365 and to arouse civil war rivalries.[1] But John did not tamely submit to Charles V. Collet castle had been captured and Brittany's south-western coastline was exposed to piratical attacks from the French-controlled Marches of Brittany and Poitou.[2] Ducal relations with Clisson, another important marcher landowner, had worsened steadily since 1370.[3] John had attempted to reinforce his position in Brittany by new alliances with his seigneurs and by new contracts for service with his castellans.[4] But their loyalty was a fragile thing when royal service offered lucrative pensions and employment.[5] In 1371 also, the movement to canonize Charles de Blois, scotched by John three years earlier, was once more set in motion. The mutual confidence established between the Duke and some former Penthièvre supporters was weakened, and the canonization process had behind it the weight of Louis, Duke of Anjou, and the approval of Charles V.[6] The Duke's only course was simultaneous negotiation with England and France.

John's envoys in England in the winter of 1371–2 found that the Franco-Breton siege of Bécherel had restored a sense of realism to Edward's Breton policy. Edward's government still thought highly of its claims on John and

---

[1] Table of Allegiances, col. 4.

[2] A.N. J 240, no. 24bis, various requests by John IV to Charles V, 1372.

[3] See above, p. 54. From the spring of 1371 Clisson kept a number of Spanish arbalesters at Blain castle (Bib. mun. Nantes, fonds Bizeul, MS. 1684, various quittances).

[4] A.L.A. E 142 (30 July 1371), Éon le Méen, ibid. (1371), Jean de Keranlouet, ibid. (14 Oct. 1371), Rolland de Guergorlé pay fealty; ibid. (18 Oct. 1371), Jean and Yvon de Launay do likewise; ibid. (9 Jan. 1372), a similar multiple homage and fealty was performed by eleven knights; ibid., Charles de Dinan, Sire de Montafiliant, promises not to fight outside Brittany; ibid. E 183 (3 Dec. 1371), Jean, Sire de la Barillière, who had fought outside the duchy, agrees to let the Duke tax him at will for this failure; ibid. (14 July 1372), Guillaume, Sire de Penhouet, promises loyalty to John IV before all others and agrees not to fight outside the duchy without permission. See also *Preuves*, i. 1641. Agreements for holding Tonquedec, Solidor, Redon (town and castle), etc., can be found in A.L.A. E 139–42 for this period.

[5] Guillaume de Saint-André recognized the lure of French gold as a solvent of loyalty (ed. Charrière, ll. 1942–3). See Table of Allegiances, cols. 4, 5. J. du Tillet, *Recueil des Guerres et Traictez d'entre Les Roys de France et d'Angleterre*, fol. 100.

[6] Plaine, *Procès, passim*; *Preuves*, ii. 2–33; A. Du Chesne, *Hist. de la maison de Chastillon-sur-Marne, Preuves*, pp. 126 ff.; Hay du Chastelet, *Hist. de Bertrand du Guesclin*, pp. 304–8. Anjou was Blois's son-in-law.

assumed that ducal compliance with its wishes would be extensive. But the English were now prepared to use Bécherel as a bargaining counter while it was still in their hands.[1] The release of Bécherel was suggested, together with the delivery of Chizé, Melle and Civray in the Poitevin Marches to the Duke. Remission of 9,000 marks of John's debts was also offered. But, considerable as these concessions appear, John's envoys were eager to exploit the English desire to win John over. They saw that John was already in a position to argue himself out of the remaining debt, whilst the castles in Poitou, which had been offered to Charles the Bad in 1370, were seriously threatened by the French advance.[2] The release of Bécherel was also linked with the handing-over of Brest, Morlaix, Hennebont, and nine other towns to English garrisons, as well as the abandonment to Edward III of all ports and castles which the King needed to prosecute his war. Such conditions were carbon copies of those of 1342.[3] Ducal power and independent initiative would have been snuffed out. The ultimate indignity was that John should do liege homage for Brittany to Edward when he gained the French crown. Admittedly, these conditions were not Edward's final offer but were the basis for negotiation. England's influence in northern France was being violently hacked away; the English could hardly avoid making extravagant gestures. But Thomas Melbourne saw through this false optimism to the hollow substance of the concessions first advanced.

The negotiations of 1372, long and hard, fall into five distinct periods. After discussions with the English Council in November 1371, Melbourne and FitzNicol probably returned to the duchy with envoys appointed to advocate the English proposals.[4] In February 1372 John IV countered by requesting the return of Richmond.[5] In March the

---

[1] *Foedera*, iii. 926–7.   [2] Cf. Delachenal, iv. 365–6.

[3] Cf. Le Patourel, *History*, xliii (1958), 187.

[4] Issue Roll 444 m. 10 (22 Nov. 1371), £66. 13s. 4d. paid to Melbourne and FitzNicol as part of 400 marks gift from Edward III for their expenses; ibid. m. 9 (17 Nov.), payment to Neville and Barry going to Brittany; Accts. For. 5 m. 27, their accounts for this journey undertaken between 17 Nov. 1371 and 18 Mar. 1372; A.L.A. E 142 (16 Feb. 1372), renewed fealty of Melbourne to John IV.

[5] A.N. J 242, no. 54 (20 Feb.), appointment of Melbourne as John's proctor for the negotiations (cf. *Foedera*, iii. 936).

Breton envoys returned to England, and by dint of hard bargaining a treaty was drafted.[1] During the next two months military preparations for campaigns on land and sea and for an auxiliary force to go to Brittany were made.[2] In June and July more negotiations in England led to a treaty of alliance.[3] From August troops were waiting to go to the duchy. They landed in October, and John then confirmed the July treaty.[4] Edward III, for his part, finalized a donation to the Duke of all lands, apart from those of the Church and royal demesne, that he could capture in France.[5]

The ultimate failure of the 1372 alliance, with its consequences of exile for the Duke and occupation of his duchy by French royal forces in 1373, should not obscure John's considerable diplomatic victory in relation to England, despite its transience. In the face of Breton desertion, John was prepared in February 1372 to reject Edward's November proposals. He did not wish to become Edward's cipher. In asking for Richmond, it may be suspected (as was the case in the 1380s and 1390s) that John was seeking insurance. There would be something for him to salvage if his efforts resulted in the loss of his duchy. He also accepted the quittances offered for Bécherel and the castles in Poitou. But he was not prepared to release the stipulated ports, and England continued to hold Bécherel. He managed to obtain the concession of mutual trading rights between Brittany and Guyenne and the interchangeability of money.[6] In this way John sought to emphasize his role as an ally, not as a mere client.

When Melbourne returned to England in March 1372, the Duke's desire for equal status was borne home to the Council. The initial parrying of the French offensive since 1369 had turned into a long rearguard action as the English tried to defend the territories won at Brétigny-Calais. By the spring of 1372 the English hold on Poitou was tenuous.[7] Failure to come to terms with Charles II had allowed the French to re-establish their authority in Normandy. Con-

---

[1] B.M. MS. Cott. Julius B. vi, fol. 7ᵛ, draft letters patent of Edward III.
[2] Sherborne, *E.H.R.* lxxix (1964), 725–6.   [3] *Foedera*, iii. 943, 953–5.
[4] Ibid. 964.   [5] Ibid. 968.   [6] Ibid. 935.
[7] Delachenal, iv. 391 ff.; *Arch. hist. Poitou*, xix (1888), xiv, 41 ff.

cessions now granted to John IV suggest that the English were very anxious to make sure that Brittany would still be friendly. It might yet be used as a springboard into France. Mutual trading rights, a monetary agreement concerning Guyenne, and the promise to include John as an English ally in any future peace-talks were quickly agreed upon. He was also promised support 'by all reasonable and honest means' against his domestic enemies.[1] No mention was made of specific ports to be handed to the English. Instead, 300 men-at-arms and 300 archers were to be sent to the duchy, so that John could use his own discretion in deploying them, a freedom reinforced by his agreement to pay them. John also promised to join Edward with 1,000 men-at-arms if he should come to France, and further arrangements for the lodging and victualling of any troops the King might send were discussed. Richmond was conceded, and John's debts annulled.[2]

Between March and July both sides mulled over the proposals,[3] although few were changed in the treaty completed on 19 July. Pious verbiage apart, the framework of the treaty, which was the basis of all future Anglo-Breton treaties in John's reign, was a professed perpetual alliance against the King of France, mutual support against domestic enemies, and support for each other's rights. Troops had long been ready to go to the duchy.[4] The English Chancery drew up the necessary documents, and Edward III issued a general quittance to John. Yet for the moment the alliance was kept secret, and, in view of the serious consequences publication might entail for John, curiously indecisive terms covered this eventuality. The great seal was appended to the treaty in August.[5]

---

[1] B.M. MS. Cott. Julius B. VI, fols. 7ᵛ, 7ʳ.   [2] Ibid.

[3] A.N. J 918, no. 33 (18 June 1372), order from Edward III freeing the master and crew of a boat in which a messenger sent by Melbourne to John IV had been held up.

[4] Issue Roll 446 m. 9 (15 May), £266. 13s. 4d. advanced to Melbourne and FitzNicol for their retinue of 30 men-at-arms and 30 archers. The same amount was paid to them on 29 June (ibid. m. 22). Eventually they were supposed to lead 178 soldiers (Sherborne, *E.H.R.* lxxix (1964), 725–6).

[5] *Foedera*, iii. 955–6 (concessions), 958 (5 Aug., confirmation). The secrecy clause ran: 'La quiele chose serra notifie et publie es paiis et seigniures [*sic*] de l'un les [*sic*] et de l'autre, le pluis toste que faire se pourra, et au temps quel semblera

All that remained was to obtain John's ratification and to implement the treaty.[1] But when John, Lord Neville, leader of the English auxiliary force, arrived in October, after a long delay, the Duke wanted one significant addition. In the confirmation of 22 November a clause was added to the effect that John would not do homage to Edward if he became king of France.[2] A year before, the English had been asking for liege homage. John's insistence now is understandable. Committed as he was to the English cause after three years of deliberate prevarication, the prospective sovereign independence offered him by the alliance was a consummation devoutly to be wished. Unlike Charles II in 1370,[3] but echoing Edward's own standpoint with regard to Guyenne, he rejected the royalist view of provincial relations with the French crown. Though he was at loggerheads with his own nobility, John was essentially at one with them in maintaining the integrity of the duchy. His personal tragedy was a failure to carry his subjects along with him in his foreign policy at this point. Diplomatic victories, for in a way so the treaty was, were valueless to a deposed duke.

Between 1369 and 1372 John's relations with Charles V had been superficially polite. Quite correctly emphasis has been placed on the conciliatory attitudes of the French King. As late as September 1372 Charles was prepared to meet John some way along the road towards agreement over the execution of the terms of the first treaty of Guérande, which they had previously failed to complete. He was also willing to compromise over a number of disputed points which had arisen since 1365.[4] But equal emphasis ought to be placed

---

bon ou expediente a les avantditz deux seigniures Roi ou duc, a fin que la chose soit de plus overtement conue' (ibid. 955).

[1] A.N. J 642, no. 19 (26 July), appointment of Neville 'de requerir de par nous . . . nostre tres cher . . . Johan, duc de Bretaigne, counte de Richemond et de Mountfort quil acorde, passe, face et renouelle en sa propre persone les alliances et covenances darreinement faites a nostre palais de Westmoustier le dis et noefisme jour de cest presente mois de Juyl'; ibid. J 242, no. 55, a notarial document summarizing the course of the negotiations. Delachenal, iv. 465 ff., and below, p. 73, n. 6, for a discussion of how these documents came into French hands.

[2] *Foedera*, iii. 964.   [3] Cf. Delachenal, iv. 367.

[4] Borderie, *Rev. de l'Ouest*, ii (1855), 559; *Preuves*, i. 1636 (Jan. 1370), letter dispensing Duke from serving outside Brittany; A.L.A. E 108 (23 Jan. 1370), return of 1,000*l.t.* pension on lands in France; ibid. E 113, fol. 15ᵛ (23 Jan. 1370),

on the implications of the process to canonize Blois. If he were proved to be a saint, John would be his murderer. In the uncertainty still surrounding the ducal succession— John being childless—many might see the hand of God. Some earthly representatives of divine power, the King of France among them, had positively encouraged the inquiry.[1] It has also been assumed too readily that John was alone in his dealings with Charles V, or that where he was advised, it was by English or pro-English councillors. Clisson and Hugh Montrelais, Bishop of Saint-Brieuc, ambassadors to the French court in 1369, had both trimmed their sails to the prevailing political wind, but neither was likely to be duped into advocating a cause for which he could feel no sympathy at all.[2] Jean de Saint-Gilles, another ducal envoy to France at this time, had been a supporter of John before 1364. His change of heart after 1372 was typical of many who had less reason to be pro-English. Briant Lannion, Guillaume Lévêque, Guillaume Paris, and Guy de Roche-fort, Sire d'Assérac, other envoys, cannot be labelled pro-English by any stretch of the imagination.[3] In La Borderie's phrase, they were all 'good Bretons'—men who had a clear grasp of the duchy's needs. Yet they all advocated John's French policy.

To the King's discredit, John could cite dilatoriness in returning Montfort lands outside Brittany despite frequent regrants.[4] To complaints over the process of canonization and the seizure of Collet castle were added the King's interference in John's quarrels with his bishops, the issuing of safe conducts, supposedly valid for Brittany, by the

letters of non-prejudice for ducal acts against the Bishop of Quimper; B.N. MS. fr. 22329, p. 795 (Jan. 1370), return of appeal before *Parlement* of Paris to ducal courts.   [1] See above, p. 67, n. 6.

[2] *Preuves*, i. 1637. Montrelais had been present at the French court to assent to the acceptance of the Gascon Appeals (*Chron. des règnes de Jean II et de Charles V*, ed. Delachenal, iii. 139).

[3] A.N. J 240, no. 19 (1 Apr. 1372), ref. to Jean de Saint Gilles's embassy; ibid. JJ 105, p. 61, no. 99 (18 Sept. 1373), grant of 200*l.t.* compensation to him, for lost lands, by Charles V. See Table of Allegiances for the others.

[4] For example, the county of Montfort was given back to John at Brétigny (*Foedera*, iii. 487). Edward III appointed commissioners to receive it in Mar. 1361 (ibid. 612). But it was only in 1369 that John was able to appoint a governor (A.L.A. E 138, no. 2 and A.N. J 400, no. 64).

Charles V promised to return John's lands in Rethel and Nevers on 19 Jan. 1369

royal chancery and by the Constable (from October 1370, Du Guesclin), and other infringements of ducal rights by royal officers or simply by lawless seigneurs.[1] Such actions were certain to put the Duke on the defensive and make him wary of Charles V's offers. They might also have given Edward his cue.[2] But John continued to send envoys to France, and it is likely, though impossible to prove, that had English troops not landed in Brittany in October 1372, the Duke would have continued to play off the great powers against each other while maintaining his own *via media*.[3]

Neville's arrival sparked off an explosion which quickly led to John's exile. The French reconquest of Poitou in 1372 had already brought home to John his isolation. His friend Charles II, with whom he had not broken off relations after the failure of the 1370 triple alliance, departed in July 1372 for his southern kingdom.[4] Deserted by many of his most warlike subjects, who were now serving Charles V, John's own armed forces were depleted. In theory the English troops were a useful reinforcement, but in practice their arrival confirmed French suspicions about John's double-dealing. He had been warned about giving hospitality to Knolles's force and was left in no doubt as to what was expected of him. It is unlikely that Charles believed the excuses sent to explain away the arrival of the English soldiers or that he relied on John's promises to dismiss them.[5] The army, which had been restoring royal control in Poitou, used the opportunity of a short truce to enter the duchy to

---

(A.L.A. E 108) and to pay 6,000*l.t.* to Joan de Penthièvre for payments John had been unable to make, but in 1371–2 back payments and return of the lands were still outstanding (A.N. J 240, no. 19, 1 Apr. 1372, instructions to the Counts of Tancarville and Brienne sent to Brittany).

[1] Cf. A.N. J 240, no. 24*bis*, *c.* 1371–2, requests of John to Charles V.

[2] Borderie, iv. 17.

[3] To A.N. J 240, nos. 19, 24*bis* add ibid., no. 35 (schedule of items discussed with Tancarville and Brienne) and A.L.A. E 165, no. 15 (8 Sept. 1372), further letter from John about Franco-Breton negotiations in 1372.

[4] Delachenal, iv. 385, 391 ff. Charles II had appointed John lieutenant for his lands in France in Nov. 1371 (A.L.A. E 181).

[5] A.N. J 246, no. 133 (24 Nov. 1372), Charles to Breton seigneurs, enclosing a letter he had sent to the Duke expressing 'grant merveille' at John's excuses for introducing English troops into his duchy 'non pas pour dommagier nostre royaume, mais pour mettre a l'obeissance le sire de Clicon . . .'. John's reply (ibid., no. 130, 28 Dec.), signed in his own hand, hardly exculpates him.

remind John of his obligations. It was unopposed.[1] Meanwhile the King, realizing John's weak position *vis-à-vis* his barons, took them into his confidence and communicated to them the messages he was sending to the Duke.[2] Convinced of the justice of his case, a conviction stiffened by papal interference,[3] he hoped to avoid open conflict by persuading John to abandon his course. But the Duke appeared deaf to Charles's reasoning. He absolved himself and took refuge behind counter-charges against Clisson and against the Bishop and citizens of Saint-Malo, who had tried to shake off ducal overlordship. He asked the King for letters of non-prejudice to cover his own actions and requested Charles to fulfil his earlier promises. English troops remained in the duchy, he said, because there was no transport to repatriate them.[4] Further letters, written in February 1373, and a present of lampreys were hardly a guarantee of fidelity.[5] Already in the previous November it was rumoured that John had asked for more English troops. Whether the King was yet fully aware of John's commitment to the English is questionable.[6] It was also the winter season, so that it was not until the early spring that Charles finally moved to action.[7]

The delay could have been decisive. Taking advantage of the winter, John prevaricated. He knew that Edward III was well informed of his plight.[8] Unafraid, he confirmed

---

[1] B.-A. Pocquet du Haut-Jussé, 'Les séjours de Philippe le Hardi, duc de Bourgogne, en Bretagne, 1372, 1394, 1402', *M.H.B.* xvi (1935), 3–7; F. Lehoux, *Jean de France, duc de Berri*, i. 294–5.   [2] Above, p. 72, n. 5.

[3] *Lettres secrètes . . . du pape Grégoire XI*, nos. 1010 (28 Nov. 1372), 1161 (23 Mar. 1373); cf. Pocquet, *Les Papes*, i. 394 f.

[4] Delachenal, iv. 470.   [5] Ibid. 465, 471 n.

[6] Pocquet, *M.H.B.* xvi (1935), 3–5, accepts as broadly true the story in *La Chronique du bon duc Loys de Bourbon*, ed. Chazaud, pp. 38 ff., of the capture of documents by the invading French force in Oct. 1372 which revealed John's treachery. Delachenal, iv. 466 ff., assigns the events in the chronicle to 1373. But there is no insuperable problem in accepting that A.N. J 242, no. 55 and 640, no. 19 came into French hands in 1372. Alternatively, they might have been found at Vannes in 1373 (see above, p. 30, n. 3).

[7] Delachenal, iv. 472 ff.; *Lettres secrètes . . . du pape Grégoire XI*, nos. 1271–90.

[8] Accts. Var. 179/13, accounts of Walter Leicester, Sergeant at Arms, accompanying Neville to Brittany and returning on 1 Nov. 'quo die idem Walterus applicuit apud Plymouth causa renunciandi domino Regi et consilio suo de statu Britannie'; ibid. 30/8 m. 4, accounts of Walter Hauley and others, 'secum laborantur versus partes Britannie et ibidem commorantur in comitiva Johannis de Nevil et abinde redeundo a tercio die Octobris anno quadragesimo [1372] usque vicesimo quinto die Januarii '.

the July treaty and accepted Edward's charges. His pose as an aggrieved subject, and his attempt to arouse Charles's sympathies at the way in which regal and ducal rights were being flouted at Saint-Malo, were both artificial. In England, William Montague, Earl of Salisbury, indented to serve for six months from 1 March 1373 with 600 men. Under him were the two admirals, William Neville and Philip Courtenay, and several smaller retinues. The combined total of soldiers and sailors in his force approached 5,000, but they were too late to do much to remedy John's position.[1] By the end of March 1373, Du Guesclin was finally victorious in Poitou. He moved to Brittany and was soon attracting Bretons to his standard.[2] John's administration had switched to an emergency basis, and payments were being made only to those officers who could be depended upon to support the Duke. Attempts to obtain the favour of leading noblemen were desperate and unsuccessful throws of the dice.[3] By the end of April John could see no alternative to flight.[4]

The forces left behind in the duchy gallantly defended the Duke's few remaining fortresses, but the majority of Bretons accepted the French occupation without protest. Brest was the most important stronghold left to the Montfortists, although they continued to hold Derval, Auray, and Bécherel for the time being. Du Guesclin, who had obliterated most other points of resistance throughout Brittany, laid siege to Neville's troops in Brest in June 1373.[5] And French Chancery registers tell of the expropriation of

---

[1] *Foedera*, iii. 971 (Salisbury's indenture); Issue Roll 447, *sub* 18 Feb. and ff., for prests to retinues in his force. J. W. Sherborne, 'The English Navy: Shipping and Manpower, 1369–1389', *Past and Present*, 37 (1967), 172, using B.M. Add. MS. 37494, the account book of William Airmyn, controller of the King's clerk for the navy. See especially fol. 10 for retinues with Salisbury; cf. Delachenal, iv. 471.

[2] Since arms were still being provided for Salisbury on 20 Mar. (Accts. Var. 30/13, no. 7), he probably did not arrive off the Breton coast until the end of the month. Delachenal, iv. 439, 472. Jean, Vicomte de Rohan, joined Du Guesclin with 40 knights and 185 esquires in May 1373 (*Preuves*, ii. 65).

[3] A.L.A., Répertoire des chartes de . . . Jean IV, fol. 88, 29 Mar., order from John to his receivers to pay soldiers and officials only for the quarter just begun, as Melbourne would make future payments from Auray; ibid., fol. 90, 16 Apr. 1373, at Vannes, agreement of Duke with Vicomte de Rohan not to treat with Geoffroi de Lanvaux, Rohan's enemy (cf. previous note).

[4] *Chronicon Briocense*, ed. Lobineau, 838.   [5] Delachenal, iv. 477.

Englishmen who had settled in the duchy.[1] They also reveal the typical temper and attitudes of the Bretons themselves. The men whom John had entrusted with important captaincies had simply turned against him. Guillaume Kaermartin, for example, controlled four towns, including Carhais. He had not followed the Duke but

. . . ja soit ce que le dit duc de Bretaigne de puis quil ait baillee en garde au dit Guillaume les dis chasteauls, villes et forteresces se soit mis et tourne au parti de nos ennemis les Anglois. Neantmoins le dit Guillaume ne se soit mie tournez avecques lui mes ait tousjours resiste a la male voulente . . . dudit duc le quel avoit voulente et propos de les livrer aus dis Anglois . . .[2]

The places left to John could be numbered on the fingers of one hand. His hopes of a return to Brittany now depended on the amount of military aid his English ally was prepared to give him. In the duchy some officials tried to maintain their positions by exploiting the uncertainty which existed and Charles V's obvious wish to be conciliatory.[3] A few remained true to their late master; most, like John's *noblesse d'épée*, sold their services to France.[4]

The Duke had made a series of miscalculations. Above all he had misjudged his subjects, relying too much on contracts that were worthless and on English promises of

---

[1] A.N. JJ 104, p. 86, no. 199 (5 May 1373), confiscation of lands of W. Sequelton, W. Piont, W. Kingston, and their wives; above, p. 50, n. 5, for lands of H. Peyntour, J. Pich, J. Ros, and H. Thorp; A. N. JJ 104, p. 116, no. 273 (23 Apr.), lands of Adam Jehanin and wife confiscated on condition that if they returned to French allegiance they would be restored.

[2] Ibid., p. 89, no. 208 (25 May 1373).

[3] Ibid., p. 125, no. 299 (10 Aug. 1373), Charles V pardons John de Valence, who had been in John IV's service but who claimed that he had remained loyal to France. But on 2 Dec. 1373 new letters were issued stating that Alain Dupont and his sister Margaret, children of the late Nicolas Dupont and of Pleson de Penbual, wife of John de Valence (an Italian living at Brest with 'our enemies', who had asked his wife to join him there), had petitioned that if their mother joined John and her lands were confiscated, then they would be invested with their parents' lands for their good services (ibid. JJ 105, p. 22, no. 25). On Valence see below, p. 153.

[4] Ibid. JJ 104, p. 99, no. 233 (22 June 1373), in letters of confiscation of lands belonging to Jean le Barbu 'le dit maistre Jehan l'ait continualement servi [i.e. John IV] et reste avec lui estant en rebellion et en son conseil iusques a tant que il est alez devers nostre dit adversaire'. An attempt to bribe Barbu failed (ibid., no. 234). He was still in the Duke's household in 1381 (*Preuves*, ii. 274). See Table of Allegiances for Bretons in Charles's armies.

aid, which had first proved too small and latterly too late, serving only to agitate opposition. He found himself in a position analogous to his father's in 1341, with few supporters in the duchy, little territorial hold, and without resources to re-establish his authority. He was thrown back on Edward III, the ally whose own personal schemings and ambitions had drawn John actively into the Anglo-French war. John had gambled for high and not too illusory stakes, as far as his duchy was concerned, but he was sadly disillusioned by Edward's war prospects. The Duke had allowed himself to be drawn into an alliance which had more than diplomatic obligations.

(ii) THE ANGLO-FRENCH WAR AND NEGOTIATIONS 1373–1381

John IV presented himself at Edward III's court in May 1373. His sorry plight as a landless and poverty-stricken exile stirred Edward to pity and thoughts of revenge.[1] Already the King had one large fleet at sea, but a decisive show of English strength in France was desirable. John's presence in England, far from disheartening his allies, served only to encourage them to act more swiftly. The army being prepared under the leadership of John of Gaunt was destined for Brittany; it was to assemble at Plymouth by 1 May for a year's service. Even at the end of that month it was reported that the Duke was shortly to return to Brittany.[2] But the worsening situation in the duchy caused a change of plan. After the delays almost inevitably associated with medieval expeditions, Gaunt finally crossed to Calais in July. Whatever the ultimate plans of the English army were, any prospect of its marching directly to aid the few garrisons holding out for John was dashed when it moved off in a south-easterly direction through some of the richest provinces of France. Harried by forces sent out against them by Charles V, the army leaders were forced to march ever further southwards. The rest of the summer was thus

[1] Froissart, ed. Luce, viii. 125; John was still able to loan the Princess of Wales 200 marks (A.L.A. E 209, 20 June 1373).

[2] Most of Salisbury's fleet stayed at sea until late Sept. or early Oct. 1373 (B.M. Add. MS. 37494, fol. 10); Sherborne, *E.H.R.* lxxix (1964), 727.

spent cutting a damaging swathe of destruction and rapine through the eastern and central regions of the Valois kingdom.[1] Since Charles V had to withdraw some troops from Brittany to chase Gaunt, the *chevauchée* did help to relieve some of the pressure on the Anglo-Montfortist garrisons. But for John it only increased the enmity of his ex-sovereign. Diplomatically it was a suicidal venture, finally condemned by its lack of military success. What was more, John temporarily quarrelled with Gaunt. Leaving the main force before it reached Bordeaux, he paid a brief visit to Brittany early in 1374. This did little to restore his prestige and, as in the previous year, the late spring saw John a suppliant in England.[2]

Apart from this secret journey, John's affairs in Brittany were directed by lieutenants from April 1373. Their main task was the defence of Brest, which soon exhausted ducal resources there.[3] The English government then had to subsidize the garrison and that of Auray. The principal gain from the 1372 treaty, Richmond, was mortgaged by the Duke in order to pay the wages of Neville and his troops.[4] The Anglo-Montfortist fortresses, like several other English castles in Poitou and Normandy, were isolated in the French-controlled countryside. Brest was besieged on and off for six years (1373–9). Other forts fell more quickly. Hennebont was captured by Du Guesclin in 1373. In 1374 Bécherel fell to the Franco-Breton forces. By the time Auray was captured by Clisson in 1377, only Brest and a small area of the Finistère peninsula were left to the Duke.[5]

These French successes in Brittany and elsewhere in northern France demanded English retaliation. But English reactions were dulled. It was well known in the summer of 1374 that Bécherel in eastern Brittany and Saint-Sauveur-le-Vicomte in the Cotentin were seriously threatened. Preparations were in hand by August to dispatch a relieving force under the command of John IV and the Earl of March,

---

[1] Delachenal, iv. 485 ff.   [2] Cf. *Chronicon Briocense,* ed. Lobineau, 840.
[3] Below, p. 147, n. 4.   [4] *C.P.R. 1377–81,* 74.
[5] *Chronicon Briocense,* ed. Lobineau, 840, and H. Moranvillé, *Jean le Mercier,* p. 311, for Auray; Saint-Mathieu was in French hands in 1374 (*Preuves,* ii. 81) but back in English ones by 1376 (*Foedera,* iii. 1062); Froissart, ed. Luce, viii. pp. lxxi ff.

but inexplicably the sailing date was continually postponed.[1] Edward III impatiently hectored his officials, yet it was not until three weeks after Bécherel had fallen that he commissioned John IV and March as his lieutenants in France. Even then there were further delays, and they did not sail until April 1375.[2]

The results of the campaign, which began in northern Brittany with a large force of 4,000 men, were disappointing. A few towns fell, giving the invaders a useful *pied-à-terre*, but there was no general rallying to the ducal standard by Bretons. The walls of Saint-Brieuc soon halted the expedition and the opportunity for speedy action was lost. Personal rancour clouded the Duke's judgement as he lost sight of the strategic objectives of his campaign. Hearing of an opportunity to capture four of his personal enemies, he gave up the siege of Saint-Brieuc, which was on the point of success, and pursued his enemies in a wild-goose chase to Quimperlé.[3] He was followed in a few days by other contingents of his army. But even at Quimperlé he was thwarted of success. The prompt dispatch from Bruges of news of an Anglo-French truce which was to include Brittany allowed his enemies a respite. The garrison of Saint-Sauveur, who had made a local truce with the French army besieging them when they heard of John's arrival in Brittany, were left with no alternative but to surrender. By mid-July John, furious at the way events had conspired against him, could do little to halt the withdrawal of English troops.[4] Although he remained in the duchy, his forces were inadequate for anything but garrison duties.[5]

This fiasco of English arms has been attributed to the

---

[1] Sherborne, *E.H.R.* lxxix (1964), 730; C. C. Bayley, 'The Campaign of 1375 and the Good Parliament', *E.H.R.* lv (1940), 370–83.

[2] Cambridge Univ. MS. Dd. iii. 53, no. 157, letter of Edward III to those responsible for mustering troops; *Foedera*, iii. 1018 (24 Nov. 1374, appointment of lieutenants); Accts. Var. 33/33, accounts of Guy de Brian supervising musters at Plymouth 7 Jan.–3 Apr. 1375.

[3] Bayley, *E.H.R.* lv (1940), 375. Edward, Lord Despenser, was at Saint-Brieuc on 10 June (A.L.A. E 119, no. 18, quittance).

[4] Accts. Var. 34/6, no. 3 (20 July 1375), and Treaty Roll 58 m. 5 (24 July), Edward III to March and John IV telling of truce and that the Admiral to the south and west would be coming to assist their repassage. Despenser was at Saint-Mathieu on 3 Aug. (B.N. MS. Nouv. acq. fr. 5216, no. 15).

[5] 200 men-at-arms were allowed for this purpose by the truce (*Foedera*, iii. 1033).

'badly dove-tailed' policies of aggressive militaristically-minded generals and those who fancied themselves as diplomatists.[1] In Edward III's dotage, England lacked a strong centralized government with definite ideas on the conduct of war and peace. Half-hearted efforts in both directions at once had resulted in the sacrifice of the few military objectives achieved by John's expedition. Whilst the Duke remained in high dudgeon, arguing with Du Guesclin and Clisson about the application of the Bruges truce in the duchy,[2] a domestic crisis in England brought both war and peace policies under review in the Good Parliament of 1376. For the moment there was little support for John IV.

In August 1373 John wrote a letter of defiance to Charles V.[3] In it he claimed that Charles's aggression had driven him into exile and that there was no course open to him but to renounce his allegiance to the French crown. Charles V had not been slow to point out the consequences of John's own actions. The suspected treason of November 1372 had been made apparent by more English aid in 1373. Whether John held his duchy by liege or simple homage, his alliance with Edward III conflicted with his French obligations. The Duke was a rebel who 'ait fait venir les anglois nos enemies en nostre royaume et leur ait baillee pluseurs de ses chasteaux, villes, fortresses . . .'.[4] His lands and those of Englishmen in the duchy were at the King's disposal. But after the first rush of sequestrations, royal lawyers had to deliberate on the exact nature of John's crimes and on his punishment. Unfortunately the advice of the members of the *Parlement* of Paris, who debated whether John could be appealed before them and whether his duchy could officially be declared confiscated, does not appear on their registers.[5] Maybe they advised caution for what was an unprecedented situation. As the literary debate in the *Songe du verger* between the clerk and the knight was to

[1] Bayley, *E.H.R.* lv (1940), 380.   [2] *Preuves*, ii. 99.
[3] Hay du Chastelet, *Hist. de Bertrand du Guesclin*, p. 452; *Preuves*, ii. 67, and Froissart, ed. Lettenhove, viii. 451; cf. B.-A. Pocquet du Haut-Jussé, 'La dernière phase de la vie de Du Guesclin; l'affaire de Bretagne', *B.E.C.* cxxv (1967), 151–2.
[4] A.N. JJ 104, p. 99, no. 233 (22 June 1373).
[5] Delachenal, v. 237.

show a few years later, there was much to be said on both sides.[1] Charles V was in no hurry. Although he appointed Anjou lieutenant in the duchy in October 1373, he, in turn, left most affairs in the hands of Du Guesclin, Clisson, and other Breton notables.[2]

The appointment of Anjou was a sop to the Penthièvre party, who, despite their eclipse at Auray, were the legal successors to the Montfort dukes should their male line fail. Treason could well be construed as a disqualification. But Charles V was equally determined neither to compromise with John IV nor to pronounce in favour of a Penthièvre successor in accordance with the terms of the first treaty of Guérande. John's participation in Gaunt's *chevauchée* only served to harden Charles's resolve. Further, the papacy's role as a mediator in Franco-Breton disputes, apparent in 1360–4, had been destroyed by its encouragement of Charles V in 1373, and the Pope was lucky to obtain a local respite for his possessions directly threatened by the Gaunt expedition in 1373–4.[3] Between 1373 and 1375 John IV was firmly in the camp of the English war party.

The slight to John's interests by the Anglo-French diplomats at Bruges in 1375 forced John to turn to diplomacy. Although he was not present in Flanders in January 1376, the draft of a forty-years' truce, drawn up by the Anglo-French negotiators, vitally affected him.[4] It was suggested that machinery somewhat similar to that established at Brétigny-Calais should be set up to deal with all Breton problems. Alternatively it was suggested that the Duke might like to submit his case to the arbitration of Charles V and his peers in *Parlement*. In the meantime the Duke was to hold Brest, Auray, and Saint-Mathieu with a stipulated number of men. Certain goods and jewels captured in 1373 were to be returned to him. He was to be offered

---

[1] *Songe du verger*, ed. Brunet, Bk. 1, chs. 143–4; Bodl. MS. Auct. 204. 1, sigs. i–iii. Although the *Songe* deals with John IV's specific crimes, it presents arguments on the nature of the duchy of Brittany taken from the legal claims put forward by both contestants in 1341 (see above, p. 3, n. 2).

[2] *Preuves*, ii. 78–9.

[3] *Lettres secrètes . . . du pape Grégoire XI*, nos. 1447, 1449, 1460; 'Anglo-French Negotiations', ed. Perroy, *Camden Miscellany*, xix (1952), p. xiii.

[4] Ibid., pp. 26–35, esp. 34, nn. 6, 7.

a pension during the truce and, in order to facilitate the execution of these clauses, he was to leave Brittany without delay.

By the time this draft was discussed again in March 1376, John had travelled to Bruges.[1] The suggested commission was dropped. His pension was to be paid at Bruges, not Vannes, although the amount of it was now in dispute. He was still to hold the three towns agreed upon in January, and the terms on which he could raise certain ducal and extradomanial revenues by ransoming were all regulated. But although these terms were slightly more favourable than the January ones, they were hardly sufficient to compensate him for the loss of his duchy. Neither he nor his allies could be satisfied with the prospect of his exile continuing almost certainly for the rest of his lifetime if the truce became a reality. So far his diplomacy had remained as ineffectual as his military efforts.

Returning to England somewhat frustrated and, no doubt, angry, John did not hesitate to bring to Edward III's notice infringements of his few remaining rights.[2] He also seems to have decided to play a lone hand in diplomacy. The figureheads of the Anglo-French delegations had no sooner departed from Bruges, leaving the regulation of the truces to their subordinates,[3] than John paid a second visit to Flanders.[4] Edward III was puzzled by this move, and it is impossible to do anything but speculate on John's intentions. Possibly, as Guillaume de Saint-André suggests,[5] he was exploring the means to a private accommodation with Charles V. But his visit to Flanders complicated his relations

---

[1] Ibid., pp. 37–41.

[2] Memoranda Roll (E. 159), 155, Recorda, Michaelmas Term 2 Ric. II, m. 25, a petition from John IV complaining about disregard of ducal *brefs*, presented at the time of the Good Parliament (cf. Anc. Pet. file 291, no. 14503, a similar petition), and A.L.A. E 201 (Dec. 1378), inquiry held at Bordeaux which upheld the Duke's claims to issue *brefs*. John was not yet in full possession of his rights as Earl of Richmond, see below, p. 176.

[3] 'Anglo-French Negotiations', ed. Perroy, *Camden Miscellany*, xix (1952), pp. xviii, 44–7.

[4] *Foedera*, iii. 1062 (23 Aug.), Edward III informs castellans in Brittany that 'nostre tres cher filz Johan, duc de Bretaigne, par consail et abetement des auscuns Bretouns est alez en Flandres sans scieu de nous et ne savons a quele entente . . .' . John had been at Robertsbridge Abbey, Sussex, on 10 Aug. (*C.P.R. 1381–5*, 407).

[5] Ed. Charrière, ll. 2398–2409.

with Edward III. After the recriminations of the spring,
Edward again appears to have ignored ducal rights by
sending conservators of the truce to Brittany without the
Duke's consent. When this was pointed out to him, in order
to avoid a misunderstanding he invited John to send his own
representatives.[1] There was a considerable correspondence
between the estranged allies in the winter of 1376–7. But
whatever hopes Charles V may have entertained of driving
a wedge between Edward and John and thus arriving at a
peaceful solution of the Breton question were destroyed
when, in May 1377, John was lured back to England by
plans for a large-scale campaign.[2] The Duke forsook the
way of negotiation and placed his hopes once more in an
English army.

For nearly two years the military situation in Brittany had
been frozen by the moratorium imposed at Bruges in 1375.
Both sides were kept on the alert, and neither England nor
France held out much hope that the truces would be continued for long. By the beginning of 1377 France put her
cards on the table, while preparing for the eventuality that
her terms would be rejected.[3]

Although the English were not quite so well prepared to
deal with the renewal of war, which threatened after the
expiration of the general truces on 24 June 1377, plans had
been laid. Most significantly, a force which included Gaunt
and Woodstock, the old King's sons, his grandson Prince
Richard, and John IV, as well as a number of senior English
generals, including Lord Latimer and Michael de la Pole,
had been paid prests on their wages in June.[4] Two possible

---

[1] 'Anglo-French Negotiations', ed. Perroy, *Camden Miscellany*, xix (1952), 78–
80. The two letters from Edward III, one to John IV, the other to Thomas Percy,
dated post-Sept. 1376 by M. Perroy, can perhaps be dated Jan. 1377. Percy
received £40 on 5 Jan. to go to Flanders on secret negotiations (Issue Roll 461 m. 25).
John Fastolf, noted by Perroy as being abroad for the enforcement of the truces
between 5 Nov. and 31 Dec. 1376, had been to Brittany (Accts. Var. 317/16,
Accts. For. 13 m. E^v; cf. *Foedera*, iii. 1066).

[2] Cf. Accts. For. 12 m. 6^r, accounts of George Felbrigge, king's esquire 'misso
in secretis negociis predicti Regis avi versus partes Flandrie Johanni duci Britannie'.
He left London on 17 May and had returned by 1 June 1377.

[3] 'Anglo-French Negotiations', ed. Perroy, *Camden Miscellany*, xix (1952), pp.
xviii–xix; A. F. O'D. Alexander, 'The War with France in 1377', London Ph.D.
thesis, 1934 (summarized in *B.I.H.R.* xii (1934–5), 190–2), p. 14.

[4] Ibid., pp. 41–2; Russell, *English Intervention in Spain*, pp. 238 ff.

policies have been posited for this force.[1] It might sweep the Channel and contain the French fleet, or it might have been intended to relieve Brest and extend the Duke's rule in Brittany. But the death of Edward III (21 June) and a series of French naval raids on the south coast called for temporary defence measures. The large expedition was postponed, and it was not until a second French sea-borne attack on England in August 1377 had been stayed that the Government was able to return to its original plans. Some small assistance was sent to Brest while the fleet was reforming.[2] Now under the leadership of Thomas, Earl of Buckingham, and John IV, the fleet had the same objectives as those proposed for June. Part of the fleet, setting out from ports around the mouth of the Thames, was to damage shipping in the ports of Flanders and north-eastern France before sweeping down the Channel. The Thames fleet would then join up with ships fitted out in the western ports and continue jointly to the relief of Brest. A show of force in Brittany may also have been intended.

These ambitious plans were put in jeopardy almost at once by a storm which caught the Thames fleet soon after it had set out.[3] Considerable damage necessitated a refit. Putting to sea again towards the end of November 1377, the fleet was joined by John IV in the second week of December with his personal retinue of about 400 men.[4] But there was much discontent amongst the crews, which broke out in mutiny in Lord FitzWalter's squadron. Even so, some limited success, mainly against merchantmen, was achieved, and the combined fleet eventually sailed to Brest where a small force was put ashore in January 1378.[5] Heartened by this, the Government planned an extensive tour of duty for the fleet, which was to convoy ships from Bordeaux; but before it could act, the fleet had returned to port. The expenses of the expedition and Buckingham's obligations towards the garrison at Brest were heavy, but

---

[1] Alexander, loc. cit.

[2] Ibid., p. 216. [3] Ibid., p. 221.

[4] Accts. Var. 68/7, no. 149 (John's indenture). He was at Burwash, Sussex, on 1 Dec. and back at Swineshead, Lincs., on 5 Feb. 1378 (A.L.A. E 117, E 206, various household accounts). His retinue had mustered at the sea on 27 Oct. (Accts. Var. 42/13). [5] Alexander, op. cit., p. 226.

there was some gain to be shown.[1] Several prizes had been
taken and, more importantly, French ascendancy in the
Channel, which had allowed them to launch their attacks
in the previous summer, had been checked. As for John IV,
he was now chronically short of finances and had agreed to
give up Brest to the English for the duration of the war with
France.[2] He had played one of the few cards left in his hand,
and his fortunes were even more dependent on the success of
English arms.

If 1378 opened with a minor success for John's allies,
their good luck did not long continue. Once more, ambitious
plans were conceived to extend English influence in France.
These were best summarized in the speech of Richard
Scrope, Chancellor of England, to Parliament, which met
at Gloucester towards the end of this year, in which he explained the 'barbican' policy the Government now favoured.[3]
By obtaining and maintaining a ring of castles around the
coast of France from Guyenne in the south to Calais in the
north, it was hoped to place England's first line of defence
across the Channel. To this end the lease of Brest had been
formalized in April 1378 and a similar arrangement for the
lease of Cherbourg had been agreed with Charles II of
Navarre in July.[4] Gaunt's abortive expedition to Saint-Malo
in this year can likewise be seen as an attempted extension
of this scheme.[5] But the French siege at Cherbourg and
countersiege at Saint-Malo, the mounting expense of keeping Calais and the other forts, and the government's hasty
actions over the Hawley–Shakell affair all helped to vitiate

---

[1] *Foedera*, iv. 36; Sherborne, *Past and Present*, 37 (1967), 171–2.

[2] A.L.A. E 120, no. 22 (1 Dec. 1377), in copy of 22 Jan. 1391, letters patent of
Gaunt, March, Arundel, and others, witnessing and guaranteeing John's agreement
with Richard II. John participated personally in the parliamentary debates for the
lease of Brest, travelling each day by water from the City of London to Westminster (A.L.A. E 117, household accounts).   [3] *Rot. Parl.*, iii. 36.

[4] *Foedera*, iv. 34–6; *Anglo-Norman Letters*, ed. Legge, no. 141. M. Rey, *Les
Finances royales sous Charles VI*, p. 379, gives 27 June as date of Cherbourg cession.
See also Delachenal, v. 211–24.

[5] The siege of Saint-Malo, although well known from chronicle sources, has
left little trace in administrative records, partly because of the loss of Gaunt's
accounts (cf. *C.P.R. 1381–5*, 124). For general naval activity of 1378 see Sherborne,
Past and Present, 37 (1967), 172. Pocquet, *B.E.C.* cxxv (1967), 160, places the siege
between 7 Aug. and 7 Oct., though it was not finally raised until Dec. (Delachenal,
v. 231–3).

English efforts and excite hostile criticism of Gaunt.[1] The
continuing ineffectiveness of English troops in the war made
it unlikely that John would be able to return to Brittany
shortly.

From Charles V's point of view a more decisive judgement on John's *lèse-majesté* was desirable after the events
of 1377–8. By July 1378 moves had been made to bring
John's case into *Parlement*.[2] With the example not only of
the expropriation of Charles the Bad's estates in Normandy
behind him but also of the confiscation of Guyenne from
Edward III in 1369 (which had turned out so favourably for
the French), Charles V was thinking of a similar annexation
of Brittany in the autumn of 1378.[3] His brother, Anjou, was
perhaps not quite so enthusiastic because he knew his
mother-in-law's views. Her lawyers, however, were ready
to state her case for the succession, which they did in the
second week of December 1378.[4] Breton resistance to
French interference in the internal running of the duchy
had been a feature of the Duke's exile.[5] Opposition to
Charles V's plans was confirmed when the sentence of
confiscation pronounced against John IV also set aside
Penthièvre claims. Breton envoys were quickly dispatched
to England to discuss how the crisis should be met.[6]

It seems likely that the envoys' original intention was to
rendezvous not with John IV, but with his legal heir,
John de Bretagne, still held prisoner with his brother by the
English.[7] Whether the envoys informed Bretagne of plans

---

[1] É. Perroy, 'L'affaire du comte de Denia', *Mélanges Louis Halphen*, pp. 573–80.

[2] Delachenal, v. 242.

[3] Pocquet, *B.E.C.* cxxv (1967), 162.

[4] A.N. KK 242, fol. 105, Me Guy de Cleder and Me Jean le Begut left Angers on
6 Nov. 1378 'hastivement en certaines besoignes et affaires que madame la duchesse
[d'Anjou] avont a faire pardevers madame la duchesse de Bretaigne [Joan de Penth-
ièvre] par lettres de Mondit Seigneur le duc [d'Anjou] donne le xviiie jour doctobre'.
On 6 Dec. Anjou ordered a messenger to take certain 'lettres closes secrettes' to the
Duchess of Brittany 'et dicelles raportant hastivement la response a Paris par devers le
dit Mons. le Lieutenant'. *Chron. des règnes de Jean II et de Charles V*, ed. Delachenal,
iii. 213–19, for process against John in Dec. 1378.

[5] Lefranc, *Olivier de Clisson*, p. 176.

[6] Borderie, iv. 47–53; Pocquet, *B.E.C.* cxxv (1967), 161 ff.

[7] Issue Roll 471 m. 21 (17 Mar. 1379), order to pay John de Clare on English
Council's mandate 'ad ducendum certos nuncios venientes de partibus Britannie
usque in Angliam de London usque castrum de Merleburgh ad loquelam habendam

already formed to set aside his claims, or whether he suggested this solution, their talks seem to have encouraged
the Penthièvre faction in their resistance to Charles V and
united the Breton nobility in a plan to recall John IV.[1] Only
Clisson stood aside in unrelenting opposition.[2] The English,
for their part, agreed to these new moves and facilitated
negotiations by issuing safe-conducts for the envoys. They
promised to equip John IV with a force of 4,000 men.[3]
Joan de Penthièvre and her third son, Henry, procrastinated
when Anjou tried to find out the exact nature of the leagues
of Breton seigneurs and the plans to reinstate John IV. In
this uncertain atmosphere Charles V, after contemplating a
reduction of the duchy by force, decided negotiation was the
safer course of action.[4]

John IV took some time to become fully convinced that
the Bretons' wishes for his return were sincere. Financial
difficulties, as usual, hampered the English Government's
preparations, and explain the smallness of the force which
finally left Southampton towards the end of July.[5] But the
Breton welcome was genuine. Excusing themselves to
Anjou, who did likewise to Charles V, the majority of
Breton seigneurs swore allegiance to John within three weeks
of his return.[6] The Constable of France, who controlled a
number of forts in north-eastern Brittany, actually stood by
while the Duke landed, without opposing him. Presented
with a *fait accompli* in the duchy and insurrection that

cum filiis Karoli de Bloys in custodia Rogeri de Bello Campo infra castrum pre-
dictum existentibus'.

[1] Treaty Roll 63 m. 3 (31 Mar. 1379), safe conduct for Étienne Guyon, master
of Joan's household, Berthelot d'Angoulevant, and others coming to treat for the
ransom of Blois hostages. Guyon was back in the duchy by 4 May, when he was
charged with carrying letters to John IV asking him to return (*Preuves*, ii. 218).
He, Angoulevant, and two others received new safe conducts on 22 May (Treaty
Roll 63 m. 2).

[2] Joan de Penthièvre was later excommunicated for her debts to Clisson; Bib.
mun. Nantes, fonds Bizeul, MS. 1693, no. 16 (22 May 1380).

[3] Above, n. 1, for conducts; *Preuves*, ii. 220–3.

[4] Pocquet, *B.E.C.* cxxv (1967), 170 ff.; Moranvillé, *Jean le Mercier*, pp. 319–
20; Anjou had been making repeated efforts to find out Joan's intentions (A.N.
KK 242, fol. 107, payments for messengers in Mar. and May 1379).

[5] John was just west of the mouth of the Orne (dép. Calvados) on 28 July
(Pocquet, *B.E.C.* cxxv (1967), 147); Sherborne, *E.H.R.* lxxix (1964), 730–2.

[6] Pocquet, *B.E.C.* cxxv (1967), 167 ff.; Froissart, ed. Lettenhove, ix. 510.

required Anjou's attention in southern France, Charles V accepted the offers of mediation that Anjou and the Count of Flanders made on John's behalf.[1]

Once back in Brittany, John was faced again with his perpetual conflict of dual allegiance. But conditions now differed somewhat from those obtaining in 1364. John had not regained his duchy exclusively by English aid, and what aid was forthcoming only complicated John's policy in the winter of 1379–80. The only English garrison in Brittany was the isolated one at Brest. There were even fewer important English advisers than in 1364. The Duke's household contained a number of Englishmen still, but their interests were first and foremost to him, not to wide estates in the duchy.[2] Despite some outbreaks of violence and war damage, the duchy had not lost its respect for authority provided it was exercised with due regard for Breton precedents and customs, as it had been by the caretaker administration.[3] However deferential the Breton seigneurs had been to Charles V or however eagerly they had accepted his pensions and gifts, it was his prime mistake to believe that this entitled him to interfere more closely in duchy affairs. The attempted confiscation produced a startling example of the independent spirit Bretons manifested in defence of rights they considered their own.[4] The Breton nobility, as that of Béarn twelve years later on the death of Gaston Fébus,[5] acted swiftly to ensure the maintenance of their privileges and the autonomy of the Breton duchy vis-à-vis Valois France.

Although John returned with only a handful of Englishmen, there was amongst them, as Clisson reported to Anjou,

---

[1] Delachenal, v. 266–73. John's itinerary through the duchy up to 28 Nov. can be followed in his household accounts (A.L.A. E 206).

[2] *Preuves*, ii. 230; Hay du Chastelet, *Hist. de Bertrand du Guesclin*, p. 473.

[3] When it was learnt that the Bishop of Saint-Brieuc was pro-French and supported the confiscation, he found his see untenable and was translated to Avranches (*Anciens Évêchés de Bretagne, diocèse de Saint-Brieuc*, ed. J. Geslin de Bourgogne and A. de Barthélemy, i. 28); *Cartulaire du Morbihan*, no. 583, confirmation by Charles V of certain lands acquired by Rohan, because when he obtained them the duchy was in the King's hand but 'en faisant les dits bans [i.e. publishing the transaction] n'en fut faite aucune mention', an omission which clearly demonstrates the Breton position.   [4] *Preuves*, ii. 214 ff., for Defence Leagues.

[5] Tucoo-Chala, *Gaston Fébus*, p. 339.

'un certain sage Clerc Anglois qui est dou conseil dou Roy d'Angleterre'.[1] Clisson also had knowledge of the outlines of John's agreement with Richard II. He was of the opinion that John had agreed, as in 1372, to declare Anglo-Breton solidarity once he could get his subjects to consent. This intelligence, although inaccurate in detail, was based on a firm foundation.[2] The implications of John's agreement with Richard were plain enough. England had agreed to pay for the troops that were with the Duke, and the Duke was to act, with the advice of Englishmen accompanying him, as the King's lieutenant not only for the reconquest of Brittany but also for an expedition into France.[3] The logistical terms of the 1372 alliance were confirmed by the Duke, who was to make arrangements to feed, house, and reinforce the troops from England by rousing his own subjects to the Anglo-Breton cause. By this service he would discharge renewed debts to England incurred since 1372.

In the event, the strict terms of the indenture could not be kept. John sailed with only a fraction of the suggested number of troops. There was no attempt to carry the campaign into France, and there was no need to relieve a siege at Bordeaux, for which eventuality a clause in the original indenture had allowed.[4] The Duke's primary aim was the reoccupation of his duchy, which was quickly achieved. Already, the English had reduced the numbers they proposed to send him by three-quarters, so there was no chance of a prolonged campaign.[5] By 20 September Clisson's 'sage clerc', identified as Walter Skirlaw, was back in England. On the following day safe conducts were issued for a Breton embassy to come to England.[6] In the meantime another small expedition was prepared, which finally left England in December, much to the relief of inhabitants of the southern counties and much to the embarrassment of the Duke,

---

[1] *Preuves*, ii. 230.   [2] Ibid. 220–3; *Foedera*, iv. 67.

[3] Delachenal, v. 262; Russell, *English Intervention*, p. 284.

[4] *Preuves*, ii. 221.

[5] £1,000 had been advanced as a prest for 4,000 men in April. By Sept. 1379 the numbers had been cut to 650 men-at-arms and 650 archers (Issue Roll 472 mm. 16, 19).

[6] Accts. Var. 318/21 (Skirlaw's accounts for journey to Brittany); *Foedera*, iv. 70.

because of overtures which were being made simultaneously
to come to an agreement with France.[1] If this force, under
the command of Sir John Arundel, had been intended to
unite with the Duke's own forces in a combined land and
sea attack on the Nantes region held by Clisson, it fell far
short of this objective. The indiscipline of Arundel's men,
the wintry conditions, and the lack of authoritative leadership conspired to make this one of the most disastrous
failures of English arms in the 1370s.[2]

The hallmark of the Duke's policy at this moment was
indecision. The good offices of the Count of Flanders and
the co-operation of Joan de Penthièvre were thoroughly
exploited in an attempt to come to terms with the French.
Negotiations were held in January 1380 and continued
more or less seriously for the rest of the year, although both
sides prevaricated at times.[3] Yet the Duke continued to
dally with the English. New powers were issued for ambassadors to go to England, and his continued complicity in
Gaunt's schemes is indicated by commissions to them to
treat specifically with Gaunt as well as with Richard II.[4]
Some Breton seigneurs were again won over to John's point of
view, since the noble ambassadors who arrived in England in
February 1380 were all signatories of the Defence League
of the previous year.[5] The extent of ducal compliance with
English wishes was once more made apparent in the treaty of
Westminster drafted on 1 March and confirmed by Richard II
a fortnight later.[6] Although the military terms were not as

---

[1] *C.P.R. 1377–81*, 420; Pocquet, *B.E.C.* cxxv (1967), 177 ff.

[2] Delachenal, v. 281–3; *Chronicon Angliae*, ed. Thomson, pp. 247–53. The
expedition sailed on 6 Dec. (*Anonimalle Chronicle*, pp. 131–2); Lefranc, *Olivier de
Clisson*, p. 199; Sherborne, *E.H.R.* lxxix (1964), 731.

[3] *Preuves*, ii. 232–3; Hay du Chastelet, *Hist. de Bertrand du Guesclin*, p. 469, a
letter (31 Jan. 1380) to Anjou, reporting negotiations. A new procuration for the
Count of Flanders to act on John IV's behalf was issued in March (*Invt. Somm. Arch.
Dép. Pas-de-Calais, série A*, i. 136 (A. 102)); Delachenal, v. 275 ff., for later talks.

[4] A.L.A. E 120, no. 18 (8 Jan. 1380), appointment of envoys 'devers nostre
trescher Seignour et frere le Roy de Castelle et de Leon et duc de Lancastre pour
nous alier a li . . .'; cf. *Gaunt's Register 1379–83*, ii, nos. 1199–1202; *Foedera*, iv. 74
(10 Jan. 1380), appointment to treat with King.

[5] B.M. MS. Cott. Julius B. VI, fol. 17 (20 Feb.), new commission.

[6] Ibid., fol. 17ʳ, as *Foedera*, iv. 77 (1 Mar.), and ibid., fol. 19, Richard's confirmation. Although the English ambassadors were not officially appointed until
5 Mar. (Treaty Roll 64 m. 14), the draft treaty was delivered to the Treasury

specific as those of 1372, the Duke offered a refuge in Brittany for any English force sent to France. If the King were personally to lead such an expedition, the Duke would make every effort to put more castles and troops at his disposal. The existing treaty over Brest was reconfirmed. The King conceded that the Duke would owe him no homage if Richard succeeded to the French crown. In view of the double negotiations with England and France at this time, it is difficult to decide the Duke's true position. Was he, perhaps, merely insuring himself in case of a further period of exile? This is suggested by the way he now waited on events.

But there is little doubt that the English took the alliance seriously and initiated its implementation. They were eager to employ the long campaigning season now before them, and preparations were in hand by the time the Breton ambassadors were ready to go home. Boats were arrested in March, and by May, Thomas, Earl of Buckingham, agreed to be ready with a large force on 4 June for a year's service.[1] John IV was informed immediately and at least passively accepted the situation, since he did not give in to those of his own subjects who favoured an agreement with France.[2] But with the change of Buckingham's landfall from Brittany to Calais, probably due to a shortage of shipping,[3] John's position improved. While Buckingham led his troops, much as Gaunt had done in 1373, through eastern France, the death of Charles V on 16 September removed the great obstacle to a Franco-Breton peace treaty. By the time

---

on 1 Mar. (Palgrave, ii. 6). Gifts to the Bretons marked the confirmation (Warrants for Issues, file 11/71, 16 Mar.), see also Issue Roll 475 m. 17. The account by J. Calmette and E. Déprez, *La France et l'Angleterre en conflit*, pp. 219-24, of these negotiations is based on a 'collage' of documents, most of which belong to other periods of negotiation. Their quotations from B.M. MS. Cott. Julius B. VI are made with little evident attempt to check internal indications of date (e.g. p. 221, quoting fol. 55, takes no account of the fact that the document mentions the 'duc de Gloucestre' and is thus post-1385).

[1] Delachenal, v. 276-7, 365-85; Sherborne, *E.H.R.* lxxix (1964), 731-3; B.M. Add. Ch. 7914 (May 1380), copy of Buckingham's indenture sent to Sir John Bourchier; Accts. For. 14 m. 20ʳ, accounts of Sir John Cheyne, who received £40 on 5 May, left London on 6 May 'versus Ducem Britannie et Barones suos ob causam affinitatis tractate inter ipsum Regem et prefatum Ducem et subditos suos', and returned at the beginning of October.

[2] Pocquet, *B.E.C.* cxxv (1967), 183, notes how few these Francophile Bretons were.   [3] *Chronicon Angliae*, p. 266.

Buckingham was able to turn westwards in Champagne and make his way towards Brittany in the early autumn, John had intensified his efforts at the French court.[1] Unbeknown to Buckingham and the English Government, who were making arrangements as late as February 1381 to send reinforcements to Brittany,[2] John's ambassadors agreed to a second treaty of Guérande—this time with the French monarchy—which was drafted in January 1381 and confirmed at Guérande in April.[3] While John was pulling off this *coup*, he kept Buckingham's troops engaged in the wasteful siege of French-held Nantes for several wearing winter months. Presented with the *fait accompli*, Buckingham was astounded. Solaced partially by liberal *douceurs*, he led his depleted and demoralized forces from Brittany at the end of April.[4]

In just over a decade seven major and two minor expeditions involving Brittany or John IV had been launched from England in one of the most intensive periods of aggression in the Hundred Years War.[5] Most variations on the theme

---

[1] Borderie, iv. 60–7; *Invt. Somm. Arch. Dép. Pas-de-Calais, série A*, i. 137 (A. 102), for damage caused by Buckingham in Picardy; by 5 Sept. his forces were near Chartres (B.N. MS. Clairambault 33, p. 2447, no. 48, quittance to French treasurers for war from Andrew de Cobestaign, esq., and eight other esquires who, under Enguerrand de Coucy and Philip of Burgundy, were pursuing the English).

[2] Issue Roll 481 mm. 8 and 12, 3 and 21 Dec. 1380, payments to messengers going to Buckingham 'in obsessu ante villam de Nantes', together with barges and reinforcements; Sherborne, *E.H.R.* lxxix (1964), 732; as late as 6 Apr. a nuncio was 'misso ex precepto consilii versus partes Devonie et abinde versus partes Brittannie cum litteris de privato sigillo directis certis personis assignatis ad conducendum X mille libras versus partes Britannie' (Issue Roll 481 m. 25).

[3] *Preuves*, ii. 285, 294, 298–303; Pocquet, *Les Papes*, i. 403–4, and id., *B.E.C.* cxxv (1967), 181 ff.

[4] A.L.A. E 120, no. 19, 8 Apr., obligation of John IV to Buckingham, Latimer, Thomas Percy, William Windsor, and John Harleston to pay 20,000 francs at Brest and/or Cherbourg by 2 June; ibid. 120/17, no. 2, 23 Apr., Percy and Latimer acknowledge receipt of 30,000 frs. and 1,000 frs. of the 20,000; ibid., no. 1, 28 July, attorneys of Buckingham, Latimer, Percy, Windsor, and Harleston, recognize receipt of 6,000 frs. of 20,000 frs. delivered at Brest.

In their Exchequer accounts, Windsor acknowledged receipt of 2,600 frs. (worth £433. 6s. 8d.) from Percy and Latimer (Accts. Var. 39/7, no. 2). Hugh Hastings received 260 frs. (Accts. Var. 39/9, no. 4). Ralph, Lord Basset, said he received nothing (Accts. Var. 39/8, no. 6). Thomas Percy accounted for 15,271 frs.; the rest was to be accounted for jointly with Latimer's executors (Accts. Var. 39/6). All these payments were from the 30,000 frs.

[5] These expeditions were those of Knolles (1370), Neville (1372), Salisbury (1373), Gaunt and John IV (1373), John IV and March (1375), Buckingham and John IV

of a *chevauchée* had been played, and amphibious actions had been tried as well. The net gain to England in territories won or defended was small; whilst the cost of the war had brought domestic controversies to a head—on their return Buckingham's troops were used to put down rebel peasants. English policy hesitated between prosecuting war on a grand scale, reminiscent of the heyday of Edwardian success, and the temporary plugging of gaps in a defensive system which placed England's first line of defence across the Channel. It was doomed to failure on both counts unless sufficient finance were available. The ambitious schemes of Gaunt and Buckingham were expensive luxuries, especially once the French had begun to put their military house in order and to avoid pitched battles.[1] With the benefit of hindsight it can be said that English military objectives were often ill-defined, schemes badly executed, and tactical advantages poorly exploited. Communications between England and an ally like John IV were often poor, and the motives of such allies were mixed or frankly contradictory. For most of this war period John was in no position to give the aid he promised and was, indeed, dependent on English charity. Once back in his duchy his interests quickly diverged from those of Richard II's uncles. He learnt that compromise, deceit, and duplicity were essential parts of his stock-in-trade as a politician. He had entered the Anglo-French war in 1372 in the hope of profit. His reward was exile, and on his return to Brittany he determined to walk more carefully the path between England and France.

(1377–8), Gaunt (1378), Sir John Arundel (1379), Buckingham (1380); all, except those of Neville and Arundel, involved over 5,000 soldiers and sailors.

[1] Contamine, *Azincourt*, pp. 147–68, and id., *Les Cahiers vernonnais*, iv. 19–32; Delachenal, *passim*.

IV

BETWEEN ENGLAND AND FRANCE
1381–1389

THE second treaty of Guérande (6 April 1381), like
the first treaty sixteen years earlier, circumscribed
John IV's limits of action in three respects. It
regulated his relations both with France and England and
with his own people.[1] With regard to France, the terms were
not so severe as might have been expected. Homage was
eventually performed with the same ambiguous formula that
had been used in 1366.[2] John specifically swore to oppose the
Kings of England and Navarre in their French pretensions,
to oust any influential Englishmen from the duchy, and to
pay France an indemnity of 200,000 francs. The treaty was,
in effect, very similar to the ransom treaties Edward III
had imposed on his victims in the 1350s.[3] It was intended
to place John at a disadvantage in his future activities, and
French success in this direction can be seen in the way in
which John tempered his policies. Few instalments of the
200,000 francs were paid; but John did not antagonize the
French, and his aim was clearly to serve them in such a
fashion that they would remit the debt.[4]

John's participation in the Flanders expedition against
Bishop Despenser's crusade in 1383 can be interpreted in
this light. Without great danger to himself or Brittany, he
was able to contribute substantially to Charles VI's force.
Always the opportunist, he had the foresight to obtain letters
of non-prejudice for this armed service, prolongation of the
terms for repayment laid down at Guérande, and the recognition of Breton currency as valid within Valois France during

---

[1] *Preuves*, ii. 298–301.   [2] Ibid. 376.
[3] Cf. Le Patourel, *T.R.H.S.*, 5th ser., x (1960), 25–7.
[4] A.L.A. E 104, letters prolonging terms for payment issued by Charles VI on
29 Sept. 1381, 24 Mar. and 30 Sept. 1382. A quittance for 12,500 frs. was issued
on 1 Nov. 1382 (ibid.).

the period of the expedition.[1] The Duke obtained relief for
the hard-pressed English troops at Bourbourg,[2] an action
which merited adverse criticism from the Religious of
Saint-Denis,[3] who also found the Duke's mediation at the
succeeding Anglo-French talks objectionable. The talks
were lengthy and expensive; for the Duke 'aliquantis namque
diebus cum hostibus tempus in vacuum tenens, multa verba
secretissima habuit super componenda pace; quam tamen,
ut promiserat, minime solidavit'.[4] But they had served John's
purpose admirably. The royal uncles were so impressed
that full remission of the outstanding Guérande indemnity
was quickly granted.[5]

Brittany's relations with France settled down into the
pattern already developed before 1373; whilst John's own
personal friendship with the royal uncles, Berry and Burgundy, buttressed his position in the duchy. The second
treaty of Guérande had been achieved through the mediation of the Duke of Anjou. His commitments in Italy
soon removed him from the scene, but his brothers stepped
into his place. Their sympathetic respect for Brittany was
engendered, we might suspect, partly by their envy of John's
independence from royal control, a freedom they wanted to
exercise within their own apanages, and partly because all
three Dukes, Berry, Burgundy, and Brittany, were threatened by the growth of Olivier de Clisson's power, either in
Brittany and Poitou or at the French court. The struggle
between John and Clisson in Brittany and between Clisson
and the royal uncles at Paris was a dominant theme of the
1380s. John found that he could never treat Clisson as a
simple subject. His inclusion in the Guérande settlement and
his alliance with John in 1382 made him almost the Duke's

[1] A.L.A. E 104 (16 July 1383), letters of non-prejudice; A.N. J 243, no. 68
(19 Aug. 1383), money concession.

[2] Froissart, ed. Lettenhove, x. 514; M. Aston, 'The Impeachment of Bishop
Despenser', *B.I.H.R.* xxxviii (1965), 127–48.

[3] *Chronique du Religieux de Saint-Denys,* ed. Bellaguet, i. 284 ff.

[4] Ibid. 296.

[5] A.L.A. E 104 (27 Oct. 1383), letters of remission. For 'des grans frais et
missions que lui convient faire en certain fait, que commis lui avons es parties de
Saint Omer et environ' John received 3,000 and then 4,000 frs. a month (B.N. MS.
fr. 20405, no. 5). 'Et il soit neccesoite que nostre dit Cousin entende a vacqer
encores es dictes besoingnes . . .', ibid., no. 6 (10 Nov. 1383). John was paid up to
Feb. 1384 (ibid., nos. 4, 7, 8, 12; MS. fr. 20590, nos. 28, 39; *Preuves,* ii. 444).

equal; whilst his exercise of the office of Constable of France was at the expense of the royal uncles' own leadership.[1] When Clisson's attempts to ransom John de Bretagne, Count of Penthièvre, brought him to the edge of civil war with John IV, the latter's friendship with Berry and Burgundy was vital to his survival.

After 1381 the Duke again followed a policy of reducing seigneurial power. On occasion this led to appeals to Paris, where John's friends helped to give him confidence in his opposition to the legal advisers of the Valois monarchy.[2] But despite the campaign against seigneurial rights, revealed in the dispossession of the Dame de Rays (1383), the ducal defence of taxation at Paris (1383–4), the licensing of castle building, the application of *fouages*, attacks on the bishops, and so on,[3] there was genuine co-operation in government. There were no longer such overt fears that John was an anglophile.

Ducal policy towards France in the first few years after Guérande was typified by bouts of defiance interspersing calm periods in which he sought to allay French fears and, by doing small services (as long as these did not restrict Breton rights), to obtain French goodwill and so escape from the most pressing of the 1381 obligations. John's position was a subordinate one. Wishing to send an embassy to England in 1382, he had to wait several months for French approval.[4] And it was not until after 1384, when the 1381 treaty had been commuted, that John became less respectful and more insistent on his claims to pensions and lands in France. The French, for their part, knew that partial satisfaction and additional promises on these scores would retain John's interest and avoid renewed opposition.[5]

---

[1] Ibid. 298, 303, 370, 379; Lefranc, *Olivier de Clisson*, p. 229.

[2] A.N. J 243, nos. 69, 70, John's defence against the Count of Alençon, 1383–4; cf. Pocquet, *B.E.C.* lxxxvi (1925), 403.

[3] *Arch. hist. Poitou*, xxviii (1898), p. cv (Rays); Pocquet, *R.H.D.F.E.*, 4th ser., xl (1962), 360–2.

[4] Treaty Roll 67 m. 30 (27 Oct. 1382), protections for Breton embassy; extended 10 Mar. 1383 (ibid. m. 9); *Preuves*, ii. 379 (5 Mar. 1383), Charles VI's permission.

[5] A.L.A. E 108 (7 June 1382), *vidimus* of 27 May grant of lands and pensions to John in France. John appointed a commission to take possession of these on 5 May 1383 (ibid.). On 26 Sept. 1384 another commission complained about failure to render the lands. Various other promises were substituted (ibid.).

Franco-Breton affairs in this period reveal the unsatisfactory and inconclusive nature of this type of diplomacy, where both sides had some aims in common, but where they also had important differences of opinion. The Duke was often powerless to secure favourable terms, no matter how cleverly he played off rivals against each other in France. It was part of the penalty he paid for his ambiguous semi-independent position between England and France.

Within Brittany, Guérande wiped the slate clean. War crimes were pardoned, and there was a return to the *status quo ante bellum*. Grievances as old as the first treaty of Guérande were finally satisfied, and few stood out against the treaty.[1] The administration began to function once more as it had before 1373, and the Duke surrounded himself in council with Bretons. Few indeed are the Englishmen to be found holding administrative posts after 1381, and if Walsingham is right (and there is reason to believe him), even the household was purged.[2] With the death of the Duchess Joan in 1384, there was little reason to recruit new English servants. The occasional differences of opinion between John and some of his subjects about the attitude Brittany should adopt towards the Anglo-French war are not to be accounted for on 'national' grounds; it was not a question of policies advocated by Englishmen domiciled in Brittany conflicting with those advocated by native Bretons. They were differing opinions held by individual Bretons. Again, as before 1373, John was not alone in the double game he was to play between England and France. His diplomatic advisers were experienced in promoting his case at both Westminster and Paris. They were supported by an increasingly efficient civil service; whilst the seigneurs played their own part in ducal government by accepting positions of power and responsibility.[3]

---

[1] The Sire de Derval got his lands back (above, p. 53). *Preuves,* ii. 273–80 (A.N. J 242, nos. 56–7).

[2] *Historia Anglicana,* ii. 46–7; *Chronicon Angliae,* pp. 331–2; Curteys (above, p. 41, n. 4) left Brittany, and by 1393 he was Gaunt's butler (*C.C.R. 1392–6,* 168). Blakemore returned to England (below, p. 197); whilst FitzNicol seems to have remained there (below, p. 185). The only important English official in John's administration was Monde Radwell, treasurer and receiver-general at various dates between 1387 and 1397 (A.L.A. E 166–7, accounts for payments to Clisson, *fouages,* etc.).   [3] Table of Allegiances, col. 9.

John's volte-face at Guérande was a blow to English war hopes. A radical reassessment of England's continental policies was called for. The massive co-operation envisaged in the 1372 and 1380 alliances had resulted in enormous expenditure for a minimal return. Whatever the Duke's personal feelings, his subjects had made it plain that they did not want an English alliance. They preferred, with suitable provisos, a subordinate position under France. Even English diplomats in 1381 had been prepared to admit that Breton matters were a domestic concern of the French alone.[1] John's homage to Charles VI in September 1381 was a further nail in the coffin of Anglo-Breton understanding. The English Government reacted by confiscating Richmond, and the situation deteriorated still further when they continued to retain Brest and Joan Holland failed to return to Brittany.[2]

In four successive years (1382–5) ambassadors arrived in England from Brittany, setting a pattern which persisted until 1397. They came to demand the return of Brest and Richmond and always raised a number of subsidiary matters.[3] Over these latter items the English were prepared to relent, if only after prevarication. Thus the Duchess was returned to the duchy, ducal *brefs* at Bordeaux were recognized, short truces for Brest castle were arranged, small ducal debts were remitted, and favours to former ducal servants were confirmed.[4] On occasion ducal initiative was reciprocated by more positive English action; so in 1382 envoys were appointed to conclude a commercial pact with

[1] 'Voyage de Nicolas de Bosc, évêque de Bayeux pour négocier la paix entre les couronnes de France et d'Angleterre', ed. E. Martène and U. Durand, pp. 309 ff.

[2] *C.F.R. 1377–83*, 274 (confiscation). In 1381 Joan was in the Tower of London when it was besieged by the rebel peasants (Knighton, ii. 132). Froissart, ed. Luce, x. 168–9, claims her exile was enforced, though it is likely that Richard II's court was more to her liking than the Breton one (cf. Borderie, iv. 134). She did, however, suffer from ill health and received papal dispensations from fasting.

[3] *Preuves*, ii. 380 (1382), 450–6 (1384); Treaty Roll 67 m. 9 (1383); ibid. 69 m. 3 (10 May–8 June 1385).

[4] Joan was willing to return in 1382 and, apparently, the Government were willing to let her (*Preuves*, ii. 380; A.L.A. E 115, nos. 4, 5, discussions of June). It was not until July–August 1383 that she finally left (Chancery Warrants, file 481, no. 2881, 3 Aug. 1383, order to pay issues of Richmond up to the day of her departure). A.L.A. E 201, 12 June 1384, recognition of *brefs*; ibid. E 120, nos. 13, 14, truces at Brest; below, pp. 105, 195, for favours and released debts.

the duchy.[1] Yet over the main issues, Brest and Richmond, the English were adamant, and nothing, in their eyes, could absolve John from his treachery in 1381.

This state of affairs can best be illustrated by reference to the Salisbury Parliament of 1384. This meeting emphasized the inconsistencies inherent in English foreign policy since the reopening of the Anglo-French war in 1369. The prosecution of the war was extremely expensive as a result of the decision taken in the late 1370s to maintain a number of barbicans in France. In the early 1380s a further extension of this defensive ring was attempted in Flanders by taking advantage of the Count's difficulties.[2] Louis de Male's death in January 1384 and the succession of Philip of Burgundy opened a critical stage in this battle for control. But English arms, as John IV knew so well, had latterly suffered a number of setbacks, and there were several Englishmen who criticized the bellicose policies of the King's uncles and would, in turn, have settled for an accommodation with France if it could have been arranged without too great a sacrifice of prestige by Richard II. Amongst these critics, it has lately been argued, can be numbered Michael de la Pole, Chancellor of England and intimate adviser of the young King.[3] Without attempting to argue here for Pole's pacific tendencies, it may be stated that, in his speech to Parliament at Salisbury,[4] he himself recognized another aspect of the tension between two divergent foreign policies of war or peace. Although it can be sensed that there was amongst the Government and commons a general consensus of opinion in favour of an exploration of the possibilities of peace, Pole stated that advantageous terms from France would only be obtained from a position of strength. Thus the Breton embassy, which was present in Salisbury, was wasting its time in asking for the return of Brest, because that was one of England's bargaining counters which could not be sacrificed at that moment.[5] Instead the English had to maintain the

---

[1] A.L.A. E 120, no. 15 (25 June 1382).

[2] English interference at Ghent can be interpreted in this way, cf. Vaughan, *Philip the Bold*, pp. 19 ff.

[3] J. Palmer, 'The Anglo-French Peace Negotiations, 1386–1399', London Ph.D. thesis, 1967, pp. 6 ff. I am indebted to Dr. Palmer for allowing me to see this thesis.   [4] *Rot. Parl.* iii. 166 ff.   [5] *Preuves*, ii. 450–6.

Duke's interest, much as the French were doing, by small immediate rewards and by holding out the prospect of much greater future recompense. They needed his technical neutrality, but the persistent complaints of the Duke were met time and time again by procrastination or by recriminations on England's part. In 1384 the only concession obtained by the Bretons was the recognition of ducal *brefs*, but not before their threat to revert to the older and more barbaric right of *brisage* had been recognized as a serious danger to England's sea-links with Guyenne. Otherwise the English were confident that they could keep John reasonably happy by offering to treat with him at greater length in forthcoming general Anglo-French talks.[1] Again Brittany's weakness in international politics is revealed. And matters might well have continued in this vein for some years, until the English had resolved their internal dissensions over foreign policy, had it not been for two deaths in the autumn of 1384.

Joan Holland, who had returned to Brittany just over a year before, drew up her will on 25 September 1384 and died a few weeks later.[2] Released from this personal tie with England, the Duke wished to use his new freedom for political ends.[3] The succession problem was still unsolved, and Joan de Penthièvre's death on 10 September had clearly established her son John de Bretagne, Count of Penthièvre, as John's rival, although he was still a prisoner in England.[4] Already Clisson had seen that the return of the Count to

---

[1] At first Gaunt showed interest, but then he told the Breton spokesman, Robert Brochereul, to write down all his complaints because he 'ne peult jamais retenir ne entendre la moitie de ce que ledit Procureur disoit, pour ce qu'il avoit la teste et la memoire de foible retenue, comme il disoit' (*Preuves*, ii. 450). Since it was less than six months before that Gaunt and John IV had met at Leulinghen (A.L.A. E 120, no. 11), Gaunt's excuses were palpably false.

[2] A.L.A. E 24 (will). A memorial service was held for her at St. Paul's, London, on 27 Nov. 1384 (E. Anstis, *Order of the Garter*, ii, p. xii, and B.M. Add. MS. 24512, fol. 97ʳ, wardrobe expenses).

[3] A.N. J 240, no. 40 (document sent to the *Chambre des comptes*, Paris, 9 July 1385), request of John IV to Charles VI that 'moy et touz mes amis avons tresgrans desire de mariage qui soit a celle que ge puisse avoir lignee et en ce touz mes subgiz me ont exorte et requis par maintesfoiz. Et a l'on parlle de pluseurs dont les unes sont si jeunes que bonnement ne seroit la lignee par elles si briefvement tromper, comme mes amis et soubgiz le desirent'.

[4] *Preuves*, ii. 481. For Penthièvre, see above, p. 85.

Brittany would dangerously embarrass the Duke. Together with the widowed Duchess of Anjou, Penthièvre's sister, Clisson was working for his release.[1] But this was not simply a question of raising a certain sum of money. In England and Brittany there was now room for diplomatic manœuvring. In November 1384 Parliament, though it kept its decision secret, declared Richmond officially forfeit. At Christmas a small private Breton embassy was in England seeking terms for the ransom of the Blois hostages, and in February the Urbanist Bishop of Nantes was licensed to go to Brittany.[2] The reasons for this pressure on John IV are not easily discoverable, since the English Government does not seem to have been planning a more active policy in north-western France, and recent tradition had been to obtain the support of the duchy, at least in theory. Even if the Government was thinking of making peace with France, the neutrality of Brittany was a useful balance, and yet there was, it seems, a deliberate attempt to provoke the Duke. The breach was to grow still wider.

In the autumn of 1384 John had taken a strong line over the problem of Penthièvre. Assured of much more broadly based support from his noblemen, many of whom had transferred to his service from that of Joan de Penthièvre since 1379, he declared the Penthièvre lands forfeit.[3] Despite the protests of Penthièvre's representatives, John was not deterred. As the Angevin Chancellor noted cryptically after the return of envoys attempting to offer homage to John for Penthièvre, 'lequel homage il ne volt recevoir se il navoit la possession des forteresces'.[4] It would have been sheer military folly to allow his rival to occupy the vantage points of that apanage. Moving to the offensive, John also confirmed his opposition to the Angevins by attacking Champtoceaux. Angevin complaints were then transmitted to Berry, who openly acknowledged his friendship for John by sending the Angevin envoys on a fruitless journey to

---

[1] Clisson was appointed Penthièvre's lieutenant on 6 Jan. 1385 (*Preuves*, ii. 482, now Bib. mun. Nantes, fonds Bizeul, MS. 1692, no. 3).
[2] *Rot. Parl.* iii. 279; *Foedera*, vii. 454, and Treaty Roll 69 m. 12; Perroy, *L'Angleterre et le Grand Schisme*, p. 106. John had accepted the Clementist leanings of his subjects in 1379 without demur.   [3] *Preuves*, ii. 481.
[4] *Journal de Jean le Fèvre*, ed. H. Moranvillé, p. 56.

Paris, thereby making them waste valuable time.[1] Meanwhile John also used evasive tactics to muffle Angevin cries and, almost simultaneously, created a smoke-screen for diplomatic approaches to England by sending a couple of embassies to Paris.[2]

In England the matter of Penthièvre's ransom was rapidly becoming one of factional dispute, and a ducal embassy received short shrift from a Government busily engaged in organizing Richard II's first major expedition, not to France, as many of his subjects desired,[3] but against Scotland. The envoys claimed that they had come 'pour certeines chargeantz matiers pour trete ove le conseil lour dit seignour le Roi' on the strength of a safe conduct issued by the Council. Yet they had lost most of their substance whilst staying at an inn in Devon, and their official reception was barely formal.[4] Was this a deliberate slight? There was a section of the Council that welcomed Breton advances and enabled the envoys to get extended protections.[5] But there was also a group, opposed to the Duke, which had gained the upper hand by the end of 1385 and issued licences for a new Penthièvre embassy seeking the hostage's release, and this group received the King's support.[6]

The effects of Richard II's personal influence on English foreign policy has always been a matter of some debate. From 1381 it is impossible to discount this influence, however much one allows for the voices of Richard's tutors and friends speaking through him. It has been demonstrated that in 1383 the young King's actions had a very decided impact on the failure to make capital out of Despenser's crusade by a direct confrontation with Charles VI.[7] It is not merely a question of the King disliking war; his Scottish and Irish

[1] Ibid., pp. 58, 66, 72–5.
[2] Ibid., p. 59; *Preuves*, ii. 483, 490; Treaty Roll 69 m. 3 (protections for envoys to England, 10 May 1385).   [3] Cf. Aston, *B.I.H.R.* xxxviii (1965), 138.
[4] Anc. Pet., file 213, nos. 10648–9, for the envoys' tale of woe; *C.Inq.M. 1377–88*, 167, for inquiry into it. Apart from the protection issued to the envoys (Treaty Roll 69 m. 3), the only other official act which may be connected with this embassy is an order for the preparation of letters for the Duke to enjoy his *brefs* at Bordeaux (Chancery Warrants, file 491, no. 3834, 20 Nov. 1385).
[5] Treaty Roll 69 m. 1, 8 June 1385.
[6] Ibid. 70 m. 32 (12 Dec. 1385), m. 26 (6 Feb. 1386 extension).
[7] Aston, *B.I.H.R.* xxxviii (1965), 145–7.

expeditions disprove that theory. But Richard's heart was not in the Anglo-French war, and it is clearly apparent from 1386 that the King was prepared to turn his back on France and on Brittany. Perhaps he was wedded to the idea of peace, although there is still much to be explained about this thesis, but certainly he was prepared to compromise, to seal truces, possibly to search for a definitive peace settlement.[1] Opposed to these views, as is known only too well, were the belligerent opinions of men like Thomas, Duke of Gloucester, and Richard, Earl of Arundel.[2] From 1386 the dissonance of these clashing policies became more strident. The release by Richard of his interests in John de Bretagne to his own favourite Robert de Vere, Earl of Oxford, seems, for example, to have been a cause of discord. The original warrant for the release was unconditional, but a later warrant stipulated that the ransom obtained was to be used to furnish a force for service in Ireland under Vere.[3] Possibly it was felt that, if the King had decided to break finally with Brittany by antagonizing John IV, the profits of the transaction should not be swallowed up by the favourite. That there was some dispute over the grant to Vere at that time (it was, of course, one of the charges against him in 1388[4]) is evidently the case, because his attorneys were not allowed to take charge of Penthièvre until July 1386.[5] Yet the King, aided and abetted by Vere and Michael de la Pole, seems to have persevered with his unpopular French policy up to the time of the Merciless Parliament, although for most of 1387 his efforts were cloaked in secrecy.[6]

There was, therefore, in England a definite anti-Breton lobby. In view of the treatment John IV's interests were

[1] 'Diplomatic Correspondence of Richard II', ed. É. Perroy, Royal Hist. Society, Camden, 3rd ser., xlviii (1933), nos. 66, 78.

[2] Cf. Perroy's Gloucester, 'harum-scarum, hot-headed and brainless', *The Hundred Years War*, p. 185.

[3] *Foedera*, vii. 503 (23 Mar. 1386), conditional grant; on 8 Apr. an unconditional one was authorized under the privy seal, only to be superseded by another warrant ordering the original conditional grant (Chancery Warrants, file 492, no. 3947, 8 Apr., no. 3949, 11 Apr.; cf. *C.P.R. 1385–9*, 132).

[4] *Rot. Parl.* iii. 232, art. 23.

[5] Accts. For. 25 m. 49[r], accounts for keeping the Blois hostages, 1380–6. These show that Guy de Bretagne had died on 22 Jan. 1385.

[6] Edinburgh Univ. Library, MS. 183 (formerly Laing MS. 351), fols. 66, 84[v]–85, for envoys sent to each other in 1387 by the Kings of England and France.

receiving, it is not surprising that in 1385 and 1386 he had indicated, quite genuinely, to the French that he was prepared to take a much tougher line against the English garrison at Brest and over other matters.[1] Diplomacy had regained neither Brest nor Richmond, perhaps force would. The Religious of Saint-Denis, as usual, read the most discreditable motives into John's siege of Brest (1386–7). The Duke was, he said, trying to camouflage his incriminating correspondence with England by this screening action.[2] It is true that the siege was not always hotly pressed, especially after Gaunt had introduced new men and supplies into the castle in July 1386.[3] It is possibly true that John was forced to take action by some of his own more warlike subjects.[4] But Brest, the subject of so much diplomatic activity since 1381, constituted a *de facto* flaw in ducal pretensions. John did not need reminding of this fact by a French king, whose own failure to recapture Calais and Cherbourg was notorious. The Religious had no monopoly of truth, and it is far more likely that John saw the siege as a means of forcing England to alter her dangerous anti-ducal course. It was only in the autumn of 1386 that England recognized the full danger from the French fleet assembled at Sluys. By then, John had sent his own contingents to join it.[5]

The Parliament of October–November 1386 rectified some of the errors recently committed in Anglo-Breton affairs. There was a lull in the fighting around Brest, and the Sluys expedition came to nothing.[6] But Parliament took no chances and, after listening to a rousing speech from Pole in which he sought to exculpate Richard from popular slanders about his passivity, secured the Chancellor's dismissal

---

[1] A.N. J 240, no. 40, John IV to Charles VI, 1385, that he was prepared 'pour resister a la malice de ceulx de Brest'. Breton troops assembled at Damme for the expected invasion of England (*Preuves*, ii. 491). Documents concerning loans for this expedition can be found in B.M. Add. Charters 40, 3348–9.

[2] *Chronique . . . de Saint-Denys*, ed. Bellaguet, i. 432 ff.; Borderie, iv. 104–6.

[3] Russell, *English Intervention*, pp. 419 f.

[4] Knighton, ii. 208–9, notes the presence of Jean de Malestroit (cf. *Preuves*, ii. 530). Geoffroi de Kerimel, Marshal of Brittany, may have been hoping to erase memories of his part in the events of 1379. The confiscation of some of his lands in France since 1379 was confirmed as late as 1386 (*Arch. hist. Poitou*, xxi (1891), 315–21).

[5] B.M. Add. Charter 3350, letters of Charles VI, Amiens, 8 Sept. 1386.

[6] Vaughan, *Philip the Bold*, pp. 49 f.

and began to implement a more realistic war policy, whilst appointing a commission to survey the domestic administration.[1] Stores and money were dispatched to Brest.[2] Arundel, financed by a subsidy granted in Parliament, was appointed Admiral in December to reply in kind to the French menace. By the spring a large fleet was ready.[3] Diplomatic contact with Brittany was re-established with a view to using the duchy as the right wing of a two-pronged attack on France; the other wing was to involve Flanders.[4]

The Commission's initiative was a belated response to a Breton approach in the previous summer.[5] But although a number of new ideas emerged from the talks in February and March 1387, especially over the vexing question of Brest, the English offer was not yet convincing enough. Arundel's two expeditions in March and May 1387 did achieve some minor successes, but co-operation with continental allies proved unreliable.[6] The siege of Brest continued somewhat spasmodically, but the Commissioners and John IV were eager to compromise, and negotiations

---

[1] *Rot. Parl.* iii. 215 ff.; Tout, *Chapters,* iii. 411 ff.; Nicolas, i. 3–6.

[2] Treaty Roll 71 m. 16 (15 Nov. 1386), order to send 500 barrels of corn from Bristol. For money, see below, p. 162.

[3] Accts. For. 21 m. 14ᵛ, for Arundel's indenture, dated 16 Dec. 1386. His troops numbered between 2,300 and 2,500 (Accts. Var. 40, nos. 33–4). For payments to his fleet, weighing more than 7,000 tons and carrying over 2,600 sailors, see Accts. Var. 40/36.

[4] *Foedera,* vii. 553, 26 Feb. 1387, the English royal council appoints John Wendlynburgh to treat with the Duke's deputies. On 20 Mar. John Roches and Philip More were similarly appointed 'per ipsum Regem et Concilium' to follow up Wendlynburgh's discussions (Treaty Roll 71 m. 6). Richard's whereabouts are uncertain (cf. Tout, *Chapters,* iii. 419 n.). Roches and More were to discuss '. . . materia discordie inter nos et ipsum ducem penitus tollatur quod omnes redempciones que ad dictam villam et castrum de Brest tempore date dictarum literarum alias factarum sint exnunc commise et posite ad unam certam summam predictam apud Brest annuatim ad certos terminos inde consuetos pro redempcionibus supradictis . . .'. The honour of Richmond was also regranted to John, although it was not subsequently effective (*C.Ch.R. 1341–1417,* 301). The Council was using spies in Flanders early in 1387 (Issue Roll 515 mm. 11, 18, 20, 25, various payments to William van Oreigne 'explorator Regis' and Brother Adam Bamford sent to Ghent); see for further details J. Palmer, 'The Anglo-French Peace Negotiations, 1386–1399', pp. 32 ff.

[5] Treaty Roll 70 m. 7 (20 May 1386), protections for twelve envoys issued on the Council's warrant, and extended on 1 July (ibid. 71 m. 24).

[6] *Polychronicon,* ix. 93 ff.; Knighton, ii. 234, and *Historia Anglicana,* ii. 153–6, for Arundel's expeditions. He was back at Orwell from the first one by 13 Apr. (*C.P.R. 1385–9,* 323).

continued simultaneously.[1] In the light of these discussions, of Arundel's voyage to Brest, and of English favours to John IV, it is difficult to avoid the conclusion that the Duke's attack on Olivier de Clisson in late June 1387 was inspired by English pressure—a fact suspected by the Religious of Saint-Denis.[2]

But in order to understand the antecedents of this attack, reference is necessary to certain other factors. For nearly a year the Count of Penthièvre had been in Vere's hands, and the Angevins had been importuning the French Government to help ransom him.[3] Vere entered into negotiations for the ransom with Clisson, probably as a method of undermining the 1386 Commission, since the ransom talks were directly contrary to the Commission's undertaking to John IV.[4] The Duke may have received this unwelcome news from Berry.[5] He was in a difficult position now that he could not be certain which faction in England to trust. The renewed siege of Brest in the late spring of 1387 may have been intended as a precautionary measure. Yet again Berry's friendship proved its value, and a new alliance was concluded between the Dukes in May which specifically opposed Clisson and Penthièvre.[6] This was an incentive indeed for John to take vigorous action against the Constable. May we not see, therefore, in John's capture of Clisson, not merely the sordid treachery of 'le serf du roi d'Angleterre', but also a master stroke of policy intended to ingratiate the Duke with Berry and Burgundy at Paris (newly secured by Clisson's disgrace) and to fulfil any outstanding obligations to England? Such a construction is not complete fantasy. John was not as eager in 1387 to participate in the proposed

[1] A. de la Borderie, 'Le siège de Brest en 1387', *Rev. de Bretagne, de Vendée et d'Anjou*, ii (1889), 200–3. Issue Roll 517 m. 2 (1 May), payment to the ducal confessor, Peter Adam, in England for discussions. Treaty Roll 71 m. 2 (safe conducts) and m. 4 (trade concessions) for Breton merchants.

[2] Accts. For. 21 m. 41ᵛ, Arundel's accounts show that he was back from Brest by 12 June. *Chronique . . . de Saint-Denys*, ed. Bellaguet, i. 480 ff.

[3] *Journal de Jean le Fèvre*, ed. Moranvillé, pp. 331–3.

[4] Nicolas, i. 48.

[5] B.N. MS. fr. 22331, p. 45 (7 Apr. 1387), messenger to John IV from Berry.

[6] *Preuves*, ii. 534 (8 May). Burgundy, who would disapprove of any alliance with an enemy who had recently raided his territories, was also in touch with John (Froissart, ed. Luce, xiii, p. lxviii).

French invasion of England as he had been in 1386.[1] The Constable's capture brought preparations for this expedition to a halt.[2] This might have made the Commissioners so grateful to John that they would have ensured that Penthièvre was not released. But the plan misfired. The concessions, forced from Clisson when in ducal hands, were quickly forgotten once he had returned to the royal court.[3] Unlike an attack in 1392,[4] this one did not lead to the Constable's disgrace. Berry and Burgundy, aware of the general shocked reaction to the Duke's deed, had to accept Clisson's return to power, and, by the autumn, they stood as sureties for part of Penthièvre's ransom money.[5] More English troops were sent to Brest as a precaution against a greater attack, and the siege was raised.[6] The Duke found himself surrounded once more by danger. His political intrigues were leading him into dangerous isolation and threatened to cause his downfall. His friends in England, the Commissioners, had been powerless to halt Vere's own machinations. By January 1388 Penthièvre, free after more than thirty years, had married Clisson's daughter.[7] Although the Duke might complain bitterly, there was no option open to him but to come to terms with his domestic enemies. A temporary truce was arranged in July 1388 under Charles VI's aegis and through the mediation of Berry and Burgundy.[8]

Parallel to these events in France, where the royal uncles and the Marmosets (Charles V's most trusted senior

[1] Jacques and Morelet Montmor, governors of La Rochelle, who were commissioned to enrol men and gather boats for the 1386 and 1387 expeditions, were unable to do so in Brittany in 1387, although they had in 1386 (B.N. Pièces originales 2030, Montmor, nos. 17, 18; MS. fr. 25765, nos. 55, 115–17; MS. fr. 26022, nos. 1041, 1043–9; MS. Nouv. acq. fr. 3653, p. 63).

[2] Froissart, ed. Luce, xiii, p. lxxviii.

[3] *Preuves*, ii. 540; Froissart, ed. Lettenhove, xii. 382 ff.

[4] Below, p. 128.

[5] *Journal de Jean le Fèvre*, ed. Moranvillé, p. 417; *Preuves*, ii. 528.

[6] *Polychronicon*, ix. 98; Knighton, ii. 240. Issue Roll 518 m. 2, 7 Oct. 1387, Thomas atte Mille was 'misso versus dominum Regem in partibus Glouc' existentem per dominos de consilio Regis cum magna festinacione cum novis de rescussu per Henricum de Percy et alios de comitiva sua de obsessu tento coram castro et villa de Brest'.

[7] *Journal de Jean le Fèvre*, ed. Moranvillé, pp. 340, 478; *Preuves*, ii. 529; *Chronique . . . de Saint-Denys*, ed. Bellaguet, i. 498.

[8] *Preuves*, ii. 552; *Chronique . . . de Saint-Denys*, ed. Bellaguet, i. 506–12.

advisers) were struggling for control at Paris and where royal and provincial policies had become dangerously mixed, a curiously similar set of circumstances existed in England between the King and his opponents. After the attempted *entente* of early 1387, Anglo-Breton relations had been confused by Vere's negotiations, part and parcel of Richard's own secret discussions with France. There is good reason to believe the rumours that Richard was seeking to sabotage the Commission's attempts to wage successful war.[1] Fear of the King's foreign policy may well have been the factor that caused the Appellants to confront the King directly and accuse the five 'traitors' in November 1387.[2] In that month the 1386 Commission should have lapsed, but its most vigorous members now attempted to sort out the tangled skein of England's foreign policy. With regard to Brittany, they were too late to prevent Penthièvre's release, and an attempt made to stop the ransom money falling into Vere's hands failed, possibly through the King's interference.[3] But once again, as in 1387, direct contact was made with John IV.[4]

In 1388 there was a renewed attempt to put into action the campaigns planned for 1387. A new subsidy was voted by the Merciless Parliament for another voyage under Arundel's leadership.[5] The over-all strategy, apparently, was for a three-fronted attack on France through Flanders, Brittany, and Guyenne.[6] As usual the difficulties of co-ordinating such ambitious plans, together with the unwillingness of some of the proposed participants to play their parts, proved too formidable.[7] But because of the light

[1] T. Favent, 'Historia Mirabilis Parliamenti', ed. M. McKisack, *Camden Miscellany*, xiv (1926), 3; *Historia Anglicana*, ii. 156–7.

[2] J. Palmer, 'The Anglo-French Peace Negotiations', pp. 77 ff.

[3] Janico Dartasso, sent to arrest Vere's attorneys at Calais, was himself held captive there for two months on the King's orders early in 1388 (Treaty Roll 72 mm. 17, 8).

[4] Issue Roll 518 m. 18 (26 Jan.), payment to Richard Fotheringhay to go to Brittany. He was absent from 27 Jan. to 20 Apr. (Accts. For. 22 m. Aᵛ).

[5] His indenture was drawn up on 24 Mar. 1388 (Accts. Var. 41/4, Accts. For. 24 m. 38ʳ).

[6] The English ally William of Jülich, Duke of Guelders, was to be a key figure in the Low Countries (cf. Vaughan, *Philip the Bold*, pp. 97–9). Gaunt was to have 2,000 troops in Guyenne, Mem. Roll (E. 159), 166, Trinity, Brev. dir. bar. m. 16ʳ.

[7] Gaunt, for example, seems to have been more concerned about his private

this throws on the Appellants' foreign policy, and because of the central position of Brittany in their schemes, it is desirable to set out the main details of Arundel's expedition of 1388.

Of the chroniclers, Froissart has the fullest account of the expedition;[1] the Monk of Westminster both confirms and complements his story, and, because of his close personal knowledge of Arundel's doings, his account must be given considerable authority.[2] Froissart recounts how Arundel, after much deliberation with his colleagues in government, crossed the Channel to the Norman coast, turned northwards to Dieppe, but found all French ports prepared against him.[3] He then sailed south and west to Saint-Malo, where Clisson had garrisoned the town and had raised a number of Breton seigneurs against the Duke.[4] Nevertheless, Arundel was able to find shelter in some Breton ports, although he found that the Duke was engaged in the complicated negotiations that led to his temporary reconciliation with Clisson in July. Despite John's machinations, or in ignorance of their true extent, Arundel remained off the Breton coast until he had confirmation of the Duke's visit to Paris. The fleet then moved to La Rochelle, where a number of profitable raids on the countryside helped to maintain English morale.[5] After putting to sea again and indulging in a little piracy, Arundel returned home. The Monk of Westminster largely confirms this narrative, adding that Arundel used Brest harbour. He also gives a number of small pieces of circumstantial evidence which tie up closely with what can be gathered from official records. His account of raids on the Bay coast seems particularly authentic.[6] According to the

---

affairs than about those of England (cf. Russell, *English Intervention*, pp. 504–5; Froissart, ed. Lettenhove, xiii. 113–16, 127–36).

[1] Ed. Lettenhove, xiii. 105 ff.   [2] *Polychronicon*, ix. 182, 187–8.

[3] B.N. Pièces originales 2030, Montmor, no. 28, 12 June, for payments to a Castilian squadron in French service in the Seine. M. Rey, *Les Finances royales sous Charles VI*, pp. 379, 382; C. de la Roncière, *Hist. de la marine française*, ii. 98–100.

[4] Pocquet, *Les Papes*, i. 414.

[5] Cf. *Arch. hist. Poitou*, xxi (1891), 380, note on Bouteville. Was Arundel hoping to rendezvous with Gaunt? If so, he was too late; for Gaunt was about to arrange a local truce for all lands in dispute south of the Loire (*Foedera*, vii. 595–6).

[6] He is only one day out (2 instead of 3 Sept.) for the date of Arundel's return; whilst his references to the knighting of men on the Île de Baas are borne out by

Monk and to Thomas Walsingham,[1] the expedition had been successful, if not quite so successful as that of 1387.

Do official records help to confirm this opinion? We may doubt it. At the moment when Arundel sailed in June 1388 the Appellants had been apprised of events in the duchy only up to April.[2] Since then the Duke had finally agreed to meet the royal uncles. On or about 2 June he had joined them at Blois for the journey to Paris.[3] This meant the reversal of his policy of the previous winter months when he seems to have made overtures to his brother-in-law, Charles III of Navarre, to enter into an alliance. Navarre was to be helped to recover his Norman heritage.[4] Certainly in an incriminating credence for a special envoy sent to England, probably during the winter, John expressed an ardent desire to ally with the King.[5] He pointed out the dangers he was experiencing as a result of his alliance with England and how little he had received in exchange. War had not yet broken out, nor did the Duke wish it to do so; but, if it did break out, 'ledit duc sera prest affaire au roy le service contenu en les articles susnommes lesquels sont en la garde dou roy'.[6] What were these mysterious articles, and why was John dealing directly with the King after Richard's obvious slight to Breton interests in 1386–7?

A partial answer to these questions can be given from another document entitled 'Articles of the wishes of the Duke of Brittany'.[7] Surprisingly, these 'Articles' do not

dates in Arundel's accounts, which show these dubbings taking place on 28 June and 16 and 27 July (Accts. Var. 41/5, Accts. For. 24 m. 38ʳ).

[1] *Historia Anglicana*, ii. 175.

[2] Fotheringhay, who had come back from Brittany in April (Accts. For. 22 m. Aᵛ), returned to the duchy, probably in Arundel's fleet, on 6 June and almost certainly carrying news of a fresh regrant of Richmond (Accts. Var. 319/33 and *C.Ch.R. 1341–1417*, 309). On 2 June Arundel received a new commission as Admiral with very full powers to treat with John and to receive any castles he was prepared to hand over (*Foedera*, vii. 586).

[3] F. Lehoux, *Jean de France, duc de Berri*, ii. 222.

[4] Froissart, ed. Lettenhove, xiii. 105.

[5] B.M. MS. Cott. Julius B. VI, fol. 65, printed in Froissart, ed. Lettenhove, xviii. 350.

[6] Ibid.

[7] Ibid., fols. 55–6, printed below, Appendix of Documents, no. 5. Both documents have been used indiscriminately by Calmette and Déprez. See above, p. 89, n. 6.

precede the credence but follow it. They can be tentatively
dated *c.* August 1388. Again, as in the credence, John
professed to desire the honour and profit of Richard II and
his realm. He wanted to maintain the alliance between them
as set out in his most recent letters to the King and Council.
The terms of the unknown letters and alliance were based
on the agreements of 1372 and 1380 and were probably first
discussed at length in the summer of 1387.[1] In return for
help against his domestic enemies, John was prepared to
release castles to the English and to take the field with them.
But the general tone of the 'Articles' was apologetic. John
excused his failure to help men who had been sent in the
'daraine flote' by saying that they had had no mounts. Any
future force would find him ready to do his utmost to aid
them, provided that they brought their own horses. Indeed,
he pressed for immediate assistance, to arrive as soon and as
secretly as possible. A body of 1,000 or 1,200 men would be
welcome, if no larger force could be raised. Other clauses
dealt with the payment of troops, the Duke's position if an
Anglo-French peace should be sealed, conditions for John's
retirement to England, regulations guarding his and his
heir's rights in Brittany, the return of his English lands,
and an annual pension of £10,000 during his retirement.
Richard II was to become John's heir if he died without one
of his own body. If there were any difficulty in implementing
these clauses, John wished to be told by letters sealed by
Gloucester, Arundel, Warwick, Derby, and the great
officers of state.

On the face of it, the 'Articles' described an alliance with
England of an extremely exact kind. In many ways it was
the most detailed Anglo-Breton contract ever contemplated
during John IV's reign. Froissart, with his usual facility for
picking up rumour, declared that there was already a secret
Anglo-Breton treaty in 1387.[2] However, he further states
that in 1388 Arundel's forces took no horses with them,
a fact which he takes pains to repeat,[3] and it is on this
evidence that the tentative date of 1388 has been suggested

---

[1] Treaty Roll 72 m. 22, 30 July and 4 Aug. 1387, safe conducts for Peter Adam
and twelve others 'nuper in regnum Anglie . . .', by Council warrant.

[2] Ed. Lettenhove, xii. 234.   [3] Ibid. xiii. 106, 147.

for the alliance. Unconvincing as this dating would appear on such evidence alone, John's own predicament in the winter of 1387–8 would warrant the desperate insurance measures summarized in the 'Articles'. Far from seeking exile in England in the winter of 1386–7, John had been pushing ahead with the siege of Brest. But in 1387–8 his feud with Clisson had taken a new turn with Penthièvre's release, and this explains the high stakes he was prepared to offer for an English alliance.[1] Hard as it must have been to find reliable information about Richard's difficulties with his magnates, John realized the importance of getting Gloucester's approval for his insurance scheme. Yet, again, as in 1372 and on other occasions, John's feelings on the subject of an English alliance are hard to fathom.

John's evident failure to co-operate in 1388 may have been based on a real fear of France. Burgundy could hardly approve an alliance between Brittany and an enemy who was seeking to stir up minor princes of the Low Countries against Flanders.[2] It may have been an accidental failure— John was delayed in Paris by the royal uncles in June–July 1388 and, by the time he had returned to the duchy, Arundel had gone elsewhere.[3] But it may have been deliberate policy on the Duke's part. With the immediate threat from Clisson parried, the Duke had no need of English help. His excuse for not aiding Arundel was a convenient if not very convincing one. If the ransom of the Count of Penthièvre was a fair indication of Richard II's wishes in a Breton policy, this policy was not a friendly one. In circumstances where the Duke could not be certain whether the proposals put forward in the King's name represented his wishes or those of the Commission or Appellants, or where he could not be certain who exercised final authority in England, he would have been unwise to get too involved in affairs that would surely alienate his friends at the Valois court. Withdrawal was his only course of action. Philip More was sent 'pro certis festinis negociis dominum Regem

---

[1] *Preuves*, ii. 543–6, and A.N. K 53, no. 68*bis* (27 Nov. 1387), for the Bishop of Langres's embassy to Brittany about the Duke's treatment of Clisson.

[2] Above, p. 104. Another important French embassy was sent to convince the Duke of the error of his ways, *c*. May 1388 (Froissart, ed. Lettenhove, xiii. 117 ff.).

[3] John was back at Vannes by 27 Aug. 1388 (A.L.A. E 166).

tangentibus' to Brittany in July 1388.[1] His journey may have had a political or diplomatic end. But it seems that by then immediate communications between England and the Duke had broken down. The English Council attempted to inform Arundel, whose rather uncertain course is explained by his poor intelligence of the way events were moving in the duchy and in Paris. Hindered by a lack of horses, like the Earl of Cambridge in Portugal seven years before, Arundel kept to the coastlands in the Marches between Brittany and Poitou.[2] He disrupted local trade by his attacks on enemy shipping, but in the long run the results expected of his expedition were not achieved. Even before he returned home early in September, there were indications that the Appellants would have to sue for peace with France.[3]

In the winter of 1388 and the early part of 1389 there were a number of important domestic changes in England and France. In France the Marmosets came to power after the return of the King from an armed demonstration in the Low Countries designed to bolster up Philip of Burgundy's overlordship.[4] This change partially extinguished the influence of Berry and Burgundy at court and promoted the interests of Clisson. It was a potentially dangerous situation for John IV now that his principal enemy could use royal resources more freely to pursue his feud with the Duke. In England, too, the composition of the Government was altered by a redistribution of royal favour after Richard declared himself of full age in May 1389 and ended the period of Appellant rule.[5] Richard had chosen his moment carefully, and skilfully exploited the royal prerogative to win a measure of popular sympathy by remitting part of a subsidy granted at the Cambridge Parliament of 1388. He was also able to make capital out of the peace talks started in the previous year by the Appellants; and by June 1389

---

[1] Issue Roll 519 m. 19 (17 July).

[2] Ibid., messenger to search for Arundel. Cf. Russell, *English Intervention*, p. 312.

[3] *C.P.R. 1385-9*, 502-3. From Nov. 1388 commissions for ambassadors were issued thick and fast (*Foedera*, vii. 608, 610-12, 614, 616, etc.; H. Moranvillé, 'Conférences entre la France et l'Angleterre, 1388-1393', *B.E.C.* 1 (1889), 355-80).

[4] Vaughan, *Philip the Bold*, pp. 42, 98-9; Rey, *Les Finances royales*, pp. 573-7.

[5] Tout, *Chapters*, iii. 454 ff.; McKisack, *The Fourteenth Century*, p. 463.

the first of a number of truces with France, which were to lead to the twenty-eight years' truce of 1396, had been sealed.[1] But towards Brittany the King had not been so generous, despite the regranting of the honour of Richmond in November 1388. Messengers hurried between the King and the Duke, but all the indications were that a return to the anomalous diplomacy of the early 1380s was imminent.[2]

For all his flirtations with England, and some of these had been dangerous episodes, the Duke was back where he had started in 1381. Brest and Richmond were still in English hands. For their failures both sides could blame themselves. The off-hand treatment of the Duke before 1386 had created an atmosphere of distrust in Anglo-Breton relations. The actions of the King's friends, in particular, had endangered the Duke by creating the opportunity for Clisson to use Penthièvre against the duchy. It was difficult for John to steer his way through the troubled waters of English factional dispute after 1386 without laying himself open to other lines of attack. For his part, although he offered considerable concessions of a diplomatic nature, John was most concerned to defeat his domestic enemies. To do this successfully he had to utilize his friendship with the royal uncles, but this, in turn, threatened to stultify his own foreign policy where independence of action was essential if Brittany's weight was to be felt in the general Anglo-French war. His intricate diplomacy could easily be upset by the greater powers ignoring his claims; whilst in Brittany the loyalty of his seigneurs was still a fragile thing, subject to the fluctuations of success and failure achieved by John in his external affairs. He was trying to avoid committing himself to obligations to England and France that would restrict him. On Brittany's small resources this was often the most he could hope for during the Anglo-French war. Would he fare better when the great powers moved towards peace?

[1] *Foedera*, vii. 620–1 (subsidy), 622 (John Holland, Earl of Huntingdon, replaces Arundel as captain of Brest), 622–30 (truce).

[2] *C.Ch.R. 1341–1417*, 312; Issue Roll 521 m. 10 (4 Dec.), Fotheringhay sent to Brittany for the third time within a year. He returned by Mar. 1389 (Accts. Var. 319/36).

V

ENGLAND, FRANCE, AND THE DUCHY OF BRITTANY
1389–1399

At an inquiry held in 1455 into the Duke of Brittany's rights, an aged witness remembered his youth and a conversation with his uncle Eustace de la Houssaie. Eustace, he said, had declared that 'le duc n'estoit point suget au Roy quel le Roi estoit au Duc'.[1] Although these sentiments aptly characterize the attitudes of fifteenth-century Breton Dukes towards their obligations to France, they were not out of keeping with Breton ideas in the 1390s. Another octogenarian cross-examined at a similar inquiry in 1392 had stated on the subject of liege homage that 'Nos seigneurs les Ducz sont Princes et Seignours souverains au duche de Bretagne et ne souloint recognoistre aucun soverain . . .'.[2] Only if the Duke refused to do justice or gave a false judgement could a plaintiff appeal to Paris, provided that he had already exhausted the legal methods of redress open to him within the duchy. This right of appeal was used but rarely and almost invariably produced a violent reaction from the Duke. The two Breton clerks who asserted at Avignon in 1394 that in his duchy the Duke was like a king, and the seneschal of Nantes who informed royal officials that his master had the same freedom to act in Brittany as the King had in Paris, echoed John IV's views on his relationship with his sovereign.[3]

Without exaggeration it can be said that in the last ten years of his reign John IV acted as though he were an independent prince whose state was contiguous with, and not within, the bounds of Valois France. His claims were most emphatically countered by the monarchy. But despite innumerable domestic upheavals and rapid changes on the

---

[1] *Preuves*, ii. 1668.　　　　　　　　　　[2] Ibid. 595.
[3] A.N. J 243, no. 76 (*Preuves*, ii. 631).

international scene, John managed to maintain, with some success, the position he had adopted. Sometimes he overstepped the mark and found that it was expedient to compromise with Charles VI. But by his awareness of, and defence against, the encroachments of an interfering monarchy, John was able to foster Breton independence. In earlier chapters we have seen how the idea of Breton independence was grounded on a historical appreciation of the duchy's former glories as a kingdom (albeit a rather inaccurate appreciation) and, more practically, on an increasingly efficient administrative machine with sound financial resources. Suffice it to say here that, despite political disturbances in Brittany and continuing alarms in the general Anglo-French war, the 1380s and 1390s were a period of increasing economic prosperity for several sectors of Breton society. This partly helps to explain the Duke's confident assertions of independence from Valois France. By his policy of neutrality in the general war, the Duke of Brittany helped to create the conditions that enabled his subjects to benefit from an expansion of commerce. This expansion, insignificant though it was when set against the general contraction of markets in western Europe at this period, continued well into the fifteenth century and must be counted as a significant factor in Breton history at this point.[1]

But as the independence issue coloured Breton relations with France, so it also coloured relations with England. A small state likely to find itself overrun or ignored by England and France needed to exercise whatever influence it possessed carefully and, often, deviously. About the sovereign states of Scotland and Portugal at this period it has been remarked that

it was easy for great powers [i.e. England and France] to gather clients and promises in such relatively poor and feeble states. But the political divisions and institutional weaknesses which made this easy made it equally difficult to induce the small states to give more than passive and ambiguous help. They were capable of effective action on a large scale only under the stimulus of great danger or great opportunity.[2]

[1] Touchard, Le Commerce maritime breton, especially pp. 87 ff.

[2] J. Campbell, 'England, Scotland and the Hundred Years War', Europe in the Late Middle Ages, ed. Hale et al., p. 214.

The same holds true for Brittany. For John and his duchy in the 1390s it must often have seemed that they were caught between two great millstones whose slightest turn would crush the fragile seeds of independence. All the vacillations of John's policy cannot be followed; its complexity can only be understood in the light of the Breton desire for independence. This desire sometimes made it impossible to apply one constant policy because of the swiftly changing diplomatic balance. The interplay of conflicting interests is nowhere better seen than in Anglo-Breton relations in this period of the Hundred Years War. In the 1380s England had attempted to use Brittany when it suited her. Would John continue to accept such treatment? By exploiting the situation where England and France were so evenly matched, he might gain political victories which up to the present had eluded him. In particular, his aim was to regain Brest and Richmond from England and to recover from France the lands and pensions that had been granted to him or his predecessors by successive kings of France. By gaining these practical objectives John's powers would be noticeably increased to match his theoretical pretensions. His main concern was to win concessions without having to give anything other than 'passive and ambiguous help' to either great power.

The English Government recognized John IV's position, but was more concerned with greater problems arising from the Anglo-French negotiations, which continued almost without ceasing from the end of 1388 until November 1396.[1] Occasionally at these general talks Breton problems were raised, but the main discussions were over the problems that had bedevilled Anglo-French relations since the treaty of Paris in 1259. Issues concerning such matters as the sovereignty of Guyenne, the extent of that duchy, and the extent of other French territorial concessions were not to be easily solved. Nor were problems arising from the uncompleted treaty of Brétigny-Calais (1360) to be lightly dis-

[1] H. Moranvillé, B.E.C. l (1889), 355–80; J. J. N. Palmer, 'The Anglo-French Peace Negotiations, 1390–1396', T.R.H.S., 5th ser., xvi (1966), 81–94, and id., 'Articles for a Final Peace between England and France, 16 June 1393', B.I.H.R. xxxix (1966), 180–5.

missed. The sincerity of each party's wish for a settlement at the talks at Leulinghen in 1389 and in the succeeding years has not yet been convincingly demonstrated, although it is agreed that the successive armistices until the twenty-eight years' truce of 1396 provided a very necessary breathing-space for the protagonists.

According to M. Perroy[1] it was the English King who assumed the lead in a policy of reconciliation. His object was to imitate the French monarch's absolutism, since only through a successful foreign policy could Richard hope to overcome the resistance of his own nobility, who had put him in leading-strings in 1386. Since the foreign policy of the 1386 Commission and of the Appellants in 1388 had been aggressive and insistent on prosecuting the war with France more effectively, Richard chose the way of peace. In this he was opposed by his uncle Thomas, Duke of Gloucester. This summary of Richard's aims and the way in which they coloured the diplomacy of the 1390s is still valuable, even if we admit that the clash with Gloucester needs much subtler delineation[2] and that Richard's admiration of France was neither slavish nor without diplomatic wisdom. But, being a summary, it glosses over certain points at which events might have taken a different turn. Inevitable as the long truce of 1396 may seem, the path to it was circuitous and strewn with the branches of lopped policies. Numerous dated and undated documents concerning Anglo-Breton relations in the 1390s mirror the changing attitudes and policies of the diplomats who had to juggle with the irregular triangular relationship of Brittany, England, and France.

The contents of these documents indicate the lengths to which the Duke was prepared to go in putting his duchy at the disposal of the English, the type of aid he desired, the possible implications should he be driven into exile, his own status in the Anglo-French peace negotiations, and the status of his duchy were Richard II to succeed to the French

---

[1] *Hundred Years War*, pp. 196 ff. See also Steel, *Richard II*, pp. 188 ff.
[2] Gloucester agreed that the Marches of Calais should be held of the King of France in 1392 (Baldwin, *The King's Council*, p. 496) and agreed to the surrender of Cherbourg in 1393 (below, p. 137).

crown. Details regulating the standing of expeditionary forces to be sent to Brittany were also worked out. By interpreting these diplomatic documents in the light of other information about the Duke's personal circumstances and feelings, we may hope to demonstrate the real value of some of the documentary clauses. But before discussing these in greater detail it may be useful to sketch in the main outlines of the story to follow.

The back-cloth before which the diplomats played their parts was the Anglo-French attempt to bring the war to a conclusion by negotiation. Both sides frequently feared, and made preparations for, the renewed outbreak of hostilities, but there were no major military operations interrupting the talks.[1] These talks took place in almost every year from 1389 to 1396, and from 1392 onwards were conducted at the very highest level by the uncles of the Kings of England and France. Arrangements for a meeting of the two Kings were continually being revised, especially after August 1392, in order to take account of the French King's mental instability. But by 1393 a general solution to Anglo-French troubles seemed imminent. Although a definitive peace was not sealed, from 1395 both great powers were reconciled to a marriage and a long truce.[2] England and France in the 1390s were thus manœuvring round each other, rather like weary wrestlers, making occasional feints or threatening noises, until they agreed to withdraw to their corners after the two Kings had embraced in friendship at Ardres in October 1396.

In these circumstances Brittany's interests might be treated in a cavalier fashion by England and France as they sought to gain slight advantages over each other. The value of John IV's alliance with England (as of Scotland's with France) was as a makeweight in the complicated diplomatic struggle. But by skilful diplomacy the Duke might gain new concessions from both sides. Breton affairs might yet impinge on the course of more general Anglo-French affairs.

---

[1] *C.P.R. 1391–6*, 88–95; Aymérigot Marchès, a notorious *routier* captain nominally in English allegiance, made some interesting points about England's attitude to the truces at his trial in Paris in July 1391 (Keen, *Laws of War*, pp. 97–100); Baldwin, op. cit., p. 493. [2] Cf. p. 116, n. 1, above.

As far as England was concerned, however, John's failure to co-operate with the Appellants in 1388 had strained Anglo-Breton relations. Further, Richard II had already shown himself somewhat unsympathetic towards the duchy and tended to ignore ducal requests for the return of Richmond and Brest, although the Duke still claimed that he needed help against his domestic enemies. Paradoxically the ducal position in 1390 improved as the Duke's links with England appeared to be weakening. He was able, for instance, to increase his demands on the French, whose fears about the Duke's English policy had been relieved. Towards the end of 1391 a very complex situation developed as the Duke moved towards a marriage alliance with France —a move which seems to have warned the English of the dangers of letting their Breton policy drift. In 1392 John became implicated in an attempt to murder Clisson, and the immediate French reaction was an invasion of the duchy, which failed only because the French King was struck with madness as he made his way westward. As a result, John's friends, the royal uncles, who had been replaced at the royal court in 1388 by the influence of Clisson and his friends, were once more able to control Charles VI and protect John IV. John in turn was able to extricate himself from some very devious negotiations for English aid, and in the next few years attempted to pursue his independent course by playing off England and France. But this policy was not successful in achieving the ends he desired with regard to the great powers. It was only after and because of the 1396 general Anglo-French truce that his lands, titles, and pensions in England, France, and Brittany were fully restored to him.

The tension that had developed between England and Brittany because of the Duke's failure to support the Appellants in 1388 can be seen in the way in which the English Council in August 1389 dealt with the Duke's latest offers.[1] John wanted to exchange certain castles in Guyenne for a definitive regrant of Richmond. The Council prevaricated by saying that the castles could only be accepted in accordance with the terms of the recently arranged Anglo-French truce. Richard felt unable to restore Richmond, even though

[1] Nicolas, i. 6.

the Duke's English supporters and his confessor urged his suit.[1] In the following December another Council meeting, attended by all the old Appellants except Warwick, as well as by the Archbishop of York, the Bishops of Winchester and St. Davids (respectively Chancellor and Treasurer), Gaunt, the Duke of York, and the Earls of Northumberland and Huntingdon, likewise put off 'a final reply' over Richmond until Parliament should meet in January, when even weightier opinions could be sounded.[2] The Duke's own failure to reply to earlier Council communications was given as the reason for this delay. Using the strict letter of the Leulinghen truces to cover their actions, the English were able to ignore ducal imprecations.

When John had first started to pick up the threads of the military alliance that had failed in 1388 his domestic position had been seriously threatened, if not quite so dangerously as in 1387–8. It is not unlikely that the uneasy truce with Clisson in the duchy, agreed in July 1388, led the Duke to make overtures to England which, so one chronicler believed, brought forth an offer to dispatch 4,000 men to the duchy.[3] But disappointments suffered in attempts to recover Brest and Richmond and newly confirmed by the 1389 embassy's lack of success sapped John's confidence in the value of his English alliance and led him to reassess his policy.

This reassessment was assisted by the birth of an heir on 24 December 1389.[4] An infant life was a precarious guarantee, but John's fears that John de Bretagne, Count of Penthièvre, would succeed to the duchy under the terms of the first treaty of Guérande were alleviated. The birth of a son, the third of eight children born to John and his wife Joanna of Navarre, gave the Duke a renewed incentive to strengthen the control he exercised over his duchy.[5] For the moment Clisson was busily concerned with affairs at the French court, and the Civil War in Brittany was restricted to isolated acts of violence. So, while the Anglo-French talks in 1390 proved inconclusive, John was able to consolidate

---

[1] Treaty Roll 74 m. 18 (28 Aug. 1389), safe conduct for Peter Adam to go to Brittany and to return by Christmas. For Richard Fotheringhay and Edward Dallingrigge, see below, pp. 151, 184–5.   [2] Nicolas, i. 17–18a.
[3] *Polychronicon*, ix. 215.   [4] *Chronicon Briocense*, ed. Lobineau, 850.
[5] Borderie, iv. 135.

his own position. Minor favours were received from both great powers.[1] Heartened by this indication of his growing strength, John felt bold enough in June 1390 to complain to the French that they were not respecting his rights. In particular he asserted that they had entertained an appeal to the *Parlement* of Paris from Olivier du Guesclin, Count of Longueville, who had been forced into selling his seigneury of La Guerche to the Duke.[2]

The Duke's actions at this point can best be understood in the light of his concern for the frontiers of his duchy. Throughout the 1380s the French had been building up in Normandy a number of strong-points. That province was vulnerable to sorties from the English-held fortress town of Cherbourg and from Brittany, so Charles VI had ordered the reconstruction of seigneurial castles and had organized garrisons to protect his subjects there. This was one aspect of a more general royal frontier policy.[3] Charles VI similarly reinforced the Marches in Picardy against Calais and those towards English Guyenne, but by taking over Saint-Malo in 1387 (and later by granting Pontorson to Clisson in 1391) he was directly encroaching on ducal lands.[4] John IV retaliated by demanding the handing over of Saint-James-de-Beuvron (originally granted to John III in 1316) and seizing La Guerche, which guarded the eastern approaches to Rennes, and, in the autumn of 1390, by besieging Champtoceaux. This much disputed stronghold was the key to the Loire valley and had recently been granted to Clisson by the Duke of Anjou.[5] Just as in 1371, when the French

---

[1] Chancery Warrants, file 511, no. 5849 (7 Jan.), warrant for Armel de Châteaugiron, esquire of Duchess of Brittany, to transport arms for the Duke; ibid. 516, no. 6377 (7 June), warrant for Duke's butler to export goods for Duke; ibid. 517, no. 6464 (12 July), warrant for John to export 155 'peces desteyn coignez paiant les devoirs ent duz et accoustumez'; ibid. 518, no. 6571 (12 Sept.), warrant for Peter Adam to pursue the business of 'our dear brother' in England for a year. On 16 May Charles VI had ordered the payment of a 260*l.t.* pension to John (B.N. MS. fr. 20405, no. 13).   [2] *Preuves*, ii. 573–4; Anselme, vi. 186–7.

[3] Rey, *Les Finances royales*, pp. 378–85.

[4] Pocquet, *Les Papes*, i. 407 ff.; Touchard, *Le Commerce maritime breton*, pp. 83–5; B.N. MS. fr. 4482, p. 61, for payments to Robert de Guitté, captain of Saint-Malo, for Charles VI from 1 Oct. 1389 to 1 Sept. 1392 (cf. Table of Allegiances, above, p. 59, for Guitté's earlier career); Rey, op. cit., p. 576, for Pontorson.

[5] *Preuves*, ii. 573–4, 555 (redated to 1390). John's attack on Champtoceaux

advance had come through Poitou, the Duke had reacted
vigorously to French threats. The King, whose interest in
Italy was being fanned by the Duke of Touraine (better
known by his later title, Duke of Orléans), now feared for
these ambitious plans. He could not possibly leave his kingdom without obtaining guarantees of good behaviour from
John IV. The situation was intensified by fears of a breakdown in the negotiations with England. An embassy, led
by the Bishop of Meaux, was sent to resolve the Breton
problem.[1]

John's defence before the Bishop and his complaints of
the previous summer over Longueville's appeal may be
treated in a composite fashion to illustrate the Duke's
attitude towards France.[2] Other vassals besides Longueville,
he claimed, had appealed to the French court. Pensions
promised by Charles V in compensation for ducal losses
elsewhere had not been paid; nor had lands, pledged under
successive treaties, been released. Ducal *brefs* issued at La
Rochelle had been ignored. The crown spokesmen countered by alleging various ducal crimes; but ducal officers
affected an attitude of injured dignity and surprise that their
master should be thought capable of acting outside his legal
sphere. Ducal dealings with Longueville were a private
affair. John could not have used force against La Guerche
because his entry into the town had been at the municipal
constable's request and was effected 'si paisiblement qu'il avoit
l'oyseau sur le poing'.[3] Although it could not be denied that
force had been used against Champtoceaux, the Duke had
since returned the town to the King. He had also made
several concessions to Clisson and Penthièvre that he had

(Maine-et-Loire, ar. Angers, ch.-l. c.) caused the citizens of Angers to mount
extra watches; *Invt. analytique des Archives . . . d'Angers*, ed. C. Port, p. 179. By
Feb. 1391 Champtoceaux was in the King's hand again (B.N. MS. fr. 20405, no. 9).

   [1] E. Jarry, 'La "voie de fait" et l'alliance franco-milanaise, 1386–1395', *B.E.C.*
liii (1892), 230–2; M. Nordberg, *Les Ducs et la royauté*, pp. 76 ff.; B.N. MS. fr.
20885, nos. 77–82, for payments to the Bishop of Meaux and his colleagues from
Dec. 1390 to Apr. 1391.

   [2] *Preuves*, ii. 573–4 (1390), and A.L.A. E 104, 'Memoire de ce que les messages
du duk de Bretagne qui vont prontement en France auront a faire de par lui', a
document which summarizes the most recent examples of disregard of ducal rights,
complaints against Clisson, and the Duke's defence before the Bishop of Meaux
(1391).   [3] *Preuves*, ii. 573.

not been obliged to make. Yet their insults continued to weary and undermine his trust. Ducal complaints with regard to internal Breton matters are, in fact, summed up in a plea for a return to the terms of the first treaty of Guérande and a promise to deal personally with any subjects then seeking judgement against John in Paris.

At some point Charles VI had obviously informed John of the progress of the Anglo-French negotiations. Flattered perhaps by this, John instructed his representatives to thank the King and to ask that he be included in any peace that might be concluded in accordance with his alliance with France. Indeed the Duke even went so far as to bring his complaints over Richmond and Brest to Charles VI's notice—a move which was probably designed to allay any fears that he was closely in league with the English.[1] There is no mistaking the attitude here cloaked beneath traditional diplomatic form. This was hardly the tone of a vassal to his lord. Half respectfully and half defiantly, the Duke was articulating the Breton view of relations with the French crown. There were obvious weaknesses in this view, as the French infringements of ducal rights indicate. But Charles VI had been forced to recognize that to ignore John would be to imperil his own plans in Italy and, more relevantly, his plans for an Anglo-French settlement. This was one of the ways in which Brittany could make its independence felt in international affairs.

John emerged from the discussions with France in 1390–1 relatively unscathed. There is no denying the skill with which he glossed over his own faults and brought his various claims to Charles VI's notice. Without becoming sycophantic, he assured Charles that he had forsaken his earlier treasonable ways. His policies were endorsed by his leading councillors. He was soon able to strengthen his position still further in two respects. First, in 1391, he formed a politico-military agreement with the Count of Armagnac, which was to be consolidated by the marriage of the Duke's heir and the Count's daughter, and by a pact with the Count of Charolles, Armagnac's brother.[2] Later, in 1393, a similar agreement was reached with Archambaud,

---

[1] A.L.A. E 104.   [2] Ibid. E 8 and E 181 (19 Apr. 1391).

eldest son of the Count of Périgord, in which clauses for mutual military aid were stipulated.[1] Secondly, John remained on good terms with the royal uncles.

The Duke of Berry's mediation in Breton internal quarrels was almost inevitable. Once some difficulties arising from their respective limits of jurisdiction in the Brittany–Poitou Marches had been amicably settled in April 1390,[2] Berry and Brittany remained on terms of the closest friendship. Berry's apanage interests in Poitou and his connections with the Angevin party, protectors of Penthièvre, reinforced his natural inclination towards compromise and peace. Berry also realized that Breton domestic quarrels might jeopardize the success of the Anglo-French peace talks. His influence at the royal court had never been entirely replaced by the Marmosets, and in 1390 he had used this influence to persuade the King to treat over Champtoceaux.[3] Towards the end of 1391 it was Berry again who brought John and his domestic enemies face to face before the King at Tours.[4] Likewise Philip, Duke of Burgundy, whose interests were best served by a cessation of the Anglo-French conflict, recognized that general peace depended on bringing John and Clisson to terms and thus destroying any justification for English intervention in Brittany in support of John IV. His mediation in John's quarrels with Clisson and Penthièvre was decisively exercised in 1394–5, when the breach opened by Clisson's homage to Charles V for Château Josselin in 1370 was finally healed and Penthièvre was allowed to possess most of his hereditary lands.[5]

That the royal uncles' fears about John's relations with England were not groundless is proved by good evidence that diplomatic exchanges continued between Brittany and England in these years. Important ducal household officials received favours when in England in the spring of 1391,

[1] A.L.A. E 181 (12 Mar. 1393).

[2] Lacour, *Le Gouvernement de . . . Jean, duc de Berry*, p. 137.

[3] *Preuves*, ii. 555–6. The royal uncles were in a difficult position with regard to the Anglo-French peace, since its successful conclusion might entrench the Marmosets even more firmly in control at Paris. They were thus forced to use delaying tactics, although they generally favoured peace talks (cf. Froissart, ed. Lettenhove, xiii. 352–4).

[4] *Preuves*, ii. 577; *Chronique . . . de Saint-Denys*, ed. Bellaguet, i. 720 ff.

[5] Below, pp. 131 ff.

although tantalizingly their business there is unspecified.[1]
A more important embassy was appointed in the summer to
ask, it goes almost without saying, for the return of Richmond and Brest. It was also to treat 'pur le fait du traite
dentre Monseigneur le Roy et nous'. There was an impressive show of solidarity from ducal advisers of all shades
of opinion who gathered to witness the appointment.[2] Unfortunately, the embassy does not seem to have left the
duchy.

There was, however, some English reciprocation. The
general trend of English foreign policy at this moment was
pacific. A devoted group of diplomats, backed up by the
royal Council as well as by Richard II, were hopefully working towards a solution of Anglo-French problems.[3] But
there was also some concern at the possibility of French
intervention in Italy, and it is probably in line with this
fear that the English were using a number of minor allies to
divert French attention. There was English support for the
Count of Armagnac's expedition against the Lord of Milan
—perhaps we see here reasons for Brittany's alliance with
the Count. There were renewed English pensions and favours
to certain princes in the Low Countries[4] and approaches to
Aragon, Castile, and Navarre (this latter was also friendly
with Brittany).[5] In England emergency preparations for the
immediate dispatch of troops to the Continent should the
truces fail were continually being revised.[6] Parliament
granted subsidies in 1390 and 1391 on condition that they
should be used solely for the defence of the realm if the peace
talks failed or (as in November 1391) 'for the personal
estate and voyage of the King to France to affirm the truces
or final peace'. If the King failed to go and the truces continued, the subsidy was not to be levied.[7] It is in this context

---

[1] *Foedera*, vii. 699. Protections had been issued in Nov. 1390 and Feb. 1391
(Treaty Roll 75 mm. 4, 8).

[2] *Preuves*, ii. 576 (31 July 1391); cf. original letters, A.L.A. E 115, no. 9.

[3] Palmer, 'The Anglo-French Negotiations', pp. 118 ff.

[4] *Foedera*, vii. 695–6; *Polychronicon*, ix. 241.

[5] *Foedera*, vii. 680–2, 692–3. Charles III of Navarre was John IV's brother-in-law.

[6] Above, p. 118. In Nov. 1390 Gaunt was possibly preparing to take an army to
Guyenne (*Rot. Parl.* iii. 279, subsidy for war; Issue Roll 532 m. 27 (Jan. 1391),
£6,000 advanced to him for troops in Guyenne).

[7] *Rot. Parl.* iii. 285–6. Dr. A. Rogers pointed this out to me.

of preparation lest the peace talks fail that England realized that ducal complaints could not continue to go unanswered if Brittany was to be of any value in persuading France to give up belligerent policies.

Thus in December 1391 a commission was appointed to investigate conditions at Brest. It was to review the men and installations at the castle and regulate any breaches of the Leulinghen truces.[1] More important, however, as revealing the English dilemma over Brittany were the Council discussions to decide whether the commissioners should be entrusted with an embassy to John's court.[2] Eventually it was decided that they should be so entrusted and that their main business would be to discuss certain proposals for marriages for the Duke's children. It was recognized that the Duke might need help against his domestic enemies and that this could be turned to good account in persuading him to give up some of his castles to the English. But the King himself was instrumental in getting the aid clauses struck out of the ambassadors' instructions.[3] Only after the marriage alliances had been prepared would England consider sending the Duke help. In the meantime they hoped to bribe him by another regrant of Richmond (to be held by some of his English friends until the marriages had taken place) and by promising to look after his interests at the next Anglo-French talks. It is hardly surprising that the ambassadors, who were finally commissioned to treat '. . . tam de pace et concordia finalibus et perpetuis quam de quibuscumque treugis guerrarum . . .', seem to have accomplished little in settling the quarrels that made an effective Anglo-Breton alliance so difficult.[4]

But at the same time as the English were acting in a more conciliatory way towards John IV, the French King, probably under the prompting of the Marmosets, demanded that the Duke should fulfil his obligations towards Clisson and Penthièvre, which he had avoided doing since the truce

[1] *Foedera*, vii. 709, enrolled on Treaty Roll 76 m. 9 (14 Dec. 1391).

[2] Nicolas, i. 36–40. The original manuscript (B.M. MS. Cott. Julius B. VI) has been repaginated, and this document is now fols. 22–4.

[3] Nicolas, i. 40.

[4] *C.Ch.R. 1341–1417*, 327; Treaty Roll 76 mm. 8, 9, for commission and protections for ambassadors.

of July 1388. Charles VI also complained about the way in which John was conducting his domestic government, about his striking of money, and about the taking of homages which did not mention the allegiance of both parties to the crown. In November 1391 Charles VI arrived at Tours expecting to meet his vassal. But it was only after a visit by the Duke of Berry to the duchy in December and the offer of a marriage between the Duke's heir and a French princess that John was persuaded to meet his sovereign.[1] In some respects this could be considered a humiliation for the Duke, but it is also typical of John that he committed himself to this course of action only after assuring himself that the English were still interested in his alliance and after hiring some Anglo-Gascon and Genoese troops for service in the duchy.[2]

In January 1392 at Tours John temporarily reversed the direction of his foreign policy.[3] He was supported in this by many of the councillors who six months previously had agreed to send an embassy to England. He agreed to marry his heir to a French princess, to maintain the treaties between himself and his sovereign, to redress Charles VI's grievances, and to come to a new arrangement with his domestic enemies. But, in a document kept secret from the King, John alleged that he had been forced unwillingly into the concessions.[4] He had by no means terminated discussions with England on the basis of the marriage alliances. He was

---

[1] *Chronique . . . de Saint-Denys*, ed. Bellaguet, i. 720 ff.; *Chronicon Briocense*, ed. Lobineau, 855. The charge over homages was true. On 26 Jan. 1386, Jean Tournemine, Sire de la Hunaudie, issued letters to serve John IV against all 'Come de raison touz et chacun les habitenz et demorenz en duchie de Bretaigne soient tenuz servir et obeir a mon souverain seigneur . . .' (A.L.A. E 143). Even after an inquiry in Mar. 1392 (ibid., and above, p. 114), the Duke continued to exact homage exclusively (ibid. 20 Jan. 1398, homage of Eustace de la Houssaie).

[2] B.N. MS. Nouv. acq. fr. 5216, no. 17 (18 Dec. 1391), quittance from John Cornwall, knight, for wages of himself and 69 other soldiers in ducal service. Cornwall issued a similar quittance on 12 Feb. 1392 (A.L.A. E 120/8). On 9 Oct. 1391 Francisco de Lescasses and his troop of men-at-arms and arbalesters had been retained to serve John 'en ses guerres' (ibid. E 143). Alan Newerk, one of the English envoys of Dec. 1391, was still not back in England on 4 Mar. (Baldwin, *The King's Council*, p. 500). Philip More, another envoy, was back by 2 Apr. (Issue Roll 536 m. 23); Palgrave, ii. 42–3.

[3] *Preuves*, ii. 578–93.

[4] Ibid., 578–80. (For similar protests by John IV, see Pocquet, *Les Papes*, i. 403–4, 416, and Borderie, iv. 62.)

still employing English troops, and there was still the possibility that he would contract a new alliance which could only contradict all that he had said at Tours. This diplomatic juggling act could continue only so long as neither great power called John's bluff.

France did just this when Pierre de Craon attempted to assassinate Clisson in Paris on the night of 13–14 June 1392. Craon's motives and the extent to which John IV might have been implicated in this attack have been discussed inconclusively several times.[1] As in 1387, when John imprisoned Clisson in Ermine castle, Vannes,[2] there seems to be little doubt that John was in close contact with England, that his envoys were in England during or immediately after the time of the attack, and that an English envoy hurried to the duchy in July 1392.[3] We may suspect that these activities were not coincidental, but there is no evidence to show that there were any carefully pre-arranged plans to take advantage of the Constable's death.

As it happened Clisson was not killed. Despite the opposition of Berry, Bourbon, and Burgundy, a royal expedition was launched against Brittany.[4] Matters were made worse by the defence of Sablé castle in the Duke's name. This castle lay well outside the bounds of the duchy of Brittany. But it was Craon's chief stronghold, and about this time he had entered into some complicated negotiations to sell it to John IV.[5] It is difficult to decide what connection, if any, this transaction between the Duke and Craon had with the

---

[1] H. Courteault, 'La fuite et les aventures de Pierre de Craon en Espagne', *B.E.C.* lii (1891), 431–48; Borderie, iv. 82 ff.; J. d'Avout, *La Querelle des Armagnacs et des Bourguignons* (Paris 1943), pp. 15–18.   [2] Borderie, iv. 74 ff.

[3] Peter Adam and Anthony Rys had been appointed envoys to England on 6 June 1392 (B.M. MS. Cott. Julius B. vi, fols. 26–7, letters of John IV at Vannes). By a writ dated at Nottingham on 16 June, Rys was granted a licence to import wine into England (Treaty Roll 76 m. 1). Philip More was the messenger (Issue Roll 538 m. 8, 11 July).

[4] Courteault, *B.E.C.* lii (1891), 433–4; Rey, *Les Finances royales*, pp. 355, 367; *Preuves*, ii. 597–616; B.N. MS. fr. 4482, accounts of the French treasurer of war.

[5] Sablé-sur-Sarthe, dép. Sarthe, ar. La Flèche, ch.-l. c.; *Chronique . . . de Saint-Denys*, ed. Bellaguet, ii. 16–19. This may explain the quittance issued by Jean de Chancheuture and Jean Michel, familiars of Pierre de Craon, for the receipt of 10,000 frs. for Craon from John IV (Vannes, 25 Sept. 1391, A.L.A. E 209); cf. *Preuves*, ii. 629 (25 Sept. 1394), quittance from John IV for 800 frs. 'qui nous estoient deubz pour le rachat et retrait du chastel et chastellenie de Sable'.

attempted assassination.[1] It may be suspected that there was some link, but the defence of Sablé was chiefly important as irritating the Marmosets. Charles VI was on his way to the castle when he was seized by a bout of insanity on 5 August 1392. Craon had already fled to Spain, and John was trying desperately to improvise a defence, when the Le Mans expedition was called off and the royal uncles came back to power.[2]

It is in these panic conditions that once more we find hints of an Anglo-Breton alliance. There are even a number of draft schedules, though there is no proof of their implementation. Such evidence is tantalizing. The *Chronicon Briocense* says that at the height of the crisis Breton envoys were in England, with large sums of money, trying to hire 5,000 troops who, according to the chronicler, were ready to sail to Brittany.[3] This estimate accords roughly with that suggested by another chronicler for the year 1389[4] and, more suggestively, with the 4,000 men requested in an undated document of these years.[5] Another comprehensive schedule for a treaty with John IV, based on the treaties of 1372 and 1380, might date from this period.[6] In it, too, the Duke was to be offered troops, protection of his rights at the Anglo-French peace talks, and the return of lands which had been severed from the duchy in the last hundred years. It also

---

[1] An equally valid reason for Craon's attack on Clisson may be found in his quarrel with the Duchess of Anjou. An action was brought before the *Parlement* of Paris on 10 June 1392, only four days before the attack (E.-R. Labande, 'Une ambassade de Rinaldo Orsini et Pierre de Craon à Florence, Milan et Avignon, 1383', *Mélanges d'archéologie et d'histoire*, l (1933), 215 ff.). Dr. J. Palmer drew my attention to this article.

[2] Arnoul Boucher, Charles VI's war treasurer, had reached Josselin by 6 Aug. (B.N. MS. fr. 4482, p. 327); *Chronicon Briocense*, ed. Lobineau, 859–60. Coucy was sent to Brittany on Charles VI's behalf on 25 Aug. (B.N. MS. fr. 4482, p. 269). Trusted ducal servants like Étienne Guyon and Eustace de la Houssaie (respectively in charge of the town and the castle at Rennes; Anselme. v. 394, and A.L.A. E 139/4) were placed in posts of vital strategic importance, while John raised a general *fouage* (*Preuves*, ii. 617–18).   [3] Ed. Lobineau, 860.

[4] *Polychronicon*, ix. 215.

[5] Nicolas, i. 89–93 (B.M. MS. Cott. Julius B. VI, fols. 38–42).

[6] Exch. Dip. Doc. 289a, 'Le alliance affayre par entre le Roy et le duc de Bretaygne'. Indications of the date may be observed from amendments which make it plain that the document was drawn up after the 1389 truce, before this was extended for more than 12 years, and after Gaunt had been created Duke of Guyenne (Mar. 1390).

showed that John was prepared to give up his claims in the duchy to Richard II in return for the restitution of his English lands and a £10,000 pension if he were to retire to England. Yet another schedule specified in detail the castles which the Duke was prepared to place in English hands.[1] With the addition of Nantes, Vannes, Concarneau, Quimper, Morlaix, and the Île de Batz to Richard II's protectorate of Brest, England's barbican scheme would have been strengthened and greatly intensified.[2] These places would also be relatively easy to supply and defend from England. But the alliance was not implemented, troops were not sent, and, after some anxious moments in the summer and autumn of 1392, John no longer required assistance. His friends came to his rescue in Paris, and he found it politic to suppress any suspicion of dealings with England.[3]

He did this so successfully that in the spring of 1393 the English seemed baffled. The Anglo-French talks had reached a crucial stage. Both sides were prepared to make concessions which would help the negotiations to advance.[4] The English, for their part, were anxious to dispose of certain side issues which might distract the negotiators from their main business. They thus issued special instructions to their chief ambassador, Gaunt, on the problem of Breton representation.[5] He was to press for Breton representation on the same footing as the French wanted for the Scots. This would be a recognition of the Duke's elevated status as an ally of England on the grounds of his personal relationship with the royal family. But such recognition could only reflect new importance on the status of his duchy. The English dilemma was that they had not consulted the Duke recently. Gaunt wanted to know what he should do in the likely event of the French refusing to allow Brittany to be treated as an English

[1] Nicolas, i. 41–4 (B.M. MS. Cott. Julius B. VI, fols. 32–3). For other drafts, ibid., fols. 34–6, and Cott. Caligula D. III, fols. 130–1, 132–3, 134, 135, 136.

[2] Above, p. 84.

[3] M. Thibault, *Isabeau de Bavière*, p. 312; Pocquet, *M.H.B.* xvi (1935), 10–11; A.L.A. E 104, 24 Oct. 1392, letters of Charles VI ordering the gift of 500 'queres' of wine to John IV by the advice of Burgundy and Berry!

[4] Palmer, 'The Anglo-French Negotiations', pp. 158 ff.

[5] Nicolas, i. 45–7, and especially 46 n. (B.M. MS. Cott. Julius B. VI, fols. 48 66–7).

ally. At a time when the problem of a general peace was uppermost in English minds, would the ambassadors have been likely to sacrifice English interests in trying to maintain a case for which it had not yet been established that John IV's support would be forthcoming? Unfortunately the surviving documents do not allow us to see how this question was answered, nor to decide whether England was using Brittany as a counterweight to certain French proposals, nor whether this was a genuine recognition of Brittany's independent role.

Indeed, with the Civil War in Brittany going in John's favour and with Berry and Burgundy in control at Paris, the Duke no longer depended for his survival on help from England. Further, feeling somewhat more secure, John was able to increase his demands from the English Council.[1] No more was there talk of leasing almost the whole western coastline of the duchy. Instead there were renewed charges over the retention of Brest and Richmond. John reminded the English how much damage had been caused by Penthièvre's release in 1386. Ducal finances as well as pride had been affected by a failure to recognize or buy *brefs* and by the failure of the executors of John FitzNicol, John's receiver-general in England, to account with the Duke. At the same time John again defended himself ably before another French deputation that had been sent to persuade the Duke to relent in his struggle with Clisson and to settle some problems which had arisen from the revolt of Saint-Malo against ducal authority.[2] In this way John showed his independence of both England and France.

John's conduct of his government soon provoked a French reaction. In 1394 complaints against his incitement of royal officials, his assumption of ducal privileges, the intolerable assertions of his servants, his attacks on surrounding crown provinces, and his wilful disregard of private rights in the duchy were all subjects which angered the crown. French pressure was applied carefully. In August 1394 John was presented with the list of complaints

---

[1] Nicolas, i. 47–50 (B.M. MS. Cott. Julius B. VI, fols. 29–30).

[2] A.N. K 53, no. 76*ter* (25 Apr. 1393), instructions to French ambassadors going to Brittany; cf. also *Preuves*, ii. 620–2.

at Angers.[1] In the autumn he claimed that he had provided remedies for most of the charges.[2]

The reasons for John's compliance are not difficult to find. Philip, Duke of Burgundy, had been dispatched in July to settle the Breton domestic disputes between John and the Clisson–Penthièvre party and to bring the Duke to heel. Philip was to remind John of his homages of 1366 and 1381 and of the terms of the second treaty of Guérande. Pressure on John from the French was intensified by their fears that the general truce, recently extended for another four years, might be broken by an English invasion of the duchy. The French were by now aware of the nature of John's negotiations with the English for the use of troops in Brittany. They were patently afraid that the force which Richard II was preparing for his expedition to Ireland was really destined for France.[3] Moreover, the French royal Council had been informed of marriage proposals affecting a match between a Breton heiress and the Earl of Derby's heir. Without wishing to stop these discussions, the Council wanted to remind John IV not to infringe the terms of his agreements with the crown.[4]

French fears were partially alleviated by October. Richard II had sailed for Ireland,[5] and new instructions issued to Burgundy were more conciliatory.[6] But both sets of instructions had insisted that Burgundy remind John of royal prerogatives. Minor concessions were offered to the Duke and, although John's October answers caused the French Council to reiterate the terms of Brittany's vassalage, it was

---

[1] A.N. J 243, no. 76 (29 Aug. 1394). These complaints were included in Philip, Duke of Burgundy's instructions (ibid., no. 79) which were delivered to him early in July (B.N. MS. Nouv. acq. fr. 7621, Portefeuilles Fontanieu 103–4, p. 151; Pocquet, *M.H.B.* xvi (1935), 10 ff.).

[2] *Preuves*, ii. 629–33 (A.N. J 243, no. 77).

[3] A.N. J 243, no. 79, 'Item, se le Roy dangleterre venoit en Bretaigne pour aydier le duc le dit Mons. de Bourgogne yra pardevers lui et lui requerra pars toutes les meilleurs manieres que il pourra que il se veuille departir . . .'; Rey, op. cit., p. 383. Civil war had broken out actively in Brittany in the early summer (Argentré, *Hist. de Bretagne*, 3rd edn., p. 476; Lefranc, *Olivier de Clisson*, pp. 377 ff.). The Anglo-French truce had been extended in May, and preparations for Richard II's expedition to Ireland were in hand in early June (Tout, *Chapters*, iii. 485 ff.). [4] A.N. J 243, no. 79.

[5] He had written to Burgundy at the end of Sept. (*Anglo-Norman Letters*, ed. Legge, p. 47, no. 3). [6] A.N. J 243, no. 81.

conceded that Gaunt and his son Derby could continue their private negotiations with John. The Royal uncles' exercise of power was cautious and, as far as Brittany was concerned, was exercised very leniently.[1] And it was on Burgundy's initiative that John and Clisson finally came to terms in 1395.[2]

During the years 1393–6 John thus avoided the complications that would have ensued from a strictly political alliance with England. Desultory negotiations did not solve the semi-permanent problems embittering Anglo-Breton relations. A solution to these problems through a series of marriage alliances, already proposed in the 1390–2 discussions, received consideration from the English Government and from private individuals like Gaunt and Huntingdon.[3] But opportunities for English intervention in Brittany were limited once the Clisson feud subsided, and the international conflict was interrupted by ever longer truces. English influence was used more peacefully in making diplomatic representations at Paris on the Duke's behalf.[4] To characterize John at this time as 'le plus fidèle allié de l'Angleterre' is to misconstrue the whole tenor of ducal policy.[5] Neutrality and independence were what the Duke wanted.

Slight advantages were, however, still to be won by long and tedious negotiations. Complicated marriage settlements, for instance, were diplomatic stratagems. Until the actual marriage took place, or part of the dowry money changed hands, little store could be set by such agreements. The intrigues surrounding the marriage of John's heir, the Count of Montfort, may be used to illustrate this point and to emphasize the triangular nature of Breton relations with the two great powers. By the time young John was two

[1] Cf. Berry's letter to John IV, 24 Sept. 1394, encouraging him to listen to Burgundy very carefully, warning him of the dangers of not doing so, and reminding him of their friendship; L. Delisle, 'Pièce soustraite au trésor des Chartes des ducs de Bretagne', *B.E.C.* lviii (1897), 379–80.

[2] *Preuves*, ii. 633–43.

[3] *Anglo-Norman Letters*, ed. Legge, no. 268.

[4] *Lettres des rois*, ed. J. J. Champollion-Figeac, ii. 284.

[5] L. Mirot, 'Isabelle de France, reine d'Angleterre', *Rev. d'hist. diplomatique*, xviii (1904), 564.

years old he had been promised in one projected marriage and betrothed in another. The first match was linked to a politico-military alliance with the Count of Armagnac.[1] But its result was to lever out of Charles VI the concession, agreed at Tours in 1392, that one of his daughters would marry John.[2] But acceptance of this offer had not prevented John IV from discussing a similar project with the English royal house. The Duke saw no bar to using his son to shield himself against French threats at Tours and as a pawn in Anglo-Breton talks.

But this independence of action was curtailed when the French resorted to marriage compacts as a way of consolidating the Anglo-French truce in 1395.[3] For all the possible matches mentioned at this time, Charles VI's daughters and other well-born French princesses were the prizes. John IV was competing alongside such eligible princes as Richard II of England in 1395–6. The time had come for him to offer more than promises. In March 1396 Richard II was plighted to Isabella of France. In July John's daughter Marie (one of the children involved in John's negotiations of the previous two years with Gaunt) was married to the Count of Perche, and in December John, Count of Montfort, was betrothed to Joan of France, Isabella's sister.[4] There was some delay in the Count of Montfort's marriage; it was finally celebrated in July 1397.[5] The young Count spent most of his time thereafter at the French court. It may be suspected that the huge financial expectations of the match (since little dowry money changed hands immediately) were meant to encourage John's friendship for that court. Certainly the French had temporarily solved a number of problems by their manipulation of the marriage market in 1396–7. They had, for example, dissolved John of Gaunt's interests in Brittany.[6]

---

[1] A.L.A. E 8 (19 Apr. 1391), and above, p. 123.

[2] *Preuves*, ii. 590–3.   [3] *Anglo-Norman Letters*, ed. Legge, no. 109.

[4] Mirot, *Rev. d'hist. diplomatique*, xviii (1904), 560–2, and ibid. xix (1905), 64–5; Thibault, *Isabeau de Bavière*, pp. 191, 312; *Chronicon Briocense*, ed. Lobineau, 868.

[5] The double affiancing of John and Joan of France has caused confusion (cf. Rey, op. cit., pp. 339–42).

[6] Marie de Bretagne, the prospective bride of the Earl of Derby's son, had been married to John, Count of Perche (Thibault, op. cit., p. 191).

The renewed acquaintance between Gaunt and John IV in the 1390s had been a useful asset to the Duke of Brittany. It has been argued that, after his withdrawal from Spain, Gaunt's motive in turning his attentions to Guyenne was to establish an apanage similar to those of the French royal uncles. In this he was helped by Richard II's compliance.[1] His relations with John IV might thus have a political as well as a personal content. It has been shown already that Gaunt kept Breton interests in mind when he attended Anglo-French negotiations.[2] From his point of view the crucial attempt to impose his rule on Guyenne came with his visit to the duchy in 1394–5. Accompanied by Derby, Gaunt had landed in Brittany on his outward journey.[3] From this date, as the French Government was soon aware, there were plans to unite the houses of Lancaster and Montfort by marriage. But the scheme was not given more definite form until a year later when Gaunt returned from Guyenne, his schemes there shattered by Gascon resistance.[4] All this while the English Government was apparently ignorant of the marriage plans. Richard II, when he learnt of them, was said to be very angry, perhaps because he was encouraging his half-brother Huntingdon (Gaunt's son-in-law) to plan for his family's future along similar lines by arranging a marriage with Brittany.[5]

John IV's main reason for offering Marie to the English can be quickly gathered. His daughter's dowry was to include the castellany of Brest and the barony of Rays.[6] It is no coincidence that both these portions were in dispute. John had seized the Rays lands in 1383, and at the very moment when he sealed his alliance with Gaunt, the Dame

---

[1] Palmer, *T.R.H.S.*, 5th ser., xvi (1966), 85 ff. This view has been challenged by M. G. A. Vale, 'War, Government and Politics in English Gascony, 1399–1453', Oxford D.Phil. thesis, 1967, pp. 12 ff. Here it is sufficient to note Gaunt's responsibility for government in Guyenne in the 1390s.   [2] Above, p. 130.

[3] *Anglo-Norman Letters*, ed. Legge, no. 19.

[4] Palmer, 'The Anglo-French Negotiations', pp. 178 ff.; *Preuves*, ii. 644–5, 657. The full marriage contract is to be found (transcribed from a sixteenth-century copy) in Bodleian Library, Oxford, Carte MS. 113, fols. 226ʳ–234ʳ. An original exemplar is A.L.A. E 8 (25 Nov. 1395). On 28 Nov. 1395 John IV agreed to pay Derby 30,000 *écus* in the year after the marriage (ibid.).

[5] *Chron. de la Traison et Mort de Richart Deux*, ed. B. Williams, pp. xix–xx.

[6] *Preuves*, ii. 644–5.

de Rays was seeking a judgement in the *Parlement* of Paris
against the Duke.[1] As Richard II's captain of Brest, Huntingdon already held Brest castle.[2] John IV wanted Gaunt
to do all in his power to obtain full satisfaction for his claims
on the lands exchanged for the lease of Brest and to facilitate
the return of Richmond. If Brest were returned to the Duke
under the terms of an Anglo-French peace treaty, compensation would be granted to the young couple. On
25 November 1395 the two Dukes sealed an alliance in
which they promised to be loyal to each other, saving only
certain superior allegiances.[3] Only one thing was required
for the marriage treaty's fulfilment: the approval of Richard
II. But though this was not forthcoming, there is no
evidence that this was due to Huntingdon's influence over
the King.

It is equally impossible to say whether Gaunt advocated
John's claims as strongly as he was bound to do. Yet there
is some evidence to indicate that Gaunt's mediation did
result in more attention being paid to Brittany in 1396.
After a period in which few embassies had passed between
the duchy and England, there was a surge of activity.
Closely following Gaunt's return came an embassy asking
for the restitution of Richmond.[4] Impersonal diplomatic
representations were backed up by a chatty letter from
Joanna, Duchess of Brittany, to the English King.[5] Richard
II released the Duke from a number of small debts and
interceded for him at Paris.[6] But neither Richmond nor
Brest was returned, and, with the marriage of Marie to the
Count of Perche, Gaunt's interests in Brittany faded.

Once more, then, John IV's efforts had failed to move the
English to relent. Once more was revealed the weakness of
his state before the impassivity of one of the great powers.

---

[1] 'Cartulaire des sires de Rays', ed. R. Blanchard, *Arch. hist. Poitou*, xxviii (1898),
pp. cv ff., 12, 14, 37, and xxx (1899), 78. The seigneury was particularly desirable
because of its salines.   [2] Below, p. 148.   [3] A.L.A. E 120, no. 7.

[4] *Lettres des rois*, ed. Champollion-Figeac, ii. 279 (from B.M. MS. Cott. Julius
B. VI, fols. 71–2); *C.C.R. 1392–6*, 459.

[5] *Lettres des rois*, ed. Champollion-Figeac, ii. 280 (B.M. MS. Cott. Julius B. VI,
fol. 54, no. 2).

[6] *C.C.R. 1392–6*, 462, 471; 'Diplomatic Correspondence of Richard II', ed.
Perroy, Royal Hist. Society, Camden, 3rd ser., xlviii (1933), no. 227 and note.

In 1360 Edward III and John II had abrogated their uncompromising support for the rivals in the Breton Civil War by relegating Breton problems to a separate and uncompleted agreement. At Bruges in 1375–7 further compromises had been vitiated by ducal actions that had provoked Charles V to revenge. Although Breton problems were raised occasionally at the Anglo-French talks in the 1380s and 1390s, discussion was neither extensive nor conclusive. Conservators of the truces were appointed for the duchy,[1] but discussion of its problems was unprofitable, given the differing interests of England and France in the duchy. Each great power knew what it was prepared to do for John. Each was eager to represent the duchy in order to make sure that the other was not obtaining some new advantage there. But so often the ambiguous attitude of the Duke and the uncertainty of reliance on his promises made each side reluctant to press the other as long as the Duke remained quiescent or involved in personal struggles that left him little time to throw his support decisively into one camp. With the removal of the threat of general war by the truce of 1396, England and France could afford, at last, to treat John more considerately.

The *rapprochement* of England and France, symbolized in the marriage of Richard II and Isabella of France and in the elaborately formalized meeting between Richard and Charles VI at Ardres in October 1396,[2] allowed Richard to sanction the return of Brest immediately after his own return from Calais.[3] The way had already been partially prepared for a renunciation of the barbican policy by the restitution of Cherbourg to Charles III of Navarre in January 1394.[4] Richard was finally turning his back on policies pursued since his minority. In doing so he may well have provoked his uncle Gloucester, who had acquiesced in many of Richard's plans in the 1390s. But Gloucester's protests against his nephew's foolhardy peace policy, which may well have led to his own murder in July 1397, were out of keeping

[1] *Foedera*, vii. 421 (1384), 629 (1389), 829 (1396), etc.
[2] Cf. description in Oriel College, Oxford, MS. 46, fols. 104ᵛ–106ᵛ.
[3] A.L.A. E 120, no. 6 (21 Jan. 1397), *vidimus* of Richard's letters given at Windsor, 29 Nov. 1396.
[4] Rey, op. cit., p. 379.

with the general war-weariness of most Englishmen.[1]
Further, the release of Brest was almost inevitable once the
Anglo-French war had been brought under control. There
was little point in continuing to antagonize the Duke of
Brittany, although he was certainly made to pay for the
repossession of Brest.

Indeed, the Duke faced a number of difficulties in gaining
possession once Richard had agreed to the return. They
illustrate the weakness of his small independent duchy in
international affairs; he had to pay for his neutrality.
Richard's terms were severe. John was to pay 120,000 francs
at Hesdin in the Low Countries by Easter 1397.[2] The castle
would then be handed over within three weeks. Possibly
Richard had been persuaded by Charles VI at Ardres to
give up the castle. Perhaps, too, John IV hoped to use the
dowry of his French daughter-in-law (150,000 francs) to
offset the payment to England, since he had confirmed the
Franco-Breton marriage plans in December 1396. It was,
however, characteristic of the Duke that in the spring of
1397 he sent another embassy to England, probably with
the intention of trying to beat down Richard's price.[3] The
1378 agreement had, after all, stipulated the free return of
Brest on the conclusion of peace or a long Anglo-French
truce. But the English were adamant about the 120,000
francs even if they allowed a number of small changes in
the actual details concerning its payment and the nature of
the restitution of Brest.[4] The Breton envoys could still
achieve little when the English Council decided to refer the
question of Richmond to Parliament. They promised that
Brest would not be used against the King or his subjects,

---

[1] Steel, *Richard II*, p. 230; this account is inaccurate: Brest was not handed over
in April (below, p. 139), and neither was it handed to the French, but to John IV.
It was noted in France that Gloucester disagreed with his nephew (*Chronographia
Regum Francorum*, ed. Moranvillé, iii. 143); McKisack, *The Fourteenth Century*,
pp. 481–2.

[2] A.L.A. E 120, no. 6.

[3] *Lettres des rois*, ed. Champollion-Figeac, ii. 282 (wrongly dated May 1396).
The copy of the agreement with the English in the ducal archives is clearly dated
16 Mar. 1397 N.S. (A.L.A. E 120, no. 5).

[4] Nicolas, i. 64–9 (B.M. MS. Cott. Julius B. VI, fols. 49, 62–3, 77–8). The
payment was made in Paris in May 1397 (A.L.A. E 120/3 i, quittance from
William le Scrope to the ducal agents); ibid. E 120, no. 5.

and in return were promised that Richard would recognize ducal *brefs* and customs duties at Brest in the future. Fresh letters were sent to Paris by Richard, although there the Duke's interests were soon pushed to one side.[1]

With the return to Brittany of the ambassadors of March 1397, John started to raise a special subsidy for the various payments that he had to make to England and to the garrison. On 30 June the town and castle of Brest were delivered to the Sire de Malestroit, so ending nearly twenty years of official English occupation.[2] The main features of the military side of the occupation and the reasons for its long duration will be described in the next chapter. Here may be emphasized the fact that the English departure, although no doubt owing something to the persistence of the Duke's diplomatic approaches, must be seen in the context of the Anglo-French *rapprochement*. The settlement with the Breton envoys in March had been phrased as carefully as any such agreement could be in order to guard against future contingencies. Some, no doubt, benefited from ducal payments for the release of the castle.[3] John IV still had to be satisfied with regard to Richmond. An appreciation of this desire and a dawning understanding of the nature of John's role as an independent and neutral agent probably convinced the English that ducal self-interest would prevent his allying strictly with the French. The sacrifice England was making was more apparent than real.

---

[1] A.N. J 644, no. 20 (14 Apr. 1397), 'Cest la response fait au conte de Ruthelland . . . envoyez au Roy [de France] depar le Roy Dengleterre . . .'. This document shows that Richard II pleaded John IV's cause over the seigneury of Rays, but that the French answers were evasive.

[2] A.L.A. E 120/2 i (29 June 1397), quittance from lieutenant of the captain of Brest to the 'Receveur de la chevance ordenee en Bretaigne bretonne pour la deliverance de la ville et chastel de Brest' for 400 frs. for transport of the garrison to England. A quittance for 10,400 *écus* had been given to the receiver for ransom arrears on 16 June (ibid. E 120/2 iii), whilst on 19 June another quittance for 24,666 *écus* had been issued 'pour racaust de touz les restaz, rampczons, coustumes et autres choses qui pouroint estre deuz a nostre dit seigneur le comte [de Huntingdon] de tout le temps passe a cause de la ville, chastel et bastide de Brest'; cf. B.N. MS. Nouv. acq. fr. 5216, no. 18, similar quittance on same day for 30,000 *écus*, the full amount to be paid to the garrison; A.L.A. E 120, no. 1, for document confirming the handing over.

[3] None of the payments mentioned in the previous note can be traced through the Exchequer.

English optimism about the Duke's future behaviour was not misplaced. Favours began to flow from John's friendship with Paris, but at the same time there was growing confidence in Anglo-Breton relations, stemming from the restitution of Brest. This reached a climax in the spring of 1398 when John visited England for the first time since 1379. He was reinvested with Richmond, took up his stall as a Knight of the Order of the Garter, and concluded a military pact with Richard II. The Richmond–Brittany link and an investigation of the true value of Richmond to John IV will be examined more closely in the final chapter. As John was himself the founder of a knightly order, his personal pleasure in wearing the Garter may be taken for granted.[1] The military covenant, which provided for mutual aid of 300 men-at-arms and 300 archers, harked back to previous alliances.[2] But its terms were simple summaries of what had earlier been concluded at great length, when both sides had sworn to be true and loyal friends, to encourage no subversion by each other's enemies, to send mutual aid, and so on. There was now no mention of the legal status of the duchy *vis-à-vis* an English king of France, no escape clauses for a fugitive duke, no marriage alliance, no list of forts to be handed to an auxiliary force. All in all it was very much a political alliance of equals, despite their very different strengths.

After a turbulent reign the years from 1397–9 form a peaceful epilogue for John. In November 1397 commissioners were appointed to accept French compensation for the release of his claims in Rethel and Nevers. In 1398 he was on friendly terms with Charles VI and Berry. He concluded an alliance with Charles III of Navarre very similar to the

---

[1] Anstis, *Order of the Garter*, i. 13, 72; Beltz, *Order of the Garter*, p. 204. Very little is known about the Order of the Ermine which John seems to have founded soon after 1381 (*Preuves*, ii. 445, for endowment of Saint-Michel, Auray, the chapel of the Order). John probably used it to strengthen the political unity of his duchy by binding his magnates to him (cf. P. S. Lewis, 'Une devise de chevalerie inconnue, créée par un comte de Foix? Le Dragon', *Annales du Midi*, lxxvi (1964), 77–8). One of the most informative early documents is a letter from John V in 1437 ordering the collection of the Order's collar from the relatives of dead members (*Lettres . . . de Jean V*, ed. Blanchard, iv. 171, no. 2287, and *Preuves*, ii. 1315–16).

[2] Nicolas, i. 79.

one with Richard II.[1] Prompt payment for the evacuation of Brest reinforces the impression gained from other sources that these years were not without prosperity for the Duke.[2]

But while John enjoyed something of an Indian summer, Richard's impolitic absolutism created the opposition that caused his downfall. How far John was cognizant of Henry of Lancaster's plans or how far he helped the exiled Duke with whom he had earlier come so close to a marriage alliance are unanswerable questions. Froissart says that Bolingbroke visited his kinsman in Brittany during the spring of 1399. In one version the very boats that he used for his descent upon England were provided from the duchy.[3] But Henry sailed from Boulogne, not from Vannes.[4] The stories that Breton troops accompanying him were dismissed once he landed can be explained away by the licence granted to John's attorneys, who were in England on Richmond business, and to Pierre de Craon, who had been retained by Richard II, to return to the duchy with their entourages in October and November 1399.[5] The donation of Richmond to the Earl of Westmorland by the new King suggests that he had little reason to feel obliged to John IV.[6] If the *Chronicon Briocense* reflected on this occasion the feelings of John's court as accurately as it usually did, the usurpation by Henry and the death of Richard II were viewed with horror.[7]

One by one the personalities who have dominated the repetitive and often seemingly futile political narrative told in this and preceding chapters were now slipping away from the scene. John was ignorant of the final fate of Richard II and of the loss of Richmond, which undid his labours of the previous twenty years. The commons of England protested his rights in Henry IV's first Parliament,

---

[1] A.L.A. E 108 (compensation); ibid. E 104 (30 Jan. 1398), order from Charles VI to pay John 10,000 frs. for attending peace negotiations and marriage of Isabella to Richard II; L. Douët d'Arcq, *Comptes de l'hôtel des rois de France aux XIVe et XVe siècles*, S.H.F. (Paris 1865), p. 297 (Berry); A.L.A. E 177, no. 4 (28 Aug. 1398), alliance with Charles III.

[2] Touchard, *Le Commerce maritime breton*, passim.

[3] Ed. Lettenhove, xvi. 167–76.

[4] McKisack, op. cit., pp. 491–2.

[5] Treaty Roll 84 mm. 18, 23; Issue Rolls 561 m. 4, 562 m. 7 (Craon's fee).

[6] *C.C.R. 1399–1401*, 24.   [7] Ed. Lobineau, 869.

but it is not clear who inspired this move.[1] In his need Henry IV did not fail to use his newly won power to make his position stronger by the promotion of his lieutenants. A new chapter, if it were to be opened in the history of Brittany and the honour of Richmond, would be written for another duke in another century, for on the night of 1–2 November 1399 John IV, Duke of Brittany, Earl of Richmond died.

[1] *Rot. Parl.* iii. 427.

VI

THE ENGLISH OCCUPATION OF BREST
1342–1397

O N 19 October 1342 Edward III landed at Brest to
begin a campaign in the duchy of Brittany on behalf
of John de Montfort.[1] Apart from a short ten-year
period between 1362 and 1372, English or Anglo-Breton
troops held the castle, town, and immediate environs of
Brest until Richard II restored them to John IV in 1397.
The political situation which invited this English occupation
of ducal lands and the complications which ensued have been
described in the preceding chapters. Here, by using the
occupation of Brest as a central theme, it will be possible to
link together the two main periods of English military intervention in Brittany—the Civil War period and the years
after the 1372 alliance—in order to describe the organization of English forces in a territory which was frequently, if
only nominally, allied with England. The practical problems
of maintaining, supplying, and financing the garrison at
Brest were affected by fluctuations in the character and course
of the Anglo-French war. The choice of personnel and the
instructions to captains at Brest by the English Government
serve to illustrate not only the solutions proposed for local
difficulties engendered by the occupation, but also some
of the more general problems of Anglo-Breton relations.
The continued occupation of Brest after 1381 can be explained by the requirements of England's general war
strategy; but, even before the formulation of the barbican
policy, Edward III's motives for invading and occupying
parts of Brittany appear to have been principally military
and strategic.[2] By describing the microcosm of Brest many
of the larger problems of English war policy and administration in the fourteenth century may be illuminated.

[1] *Chronique de Richard Lescot,* ed. Lemoine, p. 207.
[2] Above, p. 9.

The strategic importance of the Finistère peninsula to the English has been mentioned several times already, but this fact may be stressed. When the Hundred Years War began, England held no footholds on the southern shore of the Channel. The early campaigns started from the lands of England's Flemish allies in north-eastern France. In the Channel, England possessed the Channel Isles, but their defence was difficult. Channel Island ports served as useful harbours for keeping ships at the ready to suppress Norman or Malouin piracy. But they were not so well placed for patrolling the northern and western Breton shoreline, nor the region that came under French influence from La Rochelle. By the time Edward III intervened in Brittany, long stretches of the vital Anglo-Gascon sea-route were threatened by France.[1] The possession of the Finistère peninsula would make communications between French bases at La Rochelle and the Channel ports of Normandy more difficult. Occupation of the Brest region above all other places in Brittany was necessary to Edward III's schemes. The reluctance of Richard II's governments to release Brest to their technical ally John IV was likewise based on a clear acknowledgement of its military and economic importance.[2]

From the first, the English occupation was not solely confined to Brest. The small neighbouring towns of Saint-Mathieu, le Conquet, and Trémazon (held by Tanguy du Chastel, a Breton supporter of the Montfortists),[3] and islands like Ouessant and Tristan (in the bay of Douarnenez), were quickly brought under English control.[4] The captain's authority spread outside the town and castle of Brest. John Gatesdene, appointed captain in December 1343, was given jurisdiction over the *vicomté* of Léon.[5] He continued to

---

[1] T. Williams, 'The Importance of the Channel Isles in British Relation [*sic*] with the Continent', *Bull. de la Soc. Jersiaise*, xi (1928), 65 ff.

[2] P. Levot, *Histoire de . . . Brest*, i, *passim*; Touchard, *Le Commerce maritime breton*, pp. 47-8.

[3] Treaty Roll 29 m. 13 (9 Mar. 1351), confirmation of grants first given to Tanguy in 1342; *Arch. hist. Poitou*, xvii (1886), 28.

[4] Treaty Roll 30 m. 10 (12 May 1352), confirmation of grant of Île Tristan to Anthony Bache by Walter Bentley. As early as 1346 Bentley's lieutenant for the island of Tresco (?Tristan) was issuing safe conducts (Exeter, City Library, Dartmouth Deed 60670).

[5] *Foedera*, ii. 1240. Appendix C for list of captains of Brest.

enjoy civilian revenues from former ducal monopolies in the fish-drying trade, and from admiralty rights and customs dues exacted at Saint-Mathieu and Brest. This combination of military and civilian duties in the captaincy of Brest is paralleled by the role of the lieutenant appointed to act for Edward III and the Duke of Brittany in the duchy at large.[1] Within the castellany the captain's powers were wide. Appointed at the King's pleasure, he was almost entirely free from official supervision. It is no surprise to find Thomas Dagworth, King's lieutenant in Brittany from 1347 to 1350, personally holding Brest.

A quittance issued by Dagworth's widow in 1350 reveals the captain's freedom of action. She had given her receiver at Brest 'plein poair de lever et de faire lever rentes et toutes leveez dues dedeinz la dite Chastelnye si bien des confiscacions come dautres choses'.[2] But the freedom of individual castellans weakened the authority of the King's lieutenant, and it was in his interest that a reaction set in after 1350. In accordance with suggestions to the King's Council in 1352 from Dagworth's successor as lieutenant, Walter Bentley,[3] John Maynard, the new captain of Brest, was held more directly responsible to the lieutenant. Stricter control of the captain's accounts was exercised, but he still could not be removed except by the King's licence. He also continued to use the forfeited lands of Blois supporters.[4]

The full extent of the captain's jurisdiction can be judged from the terms upon which Matthew Gournay accepted the captaincy of Brest in 1357.[5] The castle and town of Brest were to be held

cum toto dominio eidem castro pertinente et simul cum moneta, redemptionibus, confiscationibus et omnibus aliis proficuis ad dictum castrum spectantibus . . . etiam villam de Sancto Matheo cum brevibus et custumis ejusdem villae ac admiratu, piscariis, redditibus, servitiis et omnibus aliis exitibus et proficuis ad praedictam villam et dominium qualitercumque spectantibus . . .

---

[1] Le Patourel, *History*, xliii (1958), 187.

[2] Chancery Miscellanea, bundle 35/10, no. 60.

[3] Froissart, ed. Lettenhove, xviii. 339–43, for Bentley's memorandum. It is enrolled on Treaty Roll 30 m. 8^v.

[4] *Foedera*, iii. 247. [5] Ibid. 383.

Gournay held his captaincy at the King's pleasure, and control over his accounts, if exercised at all, passes beyond our grasp, for in 1358 he and a number of other captains in Brittany were made directly responsible to the King's Chamber rather than to the Exchequer.[1] No more captains' indentures for Brest survive before 1362, when England handed the duchy over to John IV.

Throughout the Civil War, the captain of Brest had been almost a free agent. Aware of the dangers of such independence, the English Government had taken some measures to stamp out the worst excesses of military occupation and exploitation by irresponsible captains in the duchy at large. There is no evidence that Gournay was particularly extortionate at Brest, although it is unlikely that he let easy profits slip through his fingers. In 1362 he was imprisoned in the Tower of London for his part in selling some Norman forts;[2] his connections with Brittany were still strong,[3] but it is uncertain whether he was still captain of Brest and his agreement with John IV for the farm of ducal *brefs* at Bordeaux in 1364 makes no mention of his captaincy.[4] He fought at Auray, a service which temporarily lost him his English lands, but after 1364 he left Brittany and made a profitable career in Guyenne.[5]

Sometime between 1362 and 1364 Gournay released Brest and John IV entrusted it to a Breton supporter. Its captaincy became a matter of English concern again in 1372. It was then suggested that in exchange for Bécherel (one of the sureties for John's debts to England) John would deliver Brest, along with Morlaix, Hennebont, and some other towns, to the English.[6] As in 1342, English interest in controlling the Breton littoral is manifest. After Geoffroi de Poulglou, the Breton captain of Brest, had deserted to the

---

[1] Tout, *Chapters*, iv. 250–1, 317 ff.; Accts. Var. 176/9 (accounts of the treasurer of Anglo-Montfortist Brittany, 1361–2), for a list of similar castles.

[2] *C.P.R. 1361–4*, 144; Keen, *Laws of War*, p. 35.

[3] He was one of the hostages for the truce concluded with Blois at the *Landes d'Évran* in July 1363 (B.N. MS. Nouv. acq. fr. 5216, no. 1, quittance from Gournay to John IV, 8 Mar. 1364).

[4] Appendix of Documents, no. 1.

[5] *C.Inq.M.* iii. 199; Carte, *Catalogue des rolles gascons*, i. 165 (2 Aug. 1378), grant of the *sénéchaussée* of the Landes.   [6] *Foedera*, iii. 927.

French,[1] John IV allowed an English force under Lord Neville to take over control there in October 1372.[2] In 1378 Neville petitioned Parliament over various grievances arising from his captaincy. He complained that Edward III had ordered him to go to Brest. He had there agreed with John IV to guard the castle while the Duke collected a force to relieve it, because it was closely invested by Du Guesclin from May 1373. Ducal help failed, and Neville was compelled to pay large sums to redeem hostages which he had given in order to obtain a short truce with the French.[3] Acting for both the King and the Duke, Neville had taken the remains of John's treasure at Brest to conduct the defence throughout 1373.[4] After being pressed by huge French forces the siege was lifted, and Neville appears to have handed over the captaincy to Robert Knolles and John Devereux in 1374.[5] The Bruges truces afforded further relief to the garrison, and Knolles left lieutenants in charge at Brest.[6] But because these new English captains were chiefly responsible to the Duke, no indentures of service survive. English payments to John IV between 1375 and 1378 were principally for wages he had earned by participating in various expeditions or for the wages of garrisons at Brest and Auray.[7] By the autumn of 1377 England had to assume responsibility for victualling Brest, and by December the Duke agreed on the principles of the castle's lease to the English.[8]

[1] A.L.A. E 134/2, 24 Feb. 1372, fealty of Poulglou to John IV for holding Brest; B.N. MS. fr. 22325, p. 859, 3 May 1374, holding Nantes for the French.

[2] *Anonimalle Chronicle*, ed. Galbraith, pp. 71, 178.

[3] *Rot. Parl.* iii. 53; Froissart, ed. Luce, viii, pp. lxxix, clx; in 1375 or 1376 Edward III wrote to John IV reminding him of his obligation to help the hostages for Brest pay their ransoms (Cambridge Univ. MS. Dd. iii. 53, no. 421), but these were not paid off until 1377 (Accts. Var. 37/9, nos. 1–6).

[4] A.L.A. E 212, a receipt for 20,035 frs. found at Brest.

[5] *Rot. Parl.* ii. 328–9; Knolles was active in Brittany and Normandy in 1374 (B.N. MS. Nouv. acq. fr. 3653, p. 51, no. 289, mandate from the *bailli* of Caen, 19 June 1374). John IV and Neville were in his debt (*C.C.R. 1374–7*, 102); Appendix C for Devereux. [6] *Foedera*, iii. 1062, 1066.

[7] Issue Rolls 459 m. 20, 22 Dec. 1375, 463 m. 1, 3 July 1377, supplies for Brest and Auray; 456 m. 10, 23 Dec. 1374, 460 m. 23, 8 Aug. 1376, 462 m. 14, 20 June 1377, 465 mm. 1–6, Oct.–Nov. 1377, prests to John IV.

[8] Ibid. 465 m. 8, 20 Nov. 1377, and Accts. Var. 37/23, stores; A.L.A. E 120, no. 22, 22 Jan. 1391, *vidimus* of 1 Dec. 1377, letters patent of John, Duke of Lancaster, and others guaranteeing to return Brest to John IV after its lease to the English, for the duration of the war with France, had been agreed with Richard II.

This lease was confirmed in April 1378.[1] As a result, fuller lists of captains and officials and their terms of service can be obtained from surviving indentures. Robert Knolles had re-joined the garrison in January 1378 with a small force of men when he was deputed captain by the leaders of the Buckingham expedition.[2] By April the English Government had drawn up indentures with Richard Abberbury and John Golafre. They were to be joint captains at an annual fee of 10,000 marks. They were succeeded in 1379 by Hugh Calveley and Thomas Percy, who were granted 8,000 marks for expenses. In 1381 Percy became sole captain, first at a rate of 7,000 marks a year, then, after 21 June, at 4,250 marks in wartime and 3,250 in peacetime. His final indenture, drawn up in December 1385, was only valid for a few weeks at the rate of 2,000 marks a year. John Roches, his successor in February 1386, received this same small fee. When Richard, Earl of Arundel, was made captain for life in 1388 he received 4,000 marks per annum. But he was replaced in 1389 by John Holland, Earl of Huntingdon, who took a fee of 3,000 marks per annum. In 1392 Holland was given an option on the castle for seven years or as long as it remained in Richard II's hands, although he was only to be paid in wartime or if the revenues of the castellany of Brest were insufficient to cover his expenses.[3]

Fluctuations in the captains' allowances mirror changes in the military and political situations affecting Anglo-Breton relations. In wartime, naturally, the allowances are greater— apart from the period of Roches's captaincy. We may there detect economies practised from 1386 in response to mounting criticism from both the Lords and the Commons against the cost of Brest as of the other major English garrisons in France.[4] Similar fluctuations, for example, can be followed in the wages of the captain of Cherbourg.[5] The captain was guarded against personal sacrifice by guarantees that loss of office, consequent on any Anglo-French peace, would not

---

[1] *Foedera*, iv. 34–5.
[2] Appendix C for details of this and following appointments.
[3] Accts. Var. 69/1, no. 279 (25 Oct. 1392), Holland's indenture.
[4] *Rot. Parl.* iii. 36 (1378); *Polychronicon*, ix. 85–6.
[5] William Windsor's fee at Cherbourg in 1382 was £4,000 p.a. By 1386 William le Scrope's was £2,000 p.a. (Accts. Var. 68/9, no. 226, and 10, no. 244).

mean loss of wages. As it happened, Holland received very little direct aid from the Exchequer in the time of truce. The way in which he had been reappointed to a longer period of captaincy is paralleled by indentures for the keeping of Berwick and other castles in the 1390s.[1]

But if Holland in the 1390s was enjoying greater freedom, rather like Gournay in the 1350s, his immediate predecessors had been more dependent on the Exchequer. In Abberbury and Golafre's first indenture all profits from the castle, whether by land or by sea, were to be accounted for at Westminster. The King was to take all revenues from ransoms of the land and a quarter of the profits obtained from ships captured at sea.[2] Two months later a new indenture was sealed in which the captains were to have half the ransoms of the surrounding countryside. The King still took 'la quarte partie de niefs qils gayneront sur la mier...'. The rest was to be divided amongst the garrison.[3] Later captains were allowed all ransoms and profits from the sea, although they had to account at the Exchequer and their wages were cut.[4] Unlike the captains of Cherbourg, those at Brest were not given a specific victual allowance, nor did the retiring captain have to make up stocks to the level at which they were when he first arrived at the castle. From 1380 onwards it had become usual to insert clauses guarding English captains in Marcher or enemy lands against the possibilities of siege.[5] Allowance was made for artillery expended in defence of their castles.[6] Time limits were set within which the castles were to be relieved by the King. If he failed to do so, the captains were then free to arrange terms with the enemy for evacuation. Some of these clauses were inserted into

---

[1] R. L. Storey, 'The Wardens of the Marches of England towards Scotland, 1377–1489', *E.H.R.* lxxii (1957), 600–2.

[2] Accts. Var. 37/30, no. 1 (18 Feb. 1378).

[3] Ibid. no. 2, and 68/7, no. 171 (both dated 10 Apr. 1378).

[4] Ibid. 38/8, no. 19 (7 Apr. 1379), grant to Percy and Calveley 'Tam de brevibus, sechariis, redditibus, custumis, placitis et . . . amerciamentis et forisfacturis quibuscunque, quam de redempcionibus et omnibus aliis revencionibus et proficuis que ad nos pertinent, pertinebant vel pertinere debent . . .'; *Foedera,* iv. 133.

[5] Cf. Keen, *Laws of War,* p. 125.

[6] Accts. Var. 68/9, no. 222 (1382), Calveley's indenture for Cherbourg. He did not actually take up the captaincy.

indentures of the captains of Brest, which were in most respects typical of their period.[1]

The captains had full powers to discipline the garrison and to conclude truces in the King's name with the Duke.[2] When Arundel was appointed King's lieutenant and commissioner 'in those parts' in 1388, special conditions obtained because of the political role he was playing in addition to his fulfilment of duties as Admiral of the English Fleet and captain of Brest.[3] The geographical limits of his jurisdiction were defined. From the places mentioned it can be seen that the English hoped to control a very extensive portion of the dangerous Finistère headlands and the off-shore islands, similar to the area occupied during the Civil War. The captain's authority extended for more than twenty-five miles from Brest as the crow flew.[4]

The captaincy of Brest was thus a very important post. It is possible to see in the choice of officers at Brest attempts to get men who were both experienced and acceptable to the Duke. This was not a guarantee that no dispute would arise, but it did help to smooth the path to negotiation when difficulties arose. As long as the English were determined to keep to the 1378 agreement, it was one way of trying to maintain tolerable relations with the Duke. The captains of Brest did not owe their position solely to social rank. On several occasions the captaincy was held jointly with the Admiralty to the South and West of the Thames.[5] Neville, Calveley and Percy, Arundel and Holland all combined the offices. Sometimes the captains held other important defensive posts. Calveley held the Channel Isles during his term at Brest,[6] as John Golafre, junior, held them with Cherbourg in the 1390s.[7] Percy had experience in Poitou and as Admiral to the North of the Thames before service at Brest.[8]

---

[1] For example, Accts. Var. 69/1, no. 278 (1392), Holland's indenture.

[2] Accts. Var. 69/1, no. 278.   [3] *Foedera*, vii. 578.

[4] Cf. K. Fowler, 'Les finances et la discipline dans les armées anglaises en France au XIVe siècle', *Les Cahiers vernonnais*, iv (1964), 69 n. 102.

[5] *Handbook of British Chronology*, 2nd edn., ed. Sir F. M. Powicke and E. B. Fryde (London 1961), p. 130.

[6] J. Le Patourel, *Medieval Administration of the Channel Islands*, pp. 31–2, 128.

[7] *Foedera*, vii. 759.

[8] Cambridge Univ. MS. Dd. iii. 53, no. 409, 1372, Percy as seneschal in Poitou; *Foedera*, iv. 51.

Calveley, again, in addition to his *routier* experience, had seen service at Calais.[1] John Roches had been Admiral to the South and West.[2] Though the captain could and sometimes did fulfil his duties by deputy, all of them served personally at the castle for a time. Parliament and Council kept an eye on them to see that they were accomplishing their duties adequately.[3] But they were not forbidden to hold other castles along with Brest.

When the captains were busy with other duties, they were assisted at Brest by lieutenants. They, too, were experienced soldiers, men like Digory Seys, an ex-*routier* leader, who served Percy and Calveley,[4] or like Robert Buckton, John Norbury, Richard Fotheringhay, and John Godard, who served Percy.[5] They were often pensioners of the Duke, friends from his exile, former servants, or followers of captains who were themselves personally acquainted with the Duke.[6] They were useful diplomatic agents for the English Government on occasion, for example, Philip More, who served Roches as lieutenant during the siege of 1386–7, or Edward Dallingrigge, who served under Arundel and Holland.[7] Like the captains they could conclude truces locally whenever necessary.[8] Along with the captains they were also appointed to the commissions for conserving Anglo-French truces in the 1380s and 1390s; though it may be doubted whether men like Buckton, Fotheringhay, and Norbury could always be strictly impartial.[9]

---

[1] Cambridge Univ. MS. Dd. iii. 53, no. 353, delivery of cannon to Calveley at Calais *c.* 1377.　　　[2] *Foedera*, iv. 148.　　　[3] *Rot. Parl.* iii. 213.

[4] *Arch. hist. Poitou*, xix (1899), 42 n.; *C.C.R. 1377–81*, 411, and Accts. For. 16 m. 42ʳ (Percy's accounts, 1383).　　　[5] *C.P.M.R. 1381–1412*, 45; *Foedera*, vii. 421.

[6] Fotheringhay was a pensioner from 1378 (*C.P.R. 1381–5*, 402) and had been in ducal service since 1368 at least (Plaine, *Procès*, p. 283). Dallingrigge (below, n. 7) was a ducal pensioner from 1374 (*C.P.R. 1381–5*, 55). Godard was a servant of Percy in 1374 (*Arch. hist. Gironde*, xii (1869–70), 322).

[7] Treaty Rolls 70 m. 27, 71 mm. 6, 24, and Issue Roll 517 mm. 12, 16, all 1386–7, for More; also above, p. 111. *C.P.R. 1389–92*, 118, Dallingrigge as lieutenant for Holland. In 1387 he had been victualling Brest (Issue Roll 517 m. 11). In May 1397 his son and heir thought it necessary to get a pardon on account of his father's adherence to Thomas, Duke of Gloucester, in 1386 (*C.P.R. 1396–9*, 341), although Dallingrigge eventually became one of Richard II's busiest councillors (Baldwin, *King's Council*, p. 132).

[8] A.L.A. E 120, nos. 13, 14, truces of 1 Aug. 1382 and 9 Sept. 1383 between John Norbury and John IV.

[9] *Foedera*, vii. 420–1, 714, 776; *Lettres des rois*, ed. Champollion-Figeac, ii. 291.

Under the captains and their lieutenants was the garrison. Indications from the early period of English occupation in the duchy suggest that most garrisons were small. When Brest was defended against the Montfortists in 1341 it may have been held by 300 men.[1] But there is no definite evidence for the size of the garrison until some muster lists for 1375–7.[2] At the time of the Bruges truce in 1375, when the diplomats at Bruges agreed that John IV needed only 200 men-at-arms to hold all his castles in the duchy, the garrison numbered about 100 men. Throughout the period of the truce the garrison numbers rose. In 1376 the average per quarter was about 160 men-at-arms. Just before the siege of 1377 this average had risen to about 200 men; whilst in the crisis of early 1378 about 240 men-at-arms were in the garrison.[3] Thereafter muster rolls are lacking, and the captains' accounts, although giving total receipts and expenses, do not give a breakdown of these expenses. There are occasional references to troops of from 20 to 30 men-at-arms, and an equivalent number of archers, being sent to reinforce the garrison.[4] Abberbury and Golafre took 51 men-at-arms, 71 archers, and 15 arbalesters with them in 1378.[5] Percy and Calveley took 25 esquires and 39 archers in 1379, and Percy returned home with 83 esquires and archers in 1382–3.[6] But in all these cases the numbers given are only a proportion of the garrison. Most indentures had merely stated that the captain should maintain a sufficient force in the castle. It may be suspected that the usual complement, except in times of siege, was well below 200 men.

Brest, therefore, was never staffed as fully as Calais and its March, which had a complement of over 1,000 men in wartime,[7] nor even like Berwick, the northern Marcher castles, or Cherbourg. At this last castle there were usually

[1] Froissart, ed. Luce, ii. 91; the wages of the garrison at Bécherel in 1359–60 amounted to £400. 3s. 0¾d.; whilst the wages of the treasurer of Anglo-Montfortist Brittany and his retinue of six men-at-arms and eight archers in the same year were £426. 13s. 4d. (Accts. Var. 174/4); cf. Fino, Forteresses de la France médiévale, pp. 253–4.   [2] A.L.A. E 214.

[3] Accts. For. 12 m. 4ᵛ, Knolles's accounts, 1378.

[4] Issue Rolls 515 m. 13 (12 Dec. 1386), 517 m. 16 (27 July 1387), 518 m. 7 (11 Nov. 1387).

[5] Accts. For. 13 m. Fʳ.   [6] Ibid. 16 m. 42ʳ.

[7] S. Burley, 'The Victualling of Calais, 1347–1365', B.I.H.R. xxxi (1958), 51.

350 men in residence.[1] The smallness of the Brest garrison is partly explained by the failure to develop a March district with outlying castles, like Calais, for example. Control over the surrounding countryside was ensured by sending out raiding parties from Brest, but no bridge-heads were established. Nevertheless, as will be shown later, to maintain even this small garrison required considerable resources.

After the captain and his lieutenants, the most important official at Brest was the receiver. It was his job to organize the direct supply of victuals and other necessities to feed the garrison. Like the captains and lieutenants, this man seems to have been carefully chosen. John de Valence, a former ducal official at Saint-Mathieu and, after 1379, a receiver-general of the duchy, had been employed as receiver at Brest for a period during the exile.[2] When Thomas Norwych was appointed by Richard II in 1378 as King's receiver and victualler, he may have already served there as a man-at-arms, although he was a clerk.[3] He was succeeded in 1381 by Philip Dernford, who was described as a citizen and vintner of London.[4] For a time John Godard, who has already been mentioned as a lieutenant, fulfilled some of the receiver's duties. Dernford later went to Cherbourg as victualler, only to return to Brest before the 1386 siege. Later he was accused of incompetence and replaced by John Draper, who was probably a merchant.[5] Under Holland's captaincy the receiver was no longer responsible for presenting accounts at the Exchequer, so that we lose sight of most of Holland's officials. Nevertheless, one of them, William Alyngton, was to prove himself an expert in logistics, and under Henry V became treasurer-general of Normandy.[6] Most of the receivers had experience of buying and selling stores as

---

[1] Cf. Accts. Var. 68/8, nos. 178-9, Harleston's indentures, 25 Feb. 1379.

[2] *Foedera*, iv. 36; he is referred to as receiver in the 1375-7 muster rolls (A.L.A. E 214); above, p. 75, n. 3; *Preuves*, ii. 232-3.

[3] Accts. Var. 38/8, no. 21 (1 Apr. 1378), appointment; a T. Norwych appears on the 1375-7 muster rolls (A.L.A. E 214); *C.P.M.R. 1381-1412*, 18, and *C.C.R. 1385-9*, 235, for various alleged crimes committed by Norwych, described as a chaplain or clerk.   [4] Appendix D for this and following appointments.

[5] Treaty Roll 71 m. 16 (20 Dec. 1386), order for arrest of Dernford. Draper was later in trouble also (*C.C.R. 1389-92*, 89).

[6] R. A. Newhall, *The English Conquest of Normandy, 1416-1424* (Yale Univ. Press, New Haven 1924), pp. 154-5.

merchants or as factors, although obvious connections exist
between some of them and their captains. Some had served
at Brest or with John IV before their appointment.[1] It seems
likely that this, combined with their expertise, enabled the
English to choose relatively reliable receivers and ones who
would be acceptable to John IV.

One of the best summaries of the receiver's duties is to be
found amongst the details of Norwych's enrolled accounts.[2]
Norwych was appointed by the King to receive all the
revenues due to his master, but he was under the supervision of the captain. His wages of forty francs a quarter
(£26. 13s. 4d. p.a.) were paid from the King's receipts. He
was to keep the castle well stocked by looking after the stores
and the artillery. He also ordered and arranged the transport of stores. When he obtained large quantities of goods in
England he might come under the surveillance of domestic
royal officials, but usually he acted on his own initiative.
When the Government sent provisions to Brest, Norwych
supervised their unloading and inventoried them. On his
own initiative he paid for the repair of the defences. Finally
he accounted at the Exchequer for all his actions, bringing
warrants and quittances from captains and merchants to
justify his accounts.[3]

The receiver's other duties can be gathered from comparison with the terms of appointment for receivers at
Cherbourg. In 1379 the King's victualler there was commissioned to take musters and to authorize payments from
the profits of the ransom district.[4] The same conditions are
seen in Draper's appointment to Brest in 1387.[5] He was to
take musters as often as necessary, sending to the Exchequer
lists of those present and, more significantly, of those

[1] Dernford had served with Calveley in 1379 (Treaty Roll 63 m. 4, protection)
and had been sent to Brittany with letters to Buckingham in 1380 (Issue Roll 481
m. 8, 3 Dec.). For Godard and Percy see above, p. 151, n. 6. Draper had served
with John IV in 1374–5 (*Foedera*, iii. 1010) and with Abberbury in 1378 (Accts.
Var. 37/2, 1 May 1378) as a man-at-arms.

[2] Accts. For. 18 m. 64ʳ.

[3] Accts. Var. 38/8, nos. 1–21, for example.

[4] Ibid. 68/8, no. 178 (captain's indenture at Cherbourg); Chancery Warrants,
file 458, no. 699 (8 Apr. 1379), appointment of John Walsh as victualler of
Cherbourg.

[5] Treaty Roll 72 m. 23.

defecting. Unlike the captain's wages, which were cut at about this time, the receiver's wages were increased to £50 per annum. Perhaps this was meant to improve his efficiency; if so, it is in line with the terms of the 1386 Commission's mandate to overhaul the country's defences and is a recognition of the receiver's importance.[1]

His office at Brest can also be compared with that of king's victualler at Calais, whose position and functions have been described in detail elsewhere.[2] The chief duty of this official was 'not to keep stores, but to issue them'. The victuals issued were counted as part of the wages of soldiers who received them. To help him in his daily duties, the victualler of Calais had a *familia* of soldiers and their valets, a keeper of the wine, a granger, a lardener, a tyler, labourers, and a pool of miscellaneous artisans on which he could draw, including a wheelwright, coopers, and masons. Evidence for a similar group of men at Brest is slight, although there is reference to a lardener and a granger.[3] It is to be expected that the receiver had a small army of artisans on call for repairs and the distribution of food and artillery. He hired troops of soldiers and sailors from the garrison on occasion.[4] The Calais victualler has been characterized as a 'commissariat officer supplying rations to a front-line fighting force'. Allowing for differences in size and importance between the Calais Pale and the castellany of Brest, Norwych and his fellow receivers fulfilled the same functions. But, because uneasy truce rather than open warfare was the main condition at Brest, it was simpler to supply the castle from local sources than it was at Calais. The receiver's responsibilities at Brest as at Cherbourg were heavy; for both castles were held from technically friendly allies and were infrequently supplied from home. It is no surprise that the receiver's actions were often misconstrued by the English Government. In order to maintain supplies he was often reduced to making sorties into the surrounding countryside. He also had to condone lawless acts by the garrison, who

---

[1] Cf. Tout, *Chapters*, iii. 411 ff.   [2] Burley, *B.I.H.R.* xxxi (1958).

[3] Issue Roll 471 m. 13 (1378), T. Colvyle, lardener, and Will. Barbour, granger (also Accts. Var. 37/23); in 1387 there was a butler (Issue Roll 519 m. 19).

[4] Accts. Var. 38/8, no. 14.

at Brest often found the opportunities for piracy too good to be missed.[1]

The other officers who helped to run the English administration at Brest may be quickly dismissed. In the 1350s letters from the English Government to its castellans and receivers in Brittany referred also to constables.[2] The town of Cherbourg had its English constable in the 1380s,[3] and in 1385 Thomas Ashelden was appointed to the same office at Brest during the King's pleasure. Ashelden had previously held civil office in Dartmouth and had helped to supply Brest in 1377–8.[4] At Cherbourg the constable's jurisdiction appears to have been principally limited to the town, but at Brest Ashelden also had jurisdiction in the castle. Probably in the smaller township and garrison the administration could not be rigorously departmentalized. Ashelden's earlier experience fitted him for military and civilian duties. He had mercantile connections and was also friendly with John IV during his exile.[5] The other known constable, John Hobeldod, was principally a soldier, who is known at Brest from protections issued to him between 1389 and 1395. The only other reference to him is in a document where, reading between the lines, it is possible to see him condoning, if not encouraging, intimidation of commissioners sent to inquire into some acts of piracy.[6] In this he was supported by the captain's lieutenant, but of his actual duties little is known. The same is true for a sergeant and porter of the town appointed in 1385. John Elyngham was a king's sergeant-at-arms and was to receive the accustomed fee for his office.[7] Nothing else is known of his obligations. Both the constable and the

---

[1] Cf. p. 153, n. 5, orders to arrest Dernford and charges against Draper. For demands on Walsh, victualler at Cherbourg, *C.C.R. 1381–5*, 473, 633. See also Fowler, *Les Cahiers vernonnais*, iv (1964), 70.

[2] *Foedera*, iii. 404.

[3] Masson d'Autume, *Cherbourg pendant la guerre de Cent Ans*, p. 89.

[4] Chancery Warrants, file 1351, no. 3 (appointment); Watkin, *Dartmouth*, i. 59–60, 63, 272; Accts. Var. 37, no. 1 (5 Apr. 1378), particulars of victuals bought for Brest.

[5] A.L.A. E 117, John IV's household accounts show Ashelden visiting him at Cheshunt on 7 Aug. 1377.

[6] Treaty Rolls 73 m. 3, 76 m. 11, 77 m. 11, 80 m. 19, protections, 1389–95; Privy Seal files, 1/31, c. 1388–9, charges against Hobeldod. In 1388 he had been given a licence to go to Calais for a duel (Chancery Warrants, file 500, no. 4800).

[7] Ibid., file 490, no. 3733 (18 Sept. 1385).

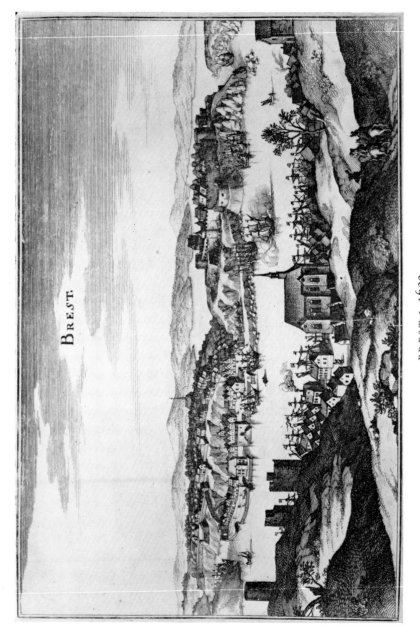

BREST

BREST *c.* 1632
Ashmolean Museum, Oxford

sergeant were originally royal appointments (Hobeldod may have been Holland's nominee). In a similar way Richard II had also appointed clerks to benefices in Brest,[1] using all the privileges that appertained to his holding of the castle, which he obviously considered to be held in full sovereignty like any other in his power.

Passing now to the defences of Brest castle, we are not very well informed about their layout in the fourteenth century.[2] Only one important remaining tower (the *tour du Midi*) has been attributed to this period, and most fourteenth-century features have been disguised in later alterations or completely destroyed. No specific work has been ascribed to the efforts of the English captains. A *donjon*, which may have been no more than a heavily fortified tower on the walls, and the *tour d'Azenor*, both thirteenth-century work, were the main defensive works on the landward and river-board sides of the castle, which was situated on the rocky left bank of the river Penfeld as it entered the *rade* of Brest. Another thirteenth-century tower (the *tour César*) faced out into the bay. The immediate advantages of the castle's position may be appreciated from the seventeenth-century print reproduced here.[3]

The 1375-7 muster lists give some indication of the way in which the garrison was apportioned.[4] The main castle was the *donjon*, and the rest of the defences were made up of the town walls—the *enceinte* of the castle included dwelling-places—and the small castle (either the *tour César* or the *tour du Midi*).[5] This 'small castle' had a complement of twenty or thirty men-at-arms and archers. A body of men twenty-five strong was referred to as 'archers of the town'.

---

[1] Perroy, *L'Angleterre et le Grand Schisme*, pp. 105-6.

[2] E. Fleury, 'Monographie du château de Brest', *Bull. Soc. Acad. de Brest* (1865), 1-64. I am indebted to M. Jean Foucher, archivist of Brest, for sending me a copy of this paper. See also Alfred, vicomte de la Barre de Nanteuil, 'Brest, guide archéo-logique', *Congrès archéologique de France*, lxxxi (1914), 3-12.

[3] Ashmolean Museum, Oxford, Sutherland Collection (cf. Zeiller, *Topographia Galliae*, p. 8, illus. no. 4). The *tour du Midi* is immediately above the tree on the right-hand side. The *donjon* and the *tour d'Azenor*, with its conical roof, are to the left-hand side, whilst the *tour César* is linked to the wall behind the *tour du Midi*.

[4] A.L.A. E 214.

[5] Cf. S. Castel, 'Brest, étude de géographie urbaine', *Annales de Bretagne*, xl (1932-3), 158-9.

The captain's household consisted of about the same number of men-at-arms and twelve to fifteen archers and other serving-men, who probably lived in the *donjon*. There are no particular distinctions drawn between the rest of the garrison, except that some were paid at slightly higher rates; though this in turn cannot be put down to a distinction between men-at-arms and archers. Nor is there any indication of any particular section of the defences being committed to their care. But there is good evidence that a large number of soldiers lived in the *enceinte* and the town, either billeted there or in their own houses. Once again the analogy of Cherbourg suggests itself. There the Government made an attempt to secure amicable relations between the garrison and the townspeople. After a petition, the Government fixed the conditions on which men could be billeted. The keynote of their instructions was that the citizens should be treated 'as if they were Englishmen'.[1] At Brest in 1382 soldiers were allowed to build their own homes. They were to pay an annual rent for them, but would be given possession for life. Ten years later Holland reported that with the continually changing captaincy and the influx of new soldiers, these arrangements had been abused.[2] Incoming captains had taken the newest houses for their troops, ousting without regard the former occupiers, whether English or native. To avoid the resultant evils of this practice the captain was empowered to grant houses at an annual rent on life tenures. The receiver's accounts show that repairs to these houses were undertaken at the King's expense.[3]

Of the three outlying *bastides* of Brest that are referred to on various occasions at the end of the fourteenth century, two very quickly disappeared. Du Guesclin might have begun to build one during his siege of 1373.[4] Another one, of wood rather than stone, and built across the river Penfeld from the main castle, was constructed by the Duke in 1386 and subsequently razed by the English. But the stone

---

[1] Masson d'Autume, *Cherbourg pendant la guerre de Cent Ans*, pp. 87–9; Chancery Warrants, file 478, no. 2557 (23 Nov. 1382); cf. Calmette and Déprez, *La France et l'Angleterre en conflit*, p. 205.   [2] *Foedera*, iv. 153, vii. 656.

[3] Accts. For. 18 m. 64ʳ, 'circa facturam et reparacionem aliarum diversarum domorum et garritarum eiusdem castri . . .'.

[4] Levot, *Histoire de . . . Brest*, i. 20.

bastide which John IV's besieging troops built in 1387 was incorporated in the English defences of Brest after it had been taken from the Bretons by Henry Percy—the famous Hotspur.[1] Its acquisition, even if the chroniclers' stories are only partially correct, must be considered a valuable asset.[2]

According to one account, this *bastide* had been equipped with guns; and this story is borne out by ducal payments to two cannoners at the 1386–7 siege.[3] Up to that time the cannons and bombards in use in Brittany had been of very small calibre.[4] In the 1380s and 1390s the Duke acquired more effective artillery, but he was in no way able to match the resources of the English.[5] They had sent relatively large quantities of gunpowder to Brest in 1378, together with a mortar and pestle 'de fer pour fere poudre pour les gones', touches, tampons, scales for weighing the amounts of powder, and pipes for feeding it into the guns.[6] As destructive agents rather than as instruments designed to inspire fear in the enemy, cannons had been first effectively demonstrated at the siege of Saint-Sauveur in 1374–5, when the French forced the English to surrender.[7] But the English were not far behind in the arms race. An inventory of the fittings at Brest, drawn up in 1381 when Norwych handed over to Dernford as receiver, shows that, besides the usual projectile weapons, there were 'ix canons dont les iiij de querere et les autres de fer'.[8] There is no evidence at Brest for monster cannons, which, like the great gun of Canterbury, for example,[9] were already symbols of municipal pride, or for prototypes of the great fifteenth-century guns.[10] But the number of small cannons there was equal to that used at castles such as

---

[1] *C.P.R. 1385–9*, 358; above, p. 106, n. 6.   [2] Cf. Borderie, iv. 105–7.

[3] Knighton, ii. 209; Borderie, *Rev. de Bretagne* (1889), 201.

[4] Borderie, iii. 427 n., 452; iv. 33, 111.

[5] Borderie, 'L'architecture militaire en Bretagne', *Association Bretonne* (1894), pp. 153–6. Pieres de Lussenbourge was making artillery for Clisson at Blain in 1392 (Bib. mun. Nantes, fonds Bizeul, MS. 1684). See also above, p. 35, n. 2.

[6] Accts. Var. 38/8, nos. 3, 16.

[7] *Mandements . . . de Charles V*, ed. Delisle, no. 1055; id., *Hist. . . . de Saint-Sauveur*, pt. ii, nos. 125, 147, 159, 160, 164, 197.

[8] Accts. Var. 38/8, no. 18.

[9] Knighton, ii. 199; cf. Hist. MSS. Comm., *Ninth Report*, i. *Appendix*, p. 140.

[10] Fino, *Forteresses de la France médiévale*, pp. 277 ff.

Porchester and Corfe[1] on England's south coast, or by the French princes, Berry and Burgundy, in their domains.[2] At Cherbourg in 1379 there were ten guns, seven casting 24-inch calibre stones and three casting 15-inch stones.[3] At Roxburgh on the Scottish border Percy, who was also captain of Brest, was using four cannons in 1384. When the siege of Brest began in 1386, amongst the first stores delivered from England were four cannons 'vocatos gunnes', 1,458 lb. of powder, and 500 round stones for the guns. These cannons were described as large, and one was double-barrelled ('dont un ove ij testes').[4] Their effectiveness is perhaps unproven, and they may not have been as large as the Cherbourg guns, but nevertheless this artillery train outclassed the ducal one. Brest carried armaments equivalent to those of the other English castles except the two greatest, Dover and Calais. Moreover, the appointment of Edward Dallingrigge as lieutenant there after the siege of 1386–7 shows English concern for the safety of the castle. Dallingrigge was one of the foremost experts on fortification of his time and, as his incorporation of artillery features in his castle at Bodiam shows, he was abreast of current developments in military architecture.[5]

Even before his appointment, earlier captains had spent quite extensively on repairs to the castle. Norwych was authorized on two occasions to spend £100. In 1382 £150 was allowed for further expenses he had incurred in this way; whilst his accounts show that in three and a quarter years his annual fabric bill averaged nearly £100.[6] This may be compared with £35 p.a. spent at Dover at this time,[7] with £200 spent at Southampton in 1377–8, or with £300+

---

[1] O'Neil, *Castles and Cannon*, p. 10; *History of the King's Works, The Middle Ages,* ed. H. M. Colvin *et al.*, ii. 594.

[2] *Inventaires mobiliers . . . des ducs de Bourgogne,* ed. Prost, i. 59; Vaughan, *Philip the Bold,* p. 124; le comte de Toulgoët-Treanna, 'Les comptes de l'hôtel du duc de Berry, 1370–1413', *Méms. de la Soc. des antiquaires du Centre,* xvii (1889–90), 115.

[3] Tout, 'Firearms in England', *E.H.R.* xxvi (1911), 686.

[4] Ibid. 688–702.

[5] O'Neil, op. cit., pp. 15–16; George Nathaniel Curzon, Marquis Curzon of Kedleston, K.G., *Bodiam Castle, Sussex* (London 1926), pp. 24–6; *C.P.R. 1381–5,* 518–19, 524–5, 588.

[6] Accts. For. 18 m. 64ʳ (£298. 12s. 9d. spent on repairs, 1378–81).

[7] *Hist. of the King's Works,* ed. Colvin, ii. 639.

p.a. spent at that important port and castle early in Henry IV's reign.[1] But this allowance was not sufficient to repair estimated damages of £1,000 caused by a storm in 1385, and the King's Council had to make special provision for the repair of four towers and a part of the wall which had collapsed.[2] Unfortunately for us the later indentures of Percy, Arundel, and Holland state that repairs are to be at the captain's own cost. It is also impossible to estimate how much had to be spent on restoring the castle after the siege. Apart, therefore, from a short period when expenditure on repairs ran at almost treble that on Dover castle, there is no way of estimating what the English spent on Brest. Most recorded payments are for moderate sums, a picture that tallies with indications of the size of the garrison and of the armaments.

Before 1362 captains at Brest and elsewhere in Brittany received nothing from the Exchequer; on the contrary, they paid an annual sum for the privilege of holding castles for Edward III and his ward.[3] Even freebooting captains who had captured castles on their own initiative were brought into a regularized organization responsible to the King.[4] But by 1370 English castellans in northern France were accountable to the Exchequer,[5] not the King's Chamber, and from 1377 Brest, too, became a national responsibility and its captains were paid from Westminster. Abberbury and Golafre received relatively prompt payment from the special treasurers for war, and their few outstanding debts were quickly liquidated after they relinquished office.[6] But their successors experienced much greater difficulties once a shortage of cash had driven Exchequer officials to the practice of assignment. The captains received regular

<hr/>

[1] Miss Hilary Turner kindly supplied these details from Accts. For. 12 m. E, 36 mm. G, H, 37 m. B.

[2] Warrants for Issues, file 14/91 (15 Apr. 1385).

[3] *Foedera*, iii. 429, 466. Edward III was pursuing Edward Twyford for sums still owed from his holding of Pymmer castle in 1363 (Memoranda Rolls (E. 159), 139, Brevia directa baronibus, Hilary 37 Ed. III, m. 22ʳ and ibid., Easter m. 1ʳ).

[4] Robert Knolles, for example; see above, p. 48.

[5] *Foedera*, iii. 917.

[6] Accts. Var. 37/27, no. 26 (2 Mar. 1378), order to Walworth and Philipot, treasurers for war, to pay Abberbury and Golafre 5,000 marks which was delivered in cash on 5 Apr. (Issue Roll 465 m. 21). The last payment to Abberbury for his service at Brest was made on 9 Dec. 1381 (Issue Roll 487 m. 12, £65. 16s. 8d.).

'payments' and allowances, but these were principally book-transactions. Money was assigned chiefly on uncollected wool subsidies and customs, and only a small percentage of their wages was paid in cash. Percy, in particular, suffered in this way, although he was gradually able to recover his due.[1] His successor Roches at first received more substantial monetary payments, but he was later forced to write off expenses incurred during the siege, because the Exchequer refused to honour its tallies to him.[2] It may be suspected that political as well as financial reasons prompted this treatment, since Roches was associated with Brest at the time of the 1386 Commission until his removal in favour of Arundel in 1388. Both the Commission and the Appellants were unpopular after 1388, and it was Roches's misfortune to have been captain with very low wages at a time of great expense at Brest. Arundel, in his turn, found difficulty in extracting money instead of tallies from the Exchequer.[3] But his successor Holland seems to have maintained the castle from its ransom district, and there are few English payments for Brest after 1389.[4] Between 1378 and 1389,

---

[1] For example, Issue Roll 511 m. 26, restoration of tallies, on 28 Mar. 1386, originally cut on 2 May 1383, 10 Feb., 2 May, 28 Oct. 1384, 16 Feb., 15 Apr. 1385. All these earlier tallies had been for £708. 6s. 8d., a total of £4,256. os. od. New tallies were cut for £923. 1s. od. On 8 Apr. 1388 Percy received new tallies for £930. 17s. 9d. (Issue Roll 519 m. 1) in restoration of tallies cut on 26 Feb. 1383, 26 Mar., 19 Oct., 12 Dec. 1386. The first two were worth £1,340. 6s. 8d. and had been cut for tallies dishonoured from the first list cited.

[2] Up to 15 June 1387 Roches received tallies worth £590. 13s. 4d. and cash payments totalling £1,662. 16s. 7d. (Issue Rolls 510–17 passim). After being relieved of the captaincy, Roches petitioned for the payment of £4,329. 19s. 9d. (Privy Seal files 5/5, 6/95), but in 1393 he accepted a final payment of £800 (Issue Roll 541 m. 20).

[3] Issue Roll 532 m. 24 (20 Mar. 1391), new assignment of tally originally cut on 15 June 1389 for £1,333. 6s. 8d. (ibid. 524 m. 7). On 23 Feb. 1391 Percy was paid £1,057. os. 8d. in cash for tallies of 15 Feb., 28 Mar. 1386, Apr. 1388 (six tallies as above, n. 1), which totalled £1,057. os. 8d. (Issue Roll 532 m. 21). The pattern of payments to the captains of Brest conforms to that described by A. B. Steel in The Receipt of the Exchequer, 1377–1485 (Cambridge 1954) with regard to the cash/assignment ratios, although it is possible to discern the preferential treatment of individual crown creditors described by Dr. G. L. Harriss, 'Preference at the Medieval Exchequer', B.I.H.R. xxx (1957), 17–40.

[4] Issue Roll 532 m. 13 (16 Jan. 1391), £266. 13s. 4d. assigned for repairs, and on 1 July bows were sent (C.C.R. 1389–92, 376). William Wykeham, Chancellor of England, was ordered to make out letters patent stating Holland's right to the ransoms on 27 June 1391 (Chancery Warrants, file 526, no. 7366).

however, the average cost of the maintenance of Brest had been about £3,500 p.a.[1] This compares with £15,000–16,000 necessary for the upkeep of Calais at this time.[2] When the costs of keeping Cherbourg and the Marches towards Scotland are taken into account, the Commons' criticisms of the barbican policy can be appreciated.[3]

Stores and supplies were delivered to Brest in time of crisis from England; in particular, cannons and the materials for their use were supplied directly from royal armouries.[4] The quality of some of the goods purveyed in England for Brest was not high. Other goods deteriorated in transshipment or in storage.[5] Already during the Civil War period the difficulties of supplying small, isolated garrisons (many of which were unofficial) from England were so great that the Government did not try to provide regular supplies for Montfortist Brittany as it did for Guyenne.[6] The garrisons were expected to live off the Breton countryside by organizing their own supplies. This exploitation of Brittany, which shocked nineteenth-century historians, has recently attracted new attention.[7] It can now be seen that it was not so arbitrary or haphazard as was once imagined. The ransom system in Brittany was rough and ready, but it followed a distinguishable pattern and showed an adaptability of approach to the problem of supply. Three phases of the 'ransoming of Brittany' by the English can be distinguished. The first lasted from the earliest military operations of the Civil War until the end of Edward III's wardship in 1362. The second stretched from 1362 to 1374, and the final period covered the official occupation of Brest by the English up to 1397.

---

[1] Appendix E. [2] *Hist. of the King's Works*, ed. Colvin, i. 425.
[3] Cf. Campbell, *Europe in the Late Middle Ages*, ed. Hale *et al.*, p. 211.
[4] Cf. O'Neil, *Castles and Cannon*, p. 5.
[5] Accts. Var. 38/8, no. 7 (1378), for stores 'que ob causam quod longum tempus fuerunt in mare per defectum venti ita calefacta et debilia devenerunt. . . . Et lxx carkoyses bovum de remanenti stauri Regis que omnes iactabantur ultra muros dicti castri in mare causa corruptionis et male odoris, perlonge iacendum in custodia infra dictum castrum . . .'.
[6] Cf. Postan, *Past and Present*, 27 (1964), 36; Hewitt, *The Organization of War under Edward III*, pp. 61–3.
[7] Fowler, *Les Cahiers vernonnais*, iv (1964), 61 ff.; id., *The Age of Plantagenet and Valois*, pp. 165–9; Keen, *Laws of War*, pp. 137–9.

Some characteristics of the pre-1362 period have been touched upon. Gournay at Brest was almost entirely free to organize and supply his castle. By 1361–2 there were twenty-five castellanies like Brest in English hands;[1] their captains were able to decide arbitrarily how they would treat the local populace as long as their actions did not disturb the Anglo-Montfortist administration based on Vannes. The treasurer of the duchy, whose resources in the 1340s had been minimal,[2] now controlled three of the largest castellanies.[3] But the rest were held by adventurers like Gournay, Huet, and Latimer's lieutenants. These men farmed their castles from Edward III and looked upon their positions as investments. In an earlier chapter examples have been cited of men who carved out seigneuries for themselves at this time.[4] The main problem facing the royal administrators in the duchy was how to bring the adventurers under control, since the royal Council, when considering similar problems arising from English intervention in Normandy in the 1350s, had already admitted that the freebooters had a right to the goods or lands which they captured.[5] A partial answer was the ransom system.

During the 1350s exactions on parishes surrounding individual castles were regularized. Bécherel castellany between 1359 and 1362 was in the hands of Giles de Wyngreworth, treasurer of Montfortist Brittany. Its ransom district comprised more than 160 parishes stretching from Saint-Brieuc eastwards to the Norman frontier, widening out southwards into a large rectangular block taking in Rennes and the communes of the eastern March.[6] From this district was exacted all manner of agricultural produce, raw materials for the maintenance of the castle, and labour services.[7]

---

[1] Cf. Map I above, p. 13.   [2] Above, p. 25, n. 2.
[3] Vannes, Bécherel, and Ploërmel, cf. Map II; Fowler, *Les Cahiers vernonnais*, iv (1964), 63.   [4] Above, pp. 48–50.
[5] D. Hay, 'Division of Spoils of War', *T.R.H.S.*, 5th ser., iv (1954), 104.
[6] Map II; E. Déprez, 'L'occupation anglaise au xive siècle en Bretagne', *Ouest France* (9 Jan. 1951), for identification of these parishes.
[7] Accts. Var. 174/5 (Wyngreworth's accounts, 1359–60) show the parishes of Fresnais, Hirel, and Mont-Dol paying in salt and Dingé in coal (all dép. Ille-et-Vilaine); Matignon (dép. Côtes-du-Nord) paid in saffron; Miniac-iuxta-Bécherel owed the services of 2 joiners and 4 labourers; Plougouac owed 2 carpenters and their mates; and Cepis-de-Lehon owed 5,000 nails.

Twice a year, at Easter and Michaelmas, each parish had to furnish a certain quota in specie or kind. These quotas were gathered by local collectors, who forwarded them to the receiver of the castle.[1] Wyngreworth's accounts show that in most cases the parishes were behind in their payments. Some were in rebellion, and their revenues could only be

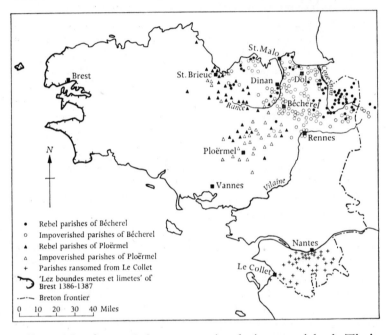

collected by force. Others were simply impoverished. Their crops and dwellings had been damaged or destroyed during the course of the war. In the short period for which accounts remain there are very comprehensive lists of arrears. At Ploërmel and Vannes, Wyngreworth collected similar ransoms, and the practice was copied elsewhere with, perhaps, less efficiency and legal form.[2] Walter Huet ransomed over thirty parishes south of the Loire from his castle at Le Collet.[3] The number of parishes reputed to be ransomed from Brest in 1384 was 160;[4] no figure survives for the pre-1362 period.

---

[1] Cf. Fowler, *The Age of Plantagenet and Valois*, p. 166.
[2] Appendix of Documents, no. 2, for other ransom districts.
[3] *Foedera*, iii. 642; Borderie, iii. 511 n.   [4] *Preuves*, ii. 454.

This system could easily lead to abuse. Over £10,000 was raised from the ransom districts of Bécherel, Vannes, and Ploërmel in 1359–60.[1] But some attempt was made to curb the worst excesses.[2] Some arrears were realistically written off. Friendly parishes received remittances. Compensation or further remittances were allowed to parishes on which troops had been billeted or where military operations had meant the requisitioning of victuals. Pension holders and a number of abbeys and convents received allowances from the ransom receipts pertaining to Vannes and Ploërmel. The administrators had some conception of responsibility to their Breton subjects; the termly sums demanded from individual parishes were always the same, and there is some slight indication that this standardization bore some relation to the ability of the parish to support its charge. Although the cases where a comparison is possible with revenues previously collected are too few to allow a meaningful generalization, there is evidence for some correspondence between the amounts demanded by the French and then by the English on the castellany of Fougères.[3]

The importance of ransoms in the pre-1362 period as a means of financing the Anglo-Breton administration can be gathered from Wyngreworth's accounts, which have been analysed elsewhere.[4] Over 75 per cent of the income at Vannes in 1359–60 was derived from the ransom district. Of the revenues for which Wyngreworth admitted responsibility in the same year, no less than 86 per cent came from ransoms, an average which fell by only 10 per cent in the next two years. The administration of Brittany in the last three years of Edward III's protectorate almost paid for itself.

The end of this administration, however, did not mark the end of ransoming or the withdrawal of the English captains. There were still two rivals for the ducal *cercle*, and the

---

[1] Fowler, *Les Cahiers vernonnais*, iv (1964), 84.

[2] Accts. Var. 175/1, nos. 48–50, 69–80, quittances and receipts subsidiary to Wyngreworth's accounts; Fowler, *The Age of Plantagenet and Valois*, p. 166, stresses only the brutality of the system.

[3] B.N. MS. fr. 26002, no. 805 (accounts of Fougères, 1357–8), where payments of a *cens* by the parishes of Bazouges, Rimoux, Antrain, and Marilly to the French corresponds roughly with the proportionate demands for ransoms by the English two years later as, for example, in Accts. Var. 174/6, 174/5, nos. 1, 2.

[4] Fowler, *Les Cahiers vernonnais*, iv (1964), 63–4.

division of ducal resources that continued until after the battle of Auray left John de Montfort no alternative but to use the expedients devised by the English. But ransoming in general ceased after Michaelmas 1365; and the payments made by John IV to the *routier* companies in 1368–9 were of a different nature from the ransoms levied for the upkeep of the English garrisons in the 1350s. The later payments were rather of protection money.[1]

It may be admitted that this distinction is a fine one, and the dividing line between the two types was blurred by the sums paid to Latimer's lieutenants at Bécherel and Plumoisan after 1365.[2] When Latimer faced charges brought against him by the Commons of England in the Good Parliament (1376),[3] the latter did not distinguish too carefully between official and unofficial payments to Latimer. He seems, for example, to have discharged quite honestly those payments of John IV's debts to Edward III that he was entrusted with conveying. But the revenues of Bécherel were another matter. In detailed charges against Latimer it was stated that in the years 1368–72 his lieutenants had raised 145,000 francs by ransoming at Bécherel and elsewhere. Evidence for this extortion was alleged to be contained in a letter from certain Breton seigneurs to the Commons—the Ragman Letter—which they were unfortunately unable to produce at the time of the trial. Surviving quittances show that some of the allegations were true, though the full extent of Latimer's enrichment at the expense of a cowed Breton populace may never be fully known.[4] In his defence, while admitting the existence of the Ragman Letter, Latimer cleared himself from its charges by declaring that the extortion, if committed, had been done by his lieutenants without his knowledge and authority. The Commons said that the ransoms were exacted in time of truce.

Yet if Bécherel was being maintained, as it obviously was, from the income of a ransom district, so was another garrison, that of Saint-Sauveur in the Cotentin. After 1370 its ransom district was regularized in the same way as the

---

[1] Above, pp. 51–2, also Appendix B.   [2] Appendix B.
[3] *Rot. Parl.* ii. 324–7.
[4] Appendix of Documents, no. 4 and Appendix B, section 4.

Breton ones of the 1350s, and it contained over 260 parishes.[1] The Commons' concern in 1376 was to destroy Latimer's influence with the ageing Edward III rather than to lighten the lot of those taxed by ransoming; they did not pursue Latimer's lieutenants. The ransom system had its virtues for English garrisons in northern France. In a period of endemic guerilla warfare the cost of maintaining these castles was transferred from England and laid on the shoulders of the native population.

Finally, Brest was the only castle in Brittany left to the English. The indentures by which the castle was held and the way in which the profits of the ransom district passed from the King to the captains have been described. Whether or not ransoms were exacted for Richard II or for his captains, they were still intended to cut the costs of maintaining the castle. The Commons in 1376 had in principle endorsed the view that victuals obtained in technically friendly areas should be paid for at normal market prices. But the official attitude encouraged ransoming. The parallel of Cherbourg is again particularly instructive.

In 1379 John Harleston agreed to do his best to ransom the lands of the King's enemies at Cherbourg and to use the money obtained for the King's profit.[2] But at Cherbourg and Brest the distinction between the King's enemies and his friends was finely drawn. In 1382 the burgesses of Cherbourg thought it necessary to get a charter confirming their rights *vis-à-vis* the garrison.[3] At Brest identical conditions existed. There were attempts to mollify the townspeople, but those of the *contado* were forced to contribute termly ransoms. Between 1378 and 1381 the receiver acknowledged receipt of £2,894. 9s. 10d., of which no less than £2,155. 19s. 8d. came from ransoms. The percentage of his income from ransoms—in this case 74½ per cent—compares with the percentages received at Vannes twenty years previously.[4] Some of the ways in which ransoms were exacted

[1] Accts. Var. 30/38, 31/19, accounts of James Treverbyn, receiver at Saint-Sauveur, 1371.

[2] Ibid. 68/8, no. 178, Harleston's indenture.

[3] Chancery Warrants, file 478, no. 2557 (23 Nov. 1382).

[4] Accts. For. 18 m. 64ʳ, Norwych's accounts, 1378–81; ibid. 16 m. 42ʳ, Percy and Calveley's accounts, 1379–81.

were traditional; Norwych was allowed expenses of
£7. 17s. 6d., which was half the cost of sending boats filled
with sailors and soldiers to compel certain rebel townships
to pay their ransoms.[1]

Ducal complaints were almost without number in the
1380s and 1390s. In 1387 a proposal was made that the
Duke should pay the English an annual fee for the upkeep
of Brest so that they would not need to take ransoms.[2] But
this arrangement was never operative. In the late 1380s and
1390s the jurisdictional control of the captain was very
extensive, geographically speaking, and the ransom district
was probably coextensive with this legal one.[3] John Holland
held Brest during the period of the Leulinghen truces on
terms which allowed him to raise revenue by ransoming. He
received little aid from the English Exchequer, and the
result of allowing him, or rather his subordinates, to obtain
their own supplies was an exacerbation of Anglo-Breton
relations. One petition from John IV has been tentatively
dated to 1394,[4] but the complaints were, *mutatis mutandis*,
traditional ones such as were first voiced by Bentley in the
1350s. The Brest garrison, like the unlicensed troops of the
1350s or the free companies of the 1360s, terrorized the
neighbourhood of the castle. They fished and hunted in
ducal lakes and woods. They had raided seigneurial estates
and assaulted Bretons. They had taken sums of money
'above agreements made earlier' and had extended the
ransoming of the land to the sea, where the rewards of their
piracy were notorious. Unfortunately, since Holland was not
responsible for rendering accounts for his captaincy, there
is no way of judging exactly the total of these extortions,
though in 1397 the payments made to obtain the return
of Brest by the Duke were themselves very considerable.[5]

---

[1] Accts. For. 16 m. 42ʳ.   [2] Treaty Roll 71 m. 6.

[3] Chancery Miscellanea, roll 6/4, no. 1 m. 1, case of *Roches* v. *Hawley* in the
Court of Chivalry stated '. . . qe meismes lez boundes, metes et limetes desuis en le
proschein article nomes par tout le temps de capitanerie de Johan de Roches furent
et unqor sount . . . en un lieu en le meer appelle Ussant devers le northwest iesqes a
la Rays de Fontenay devers le south et le dit Rays soy extendrount iesqes al Groye
devers le southest deinz le quelez boundes est Pountecroys autre foitz appelle
Odierne . . .'. See Map II, p. 165.

[4] *Lettres des rois*, ed. Champollion-Figeac, ii. 291.

[5] Above, pp. 138–9.

From 1389 one of England's barbicans was being maintained very cheaply.

In this chapter the English occupation of Brest, a single castle in fourteenth-century France, has been examined in detail. From a very early stage in the war of the Breton succession Edward III of England recognized the importance of Brest: first of all, perhaps, as a naval base to guard his own lines of supply to Guyenne; secondly, for the maintenance of his candidate's claims to the duchy of Brittany; and thirdly, as a bridge-head into Valois France. With the placing of John IV on the ducal throne of Brittany in 1364, Edward's concern for the government of the Finistère peninsula becomes less apparent, although he did remind John IV to place castles such as Brest in reliable hands in 1366.[1] The renewal of war with France in 1369 immediately caused the old King to concentrate his energies on ensuring that the peninsula was kept under Anglo-Breton supervision. From the 1370s Brest was incorporated into a tight defensive ring that the English tried to draw around the coasts of Valois France from Calais to Bayonne. For many years Brest was considered a vital English possession in the Anglo-French conflict.

Brest's importance is demonstrated by the efforts that the English made after 1372 to send men, money, and supplies to the castle, both when it was still in ducal custody and afterwards when John had leased it to them for the duration of the war with France. In the period of the Civil War in Brittany it had been impossible for the English, granted their other commitments, to maintain in quite the same way the numerous garrisons that were necessary for the struggle with Blois. Thus the ransom system had been devised as a practical method of supplying and financing the Anglo-Breton garrisons. From a relatively early stage, however, Edward III realized that alienation of the native population through blatant exploitation would serve neither his cause nor that of his protégés in Brittany. The code of conduct towards which his administrators in Brittany in the 1350s were feeling their way was amplified later in the century when Brest was held from a nominally friendly Duke. Concerned

[1] Above, p. 44.

to maintain their hold on Brest, Richard II's governments were also careful to select competent officers who would find approval with the Duke. Instructions to the captains and garrisons at Brest, and at Cherbourg, the other barbican fort that was held in a similar way, reveal more than perfunctory attempts to avoid antagonizing the native population. The English were well on the way to devising that system of discipline which was to serve them in their administration of Normandy in the fifteenth century.[1]

Difficulties did, of course, arise. Sound finance, as Walter Bentley had recognized in the 1350s, was the key to the problem. But the prosecution of an expensive foreign policy, the aim of Edward III and Richard II's advisers for so long, made it hard for the Exchequer to provide the ready cash that would keep garrisons from mutinying or exploiting their position. High ideals about provincial administration were sacrificed when the English Government was forced to turn its servants' acquisitiveness to its own advantage. The occupation of Brest posed a number of fundamental problems for English administrators, who were trying to balance the interest of the English taxpayer with those of the Duke of Brittany and his subjects. From a political point of view the English also had to balance the strategic value of Brest in the war with France against the deterioration of Anglo-Breton friendship resulting from the prolonged occupation. A study of this occupation thus illustrates the conflicting opinions held by fourteenth-century soldiers and administrators about the English conduct of the war, and emphasizes once more the delicate balance of the interests and policies of England, France and Brittany at that time.

[1] Fowler, *Les Cahiers vernonnais*, iv (1964), is sceptical of this thesis.

VII

THE LANDS OF THE DUKE OF BRITTANY IN ENGLAND

THE political negotiations which resulted in Edward III investing John IV, Duke of Brittany, with the earldom and honour of Richmond in 1372 and the subsequent attempts of the Duke to maintain his interests in England have been recounted in previous chapters. The honour of Richmond was 'one of the more prominent and enduring features of English feudal geography',[1] and the ducal family in Brittany had maintained an interest in the honour ever since William I made the original grants of land which constituted the honour shortly after the conquest of England in 1066. More immediately relevant, however, from a Montfortist point of view was the grant in 1342 to John of Gaunt, fourth son of Edward III, of the title 'Earl of Richmond'.[2] He later enjoyed the lands of the honour, and in 1361 John de Montfort, before succeeding to the ducal title in Brittany as John IV, renounced all his rights to the inheritance of Richmond.[3] However, in 1372 John IV was invested with Richmond, and John of Gaunt received the honour of Tickhill in compensation.[4] John IV's tenure was brief. In the event Richmond was confiscated by Richard II in 1381, because of John's agreement to the second treaty of Guérande between Brittany and France.[5] Although Joan Holland, Duchess of Brittany, was able to exercise some prerogatives as Countess of Richmond between 1381 and 1383, and although charters were made out for John's repossession of the honour in 1387, 1388, and 1391, it was not until April 1398 that some effect was given to these

---

[1] J. F. A. Mason, 'The "Honour of Richmond" in 1086', *E.H.R.* lxxviii (1963), 704.　　　　　　　　　　　　　　　[2] *Complete Peerage*, x. 821.
[3] Above, p. 17.
[4] *Foedera*, iii. 948; *C.P.R. 1370–4*, 183; *C.Ch.R. 1341–1417*, 224.
[5] *C.F.R. 1377–83*, 274.

regrants.[1] From 1384 until her death in 1394 Richard's queen, Anne, had maintained control over parts of the honour of Richmond. Even in 1398 the nature of John IV's tenure was confused by a simultaneous grant of the lands of the honour to his sister Joan, Lady Basset, and two co-grantees. This confusion, which probably allowed Henry IV to ignore the regrants to John IV in granting Richmond to Ralph, Earl of Westmorland, in October 1399, has still not been satisfactorily explained by experts in peerage law.[2] But what concerns us most in this chapter is to discover the reasons why John IV showed so much interest in trying to maintain or regain his tenure of Richmond. A description of Richmond and of the lands which were granted to John in exchange for the lease of Brest in 1377–8 will lead on to a discussion of their value to the Duke, his particular use of them, and their fate during the period of confiscation after 1381.

The materials for this discussion, like the lands of the honour, are scattered. A few fragmentary accounts from John's exile (1373–9), letters patent of successive grants of the honour, and a register and extent of Richmond are all that remain in ducal archives.[3] Most of the official documents concerned with the titles of the earldom have been conserved in Chancery rolls.[4] The more mundane documents, accounts from bailiffs and keepers of component parts of the honour, together with possible household accounts of previous owners, have largely perished. Some have disappeared with the ravages of time; others may have perished more violently in the conflagration which destroyed Gaunt's palace of the Savoy. He had kept the originals of muniments belonging to the earldom when it was given to John IV in 1372, possibly in expectation of its early return, and had given John IV copies. Many of the originals may have been burnt by the rebels of 1381.[5] For the rest, some accounts for various lordships in the honour survive from the time when

---

[1] Below, p. 190, for Joan Holland; *C.Ch.R. 1341–1417*, 307, 309, 312, 327, and below, pp. 194–5, for regrants.

[2] *Complete Peerage*, x. 824–5; Sir Geoffrey Ellis, *Earldoms in Fee* (London 1963), pp. 200–1; *Rot. Parl.* iii. 427. [3] A.L.A. E 114–18, 206.

[4] Conveniently collected in R. Gale, *Registrum Honoris de Richmond*.

[5] R. Somerville, *History of the Duchy of Lancaster*, i. 53, 63.

Richard II, Queen Anne, and various farmers held the honour, but these documents, too, are often isolated or fragmented.

In 1086 'Count Alan of Richmond . . . was one of the chief land owners in the whole of England', holding lands in eleven counties.[1] Only William FitzOsbern and Roger de Montgomery had held more land, and only the honour of the Count of Mortain appears to have been larger than the honour of Richmond.[2] The actual term 'honour' is first noted for Richmond in 1182, and although the value of the honour seems to have fallen as a result of the uncertain tenure of some of its holders in the twelfth century, the basic geographical units established in the eleventh century changed little.[3] The *caput* of the honour was Richmond castle in the North Riding of Yorkshire, where the lands covered most of the western half of the riding.[4] When the *Liber Feudorum* (1210) described changes in the honour since Domesday, some outlying lands in Cambridge, Norfolk, and Suffolk had contracted or changed their configuration, and some lands in Essex and Dorset had been lost entirely, but essentially the honour remained as it had been in William I's reign. Peter Mauclerc, Earl of Richmond, periodically from 1219 to 1237, gained lands in Hertfordshire, and Peter of Savoy, who held the lands of the earldom of Richmond but not the title from 1240, gained the Rape of Hastings (1262). Duke John I of Brittany was allowed to keep these gains when he regained the honour in 1268, although he then immediately handed it to his son, who succeeded him as Duke John II in 1285.[5]

By 1300 Richmond honour spread into seven counties. The Yorkshire lands centred on Richmond, Bowes, Middleham, and Gilling, the Lincolnshire lands on Boston, those of Norfolk on Swaffham Market, those of Cambridge on Bassingbourn and Babraham, those of Sussex on Hastings, and those of Hertfordshire on Cheshunt. These same lands

---

[1] F. M. Stenton, *Anglo-Saxon England*, 2nd edn., p. 621.

[2] Mason, *E.H.R.* lxxviii (1963), 703–4; P. Jeulin, 'Aperçus sur le comté de Richmond', *Annales de Bretagne*, xlii (1935), 269.

[3] C. T. Clay, 'The Honour of Richmond', *Early Yorkshire Charters*, iv (1935), 87.

[4] *V.C.H.*, *Yorkshire North Riding*, i. *passim*.

[5] *Complete Peerage*, x. 800 ff.; Jeulin, *Annales de Bretagne*, xlii (1935), 287.

comprised the honour in John IV's reign.[1] In addition, in exchange for Brest, John IV was to receive a castle or castles with a rentable value of 700 marks p.a. for the duration of the Brest lease. He received in 1378 the castle and manor of Castle Rising, Norfolk, together with the King's purparty of the toll-booth at Lynn, the manor of Sevenhampton and the hundred of Highworth, Wiltshire, and lands at Sowerby and Penrith, Cumberland.[2]

The frequent absences of the count-earls of Brittany–Richmond and of John de Bretagne, Earl of Richmond (1306–34) from their English estates meant that by the early fourteenth century the honour of Richmond was in an alarming state of decay.[3] In the troubles of Edward II's reign this parlous situation was emphasized by the siege and capture of Bowes castle by a band of robbers in 1321.[4] The Earl was in financial difficulties, and although Duke John III of Brittany was convinced of the value of the Richmond heritage when he claimed it from Edward III in 1334,[5] the evidence from the accounts of the farmers of the honour between the death of John de Bretagne and John III's succession in 1334 does not give grounds for such optimism.[6] Likewise the inquisition taken on the death of John III in 1341 gives a depressing picture, noting a fall in rents and proceeds from honorial dovecotes, vaccaries, mills, and fishponds.[7] John III had been unable to cross the Channel to do homage for the earldom and, although he had sent attorneys to represent his interests and had consulted with officials of the honour, little seems to have been done to remedy the decay of fabric either at Richmond or on surrounding manors.[8] Most services had been commuted, and little land was directly exploited by the Earl. After John III's

---

[1] Such stability of holdings was exceptional, cf. G. A. Holmes, *The Estates of the Higher Nobility in Fourteenth-Century England,* pp. 38–40.

[2] *Foedera,* iv. 34, 149; *C.P.R. 1377–81,* 284.

[3] I. Lubimenko, *Jean de Bretagne,* pp. 125–7, exaggerates common estate features such as mills to give a picture of a thriving agricultural unit.

[4] Ibid., p. 132. [5] Above, p. 4.

[6] Pipe Roll 179 mm. 18ʳ, 35ᵛ, accounts of J. Louthe and W. Squireton from 10 Mar. to 8 May 1334. They received £16. 10s.

[7] *C.I.P.M.* viii, no. 335 from Inq. post mortem, Ed. III, 65, no. 15; more fully edited in T. Whitaker, *History of Richmondshire,* i. 54–60.

[8] *C.P.R. 1344–8,* 245, 412; ibid. *1338–42,* 29, 30, 93, 110, 207, 423.

death the honour had been granted to Queen Philippa for the upkeep of her children. Once again the profits passing through her officials' hands reveal that the honour was producing a very poor return.[1] The administration of it was not made easier by outbreaks of violence and trespassing; whilst the number of orders obtained by John of Gaunt, after 1355, for repairs on both the northern and the southern estates of Richmond honour again reveals the mismanagement which had occurred when the dukes of Brittany had tried to run their English estates from a distance.[2]

During John IV's minority and in the first few years of his reign as duke, Richmond had been held by Gaunt. His administration of the honour, although difficult to follow, seems to have been reasonably enlightened.[3] John IV was invested with Richmond in 1372, and when he was exiled from Brittany in 1373 the honour assumed a much more important place in his fortunes than it had done for many of his predecessors, since he was largely dependent on income from these lands to eke out English royal charity. In the winter of 1372–3 his officers had been taking over from Gaunt's.[4] The 1372 grant allowed John IV to replace most officials, and all but a few pensions granted on honorial revenues by Gaunt were to lapse. But administrative continuity was ensured, for example, by the retention of Walter Urswick, constable of Richmond, and Roger Toup, steward of the Boston lordship, in their offices by John IV.[5] Few changes in the administration are apparent. Although John did not immediately receive full possession of all the prerogatives belonging to the honour—in 1377–8 there were complaints that he could not enjoy the franchise of return of writs—he was able to enjoy most of his rights.[6]

---

[1] B.M. Add. Ch. 40225 (25 June 1341, grant to Philippa); Accts. Var. 389/7 m. 2, accounts of J. Eston, Queen Philippa's receiver of Bassingbourn, Cheshunt, Swaffham, and Lincolnshire lands 'que fuerunt comitis Richemond . . .' from July to Sept. 1341. He received £100.

[2] *C.P.R. 1354–8*, 526, 545, 631; ibid. *1358–61*, 38, 59, 61, etc.

[3] Cf. Somerville, *Hist. of Duchy of Lancaster*, i. 52–3. Some Richmond officers held posts on Gaunt's other lordships (*Gaunt's Register 1372–6*, i, nos. 87–8).

[4] *Gaunt's Register 1372–6*, ii, no. 1174.

[5] Ibid. i, no. 13 (Gale, no. cxli); ibid. ii, nos. 1174, 1273, 1420; *C.P.R. 1381–5*, 492.

[6] Ibid. *1377–81*, 69–70; Gale, nos. cxlix, cli. The lucrative franchise of return of writs 'entailed doing everything necessary for the execution of the king's writ or

The machinery for co-ordinating the administration of the honour was small. The main link between the scattered manors and lordships during the Duke's exile was John himself as he travelled from manor to manor. The financial administration was in the hands of a receiver-general and local receivers. John used similar officials in Brittany after 1365; but even in the thirteenth century English estates had receivers-general, important household officials, to supervise the work of the local receivers.[1] With the Duke's presence in England in the 1370s the receiver-general's importance was increased by the extra-honorial moneys which he handled. There was a seneschal of Richmond, whose twelfth-century counterpart had been 'his lord's executive officer within the honour at large'.[2] But since that time the seneschal had declined in power and there is little reason to think that the seneschal of Richmond was exceptional. All the evidence tends to show that even quite senior officers at Richmond such as the seneschal or constable did not interfere with each other's duties or with the duties of officers on the other estates which made up the honour.

By 1300 there was a well-defined series of local courts in individual lordships of the honour. These were administered by local bailiffs and provosts chosen by the community under the supervision of seigneurial stewards. But this machinery had not functioned very efficiently during the Earl's absences.[3] In 1398 the register and extent of Richmond reveals that the administrative hierarchy of the honour consisted of the seneschal, the constable, and the receiver of Richmond, the bailiff of Richmond and five subordinates, the bailiff and receiver of the Lincolnshire estates, together with four more local officials, the chief bailiff of Swaffham and four subordinates, the same number at Bassingbourn and Babraham, and bailiffs at Cheshunt and Boston, and in Sussex.[4] There were eight foresters of Wensleydale, one

summons of the Exchequer. . . . It meant wide powers of distraint and the profits thereof', N. Denholm-Young, *Seignorial Administration in England*, pp. 88–9; *V.C.H., Yorks. N. Riding*, i. 12. [1] Denholm-Young, op. cit., pp. 13–15.

[2] Ibid., p. 69; John FitzNicol 'capitalis senescallis domini Ducis Britannie' quitted the provost of Cheshunt in 1378 (A.L.A. E 117, no. 23); in 1384 Robert Plessington was seneschal (Chancery Warrants, file 1342/13).

[3] Lubimenko, op. cit., pp. 131–2.

[4] A.L.A. E 116, summarized by Jeulin, *Annales de Bretagne*, xlii (1935), 296.

master miner of lead,[1] one warrener at each of Moulton, Washingborough, and Swaffham, a porter at Boston, and a parker at each of Cheshunt, Crowhurst, and Burwash. This gives a total of forty-nine domanial officials, of whom eighteen were connected directly with the administration of the lordship of Richmond.

The accounts of the King's receiver for the lordship of Richmond in 1383–4 add a few more details to the summary found in the 1398 extent.[2] The seneschal, the constable, the receiver, and the master of the New Forest all received yearly fees of £5. An auditor took a fee of 66s. 8d. p.a. and a clerk of the court 26s. 8d. A janitor and watchman were each paid 2d. a day, and another official 'de consiliis domini' was probably employed as a clerk to deal with the business of the court leet[3] or to draw up accounts, since the one known holder of this office was related to one of the receivers-general and probably served in what would now be an estate office.[4] Besides the master forester there were six other foresters; those of Arkengarthdale and Swyntonhowe receiving 20s. p.a., those of Gilling and Stainmore 13s. 4d. p.a., and those of Wycliffe and Hope 6s. 8d. p.a.[5] The number of local bailiffs and provosts (14) is larger than that in the extent; whilst some 1381 accounts add two farmers of tolls at Richmond and Bowes and a number of men responsible for the sale of wood, etc., in the different bailiwicks.[6] This gives a total of over thirty estate officials at Richmond.

In a similar way the accounts of John Bell, receiver for Richard II on the Lincolnshire lands of Richmond in 1383–4,[7] fill out the picture given in the 1398 extent, where ten officials are named. Bell received a fee of 10 marks p.a. and a livery allowance of 20s., as did a steward of the court of

---

[1] Cf. *V.C.H., Yorks. N. Riding*, i. 36, and Clay, *Early Yorkshire Charters*, iv (1935), 26, no. 24.

[2] Min. Accts. 1086, no. 2, accounts of John Darrell.

[3] First mentioned in 1341 and held until 1821 (*V.C.H., Yorks. N. Riding*, i. 12, 27).

[4] John Frithebank (Min. Accts. 1086/2 m. 2), who was acting for Gilbert Frithebank, receiver-general, as an attorney at the Exchequer in 1383 (Accts. For. 16 m. 50ʳ).   [5] Cf. *C.P.R. 1399–1402*, 546.

[6] Min. Accts. 1086/1, particulars of Gilbert Frithebank's accounts; cf. Lubimenko, op. cit., pp. 128–30.

[7] Accts. For. 18 m. 62ʳ.

the lordship, who also employed a clerk. A janitor of the court received 1*d.* a day. This small staff was responsible for collecting the fees and revenues from other local receivers. These included the bailiff of Boston and the guardian of the manor of Boston. In 1383–4 John Clerk, holder of this last office, was also collector of the seigneurial subsidy at Boston on exported wool.[1] Four provosts were in charge of the manors of Frampton, Wykes, Leadenham, and Washingborough and three bailiffs of the sokes of Kirton, Skirbeck, and Mumby-with-Gayton; a total of thirteen officials, one of whom was fulfilling his office by deputy.[2]

On the southern estates of the honour there were a steward, provost, and parker at Cheshunt during the Duke's exile.[3] The Rape of Hastings was run by a receiver and/or bailiff. The latter is once referred to as itinerant, a term which may be applied to most of these local officials.[4] On each of the Norfolk and Cambridge manors the register describes a staff of five, but only one or two of these officials appear in other surviving documents. Even less evidence survives for the organization of the manors handed to John in 1378 in exchange for Brest. The officers at Castle Rising included a constable, porter, and keeper of the chase as well as a receiver, but, apart from a custodian at Sevenhampton, nothing is known of John's officials on his Wiltshire and Cumberland manors.[5]

The functions of the receiver-general in co-ordinating the financial administration of the honour have already been touched upon. He was responsible for the muniments of the

[1] Cf. *C.P.R. 1354–8*, 545; Clerk was possibly the man pardoned for murder by service in Brittany under the Earl of March in 1375 (ibid. *1374–7*, 35), who helped to relieve Brest in 1377 (Accts. Var. 37/27, no. 32, delivery of victuals), and whose premature death was reported by Walsingham in 1379 (*Chronicon Angliae*, p. 232).

[2] Edmund Stokes; cf. *C.P.R. 1381–5*, 104, 308.

[3] A.L.A. E 117, 3 Mar. 1378, order from John IV to provost of Cheshunt.

[4] *C.P.R. 1381–5*, 532; Min. Accts. 1273/3, various documents from accounts of Walter Maunsell, receiver of the Rape, 1383–4; the 1398 register refers to errant bailiffs on several Richmond lordships (A.L.A. E 116, fol. 17ᵛ; cf. Denholm-Young, op. cit., pp. 32–5, 40).

[5] Accts. For. 12 m. 8ʳ, accounts of Robert Matthew, provost of Castle Rising, 1376; Min. Accts. 1268/2, nos. 1–11, various particulars of accounts of John Talman, receiver of Rising, 1377–8; Accts. For. 12 m. 8ʳ, Talman's accounts, 1377–8; A.L.A. E 117, no. 4, R. Russel, custodian of Sevenhampton in 'anno xxiiiiᵗᵒ' (?Edward III).

honour.[1] The actual mechanism of making a payment from Richmond revenues was similar to that used by John in Brittany—by warrants from the Duke, his receiver-general, or his personal treasurer to the local receivers—but this was common estate practice in England and France.[2]

The receipts and quittances from local receivers, provosts, and bailiffs show that there appear to be no outstanding features of accounting practice used at Richmond. English royal practice or that of other large noble households was followed. At the presentation of accounts the official brought with him quittances as justification for payments made. He may have paid locally the fees and pensions that had been assigned on his bailiwick revenues.

By the beginning of the fourteenth century many big estates followed Exchequer practice in having a system of 'view and audit', the main difference from royal practice being that, whereas county sheriffs went up to Westminster for the view at Easter and for the final audit at Michaelmas, in the seigneurial administrations the household officials (corresponding to the barons of the Exchequer) did not wait for the arrival of local officers but visited the individual manors.[3] The fragmentary Richmond accounts do not permit many glimpses of the way its accounting practices worked; but it is plain that, unlike the castellany accounts in Brittany, local bailiffs accounted, if not at regular intervals, at least for a regular financial year, which ran from Michaelmas to Michaelmas.[4] The receiver-general was able to draw up a balance sheet for the whole honour,[5] and counter-rolls,

---

[1] Cf. *Gaunt's Register 1372–6*, i, no. 241, ii, no. 972.

[2] A.L.A. E 117, no. 24, John IV to John Wodeward, receiver-general, 23 May 1378; ibid., no. 5, 1 Dec. 1377, John to John Cropwode, bailiff of Rape of Hastings; ibid., no. 21, 5 Feb. 1378, John to provost of Cheshunt; ibid., no. 27, 2 Nov. 1377, John FitzNicol, seneschal of Richmond, to provost of Cheshunt; ibid., accounts of William Windsor, personal treasurer of Duke, from 22 Sept. 1377 to 29 Sept. 1378.

[3] Denholm-Young, op. cit., pp. 131 ff.

[4] A.L.A. E 118, accounts of T. de Tynteshale, a bailiff of Richmond lordship, from 27 June 1372 (date of last account) until 29 Sept. 1374; accounts of Adam Blakemore's deputy for Norfolk manors of Richmond honour, 29 Sept. 1376 to 29 Sept. 1377; ibid. E 117, fragment of W. Windsor's accounts, starting 29 Sept. 1378.

[5] Ibid. E 118, accounts of J. Wodeward, receiver-general, from 6 Sept. 1377 to 6 Mar. 1378, including various extra-honorial moneys besides landed income, show that he received £2,114. 2s. 11d. and had expenses of £2,090. 16s. 5d.

which have been seen as springing from a need to corro-
borate the final audits, were kept for certain officials.[1] The
receiver-general also paid to the Duke's household treasurer
the revenues necessary for the upkeep of the household.[2]

This description of the history, structure, and administration of the honour of Richmond and the lands acquired
by John IV in 1378 can now serve as a basis for an assessment of the value of the Duke's lands in England. This
evaluation can be made in monetary terms, in terms of
utility in establishing and maintaining a nucleus of supporters of the ducal cause, and in terms of the more theoretical realm of prestige and honour so eagerly sought by
fourteenth-century noblemen.

Much of the evidence for the monetary value of Richmond to John IV comes from after its confiscation in 1381.
Its traditional value in rents was 2,000 marks p.a. In 1269
the executors of the future John II of Brittany had permission to receive that amount for the repayment of John's debts
if he were to die on crusade.[3] In 1341 Queen Philippa
expected the same sum from the honour, and in 1366 John
of Gaunt had permission to mortgage the honour again for
2,000 marks.[4] More detailed inquiries in 1381 ascertained
that the annual rental value was £1,796. 4s. 10¼d.; whilst
the 1398 extent estimated the rental had by then fallen to
£1,418. 8s. 4d.[5]

A piecemeal estimation of how much revenue was derived
from various estates of the honour can be established. The
different parts of the honour had traditionally been administered separately, as much for administrative convenience
as for any other reason;[6] and when Richmond was divided
after 1381 individual lordships were accounted for at the

---

[1] Denholm-Young, op. cit., p. 132; A.L.A. E 117, 206, parts of a counter-roll
kept by J. Curteys of Windsor's accounts as treasurer.

[2] A.L.A. E 117, no. 20, indenture between Windsor and Wodeward, who had
delivered £329. 1s. 3d. to Windsor for household between 13 Oct. 1377 and 29
Sept. 1378.

[3] C.P.R. 1266–72, 314, 395.

[4] B.M. Add. Ch. 40225 (25 June 1341, grant to Philippa); Delpit, *Collection . . .
des documents français*, p. 124 (1366).

[5] C.F.R. 1377–83, 274; *Preuves*, ii. 432; Jeulin, *Annales de Bretagne*, xlii (1935),
296.

[6] Cf. Denholm-Young, op. cit., pp. 41–2.

Exchequer. In 1383–4 receipts from the honorial lands in the lordship of Richmond amounted to £533. 6s. 6d.[1] The receiver in the lordship of Boston (the honorial lands in Lincolnshire) accounted for an income of £519. 16s. 10¼d. in the same financial year, and for £452. 5s. profits in the following year. Taking his expenses into account, this represents roughly the same income as in 1383–4.[2] Cheshunt manor was farmed by Henry Percy, Earl of Northumberland, and John FitzNicol for £58. 7s. 6¼d. in 1384. In 1385 the farm was down to £49. 5s., although the 1398 extent valued it at £77. 10s. 11¼d.[3] John's lands in Cambridgeshire at Babraham were let at farm in 1383–4 for £36. They were valued at £45. 5s. 6d. in 1398.[4] Those of the manor of Swaffham Market, Norfolk, were farmed by Richard Fotheringhay in 1385 for £100; the same value appears in the 1398 extent.[5] Likewise at Frampton in Lincolnshire the manor was committed to the keeping of Sir John Devereux in 1384 for £110 p.a., while in the previous year the King's receiver accounted for £105. 7s. 0½d. profits on the manor. By 1398 the manor was valued at £82. 4s. 7½d.[6] When the various pensions assigned on individual manors are taken into account, the value of this piecemeal calculation postulates an annual honorial income of £1,455 + .[7] In particular this division shows the preponderating importance of the Richmond and Boston lordships in providing two-thirds of the profits of the honour.

On the other hand, the surviving itineraries of the ducal household in England, mainly from 1377 to 1379, reveal

[1] Min. Accts. 1086, no. 2, Darrell's accounts.

[2] Accts. For. 18 m. 62ʳ, Bell's accounts, and figures derived from Receipt Roll 559.

[3] C.F.R. 1383–91, 25, 60; Receipt Roll 563 (11 Dec. 1385); A.L.A. E 116, fol. 9ʳ.

[4] C.F.R. 1383–91, 50; Receipt Roll 559 (17 Nov. 1384); A.L.A. E 116, fol. 12ᵛ. Between 29 Sept. 1397 and 23 Apr. 1398 John Hobeldod rendered £26. 13s. 11¼d. of £47. 0s. 4d. expected annual profit from Babraham (Misc. Accts. (E. 358), 17 m. 11ᵛ).

[5] C.F.R. 1383–91, 67; A.L.A. E 116, fol. 13.

[6] C.F.R. 1383–91, 64; Accts. For. 18 m. 62ʳ; A.L.A. E 116, fol. 14.

[7] The Rape of Hastings supported two pensions, one of 100 marks p.a. and another of £40 p.a. (Min. Accts. 1272/3, nos. 1–3, accounts of receiver); Min. Accts. 1280/10, nos. 1–4, quittances to Morwell and Windsor for various pensions, 1383–4, on Norfolk and Cambridgeshire manors of Richmond.

that John IV spent most of his time on his more southerly manors, and there is no evidence at all that he visited the actual *caput* of his honour.[1] This preference for the Sussex, Hertford, Norfolk, and Cambridgeshire manors was increased by the acquisition of Castle Rising in 1378. The rentable value of this latter property was £123+, and the toll-booth at Lynn was demised for 40 marks p.a.[2] The hunting at Castle Rising was good, and the close proximity to John's other manors, such as Swaffham Market, Bassingbourn, and Cheshunt, and to London made this his favourite residence in England.[3]

The income of the other lands acquired in 1378 is more difficult to estimate. In the thirteenth century the manor of Sevenhampton had yielded a handsome profit of £100–£150, principally from grain sales, and in Queen Philippa's hands in 1349–50 it had still yielded £92.[4] Under Richard II the manor could carry a 40-marks pension assigned on its revenues.[5] The value of Penrith and Sowerby in 1396 was £62 + when the lands were granted to Ralph, Lord Neville, but there is little other evidence of their value.[6] If, therefore, normal circumstances had ever obtained while John was holding the honour of Richmond and the lands exchanged for Brest, he would have received an annual income somewhere in the region of £2,000.

Circumstances were seldom normal, however. Furthermore there were a large number of expenses to be met. In the first instance there were administrative costs, wages for office holders, bills for the repair and maintenance of buildings and for the equipment of all the manor houses and castles which were included in the honour and the 1378 acquisitions. Small though some of these items appear (for example, wages of 2*d*. or even 1*d*. a day), they all ate into

---

[1] A.L.A. E 117, 206.

[2] *C.Inq.M. 1377–88*, 49.

[3] Accts. Var. 398/5, 11 Aug. 1376, orders to hunt surplus game on manor. The Duke and Duchess visited Castle Rising in Feb. 1378 before the lease of Brest was officially confirmed. It was handed to them on 14 Sept., and they were in residence by 18 Sept. 1378 (*C.P.R. 1377–81*, 284; A.L.A. E 206).

[4] Denholm-Young, op. cit., p. 79; Exch. T.R. Misc. Book 205, p. 5, summary of receipts from W. Tibote, provost, 1349–50.

[5] *C.P.R. 1389–92*, 106; *V.C.H., Wiltshire*, v. 57–9, 66, for Highworth hundred.

[6] *C.P.R. 1396–9*, 39.

the estate profits. Then during the exile there were the costs of the ducal household. In just a week over one year (1377–8) the Duke's personal treasurer received £826. 19s. 7d. from the receiver-general for household expenses.[1] John IV was not extravagant in his mode of living, and this sum was incurred during a period of straitened personal circumstances during his exile, when his household appears to have contained a very limited number of servants.[2] The Duke almost invariably had guests to dinner or to accompany him on the chase,[3] but the majority of them were men who had served him in the past and on whom he would (or at least thought he would) depend for his return to Brittany. This group of men was also further tied to him by another financially costly link: they were in receipt of pensions and annuities assigned on the Richmond lands or on the manors received in 1378.

The utility of the Duke's English lands for providing him with the wherewithal to create a coterie of followers, to reward loyal servants, to entertain or bribe influential English government advisers, and to stimulate interest in and sympathy for his cause may be quickly established.

Amongst those receiving annuities was John, Lord Neville, into whose debt John IV had fallen as a result of Neville's services in Brittany from 1372. In 1383–4 Neville was taking 100 marks p.a. on the lordship of Richmond.[4] Thomas Percy received a life pension of £100;[5] whilst John Devereux received one of 100 marks p.a., first assigned on the Rape of Hastings and then, after 1381, on the manor of Frampton in Lincolnshire.[6] All three were prominent soldiers and influential figures in the households of Edward III and Richard II, as was Edward Dallingrigge, first in receipt of a

---

[1] A.L.A. E 117, William Windsor's accounts, 22 Sept. 1377 to 29 Sept. 1378.

[2] Above, pp. 40–2, for John's household in Brittany.

[3] For example, A.L.A. E 117, various dinner accounts, 29 Sept.–17 Oct. 1378, when Knolles, Blakemore, Percy, John Clanvowe, Morwell, FitzNicol, and Wodeward were present, or ibid., 'le lundy iiie jour daoust [1377] audit Chesthonte pour Mons. et Madame et leur tinel . . . et furent mondit seigneur et madame a la chasse de Bueselt et plushours gentilz du pais Emond Fauton, sa femme et autres venours et chassours o eux . . .'.

[4] C.F.R. 1377–83, 274; Min. Accts. 1086/2 m. 2.

[5] A.L.A. E 116, fol. 20ʳ, with no indication of date.

[6] C.F.R. 1377–83, 274; C.P.R. 1381–5, 51, 53.

pension in 1374.[1] From within his own household John granted pensions to his most important English servants. John FitzNicol, Admiral of Brittany in 1370, became seneschal of Richmond and later receiver-general of the Duke's English lands. He received an annuity of 80 marks on the manor of Cheshunt.[2] Richard Fotheringhay, probably in John's employ since 1368 and prominent in his household from 1377, took a pension of £50 p.a. on the manor of Swaffham Market from 1378 and one of 40 marks p.a. from Sevenhampton in the 1380s.[3] John Austin, another soldier connected with Brest, received an annuity on Castle Rising, and Thomas Morwell, who is first found in Brittany in 1364, was receiving portions of his 100-marks pension as late as 1395.[4] John Wodeward and Geoffrey Horne were other household servants who received pensions.[5] They were trusted friends and advisers of John IV. Many of them were violent men who had made their fortunes by serving the Duke with their swords.[6] But they were also capable in other fields. Edward III and Richard II as well as the Duke employed them as diplomatists and administrators. Some were to accompany John back to Brittany in 1379.[7] Others remained in England administering ducal lands and acting as his representatives with the English Government.[8] In 1389, for example, Dallingrigge and Fotheringhay were pressing the royal council for the definite return of Richmond to the Duke. They formed part of a 'Breton lobby', which

---

[1] *C.P.R. 1381–5*, 55; Min. Accts. 1272/3, no. 2, 11 Apr. 1384, Dallingrigge drawing £20 of his annuity of £40 p.a. on Rape of Hastings.

[2] *C.C.R. 1381–5*, 46–7.

[3] Ibid. 319; Min. Accts. 1280/10, no. 4, 10 Oct. 1383, quittance for payment of pension on Swaffham Market; *C.P.R. 1389–92*, 106.

[4] Ibid. *1381–5*, 402 (Austin); ibid. *1392–6*, 329 (Morwell), also Min. Accts. 1272/3, nos. 1, 3, 17 Oct. 1383, 1 June 1384, quittances for receipt of pension on Rape of Hastings.

[5] *C.P.R. 1381–5*, 407 (Wodeward); Min. Accts. 1280/10, no. 1, 10 Oct. 1383, quittance from Horne for pension on Bassingbourn.

[6] Cf. Wodeward, pardoned for rape and murder in 1374 on condition that he served John IV 'en cest prochain viage de guerre' (Chancery Warrants, file 438, no. 30292).　　　　　　　　　　　　　　[7] *C.Inq.M. 1392–9*, 10 (Austin).

[8] Morwell acted as master of Duchess Joan's household, 1379–81 (Issue Rolls 472–87, *passim*). FitzNicol remained in England (A.L.A. E 117, no. 6, 1 Mar. 1384, order from John IV to FitzNicol to pay various arrears in England). Fotheringhay was connected with the administration of Brest (above, p. 151) and while acting as messenger for John IV in 1385 was attacked in Devon (*C.Inq.M. 1377–88*, 167).

was consulted whenever the English Government was dealing with Anglo-Breton problems.[1]

Apart from the annuitants, there were two other groups which had attached themselves to the ducal entourage during the exile. It is possible that some of the former soldiers and administrators of pre-1362 Anglo-Montfortist Brittany were annuitants rewarded by John IV from his English estates and that documentary evidence for this has disappeared.[2] Nevertheless, men like Thomas Prior, Ralph Barry, and William, Lord Latimer, received some hospitality from the exiled Duke. Prior was serving in Brittany as early as 1347.[3] Together with Latimer, Barry, and Robert Knolles, Prior can be considered as one of a group of experienced older men whom John consulted during his exile.[4] There were other men in and around the household who had served the Duke or his mother or his Duchess for several years but for whom no settled pension is recorded. The most important was Adam Blakemore, the ducal marshal, who returned to Brittany in 1379. In 1372–4 he was a bailiff on the Richmond lordship and in 1376 'custos feudorum' for John's Norfolk lands.[5] Thomas Bradwell had been in the ducal household in 1361.[6] John Cornwall, William Neville, John Clanvowe, and William Tindale were all soldiers who had been linked with the Duke by service in the duchy.[7]

The other influential group who accompanied the Duke or were recruited by him in his exile, were the clerical staff in his household, as opposed to the clerical and administrative

---

[1] Above, pp. 119–20. FitzNicol was present at Salisbury in 1384 (*Preuves*, ii. 450 ff.). In 1391 a messenger was sent to Devereux to inform him of various matters being discussed by the King's Council in regard to Brittany (Issue Roll 536 m. 11).

[2] Cf. Holmes, *The Estates of the Higher Nobility*, pp. 60–2.

[3] Accts. Var. 25/18, 175/5; *Preuves*, i. 1598; A.L.A. E 117 (15 Sept. 1377), for Prior.

[4] Prior, Barry, and Cornwall dined with John IV on 15 Sept. 1377. Latimer dined with him on 6 Sept., and Austin, Knolles, Percy, and Cornwall were with the Duke in Oct. 1378 (A.L.A. E 117). Barry was captain of Hennebont in 1359–60 (Accts. Var. 174/5).

[5] *Foedera*, iii. 981; A.L.A. E 118, acting in Richmond and Norfolk; ibid. E 206, Blakemore's counter-roll for Duke's journey through Brittany, Aug.–Nov. 1379.

[6] Issue Roll 407 m. 26. He served John in 1373 (Treaty Roll 56 m. 11, protection) and may have been a brother-in-arms of Morwell (Gascon Roll 83 m. 2, 1369).

[7] *Foedera*, iii. 1062 (Cornwall); Treaty Roll 55 m. 32 (Neville, and above, p. 74); *C.P.R. 1381–5*, 113 (Tindale).

staff who looked after the ducal lands. Amongst the most important of the clerks was William Windsor, found serving John in 1373. He later became personal treasurer to the Duke and, after 1381, co-farmer of Richmond with Thomas Morwell.[1] Richard Clerk, who was amongst the Duke's household staff in exile, later became an important official in Brittany.[2] William Wells, the ducal confessor, and Guillaume le Briz were active during the exile.[3] Thomas Melbourne, the man who was perhaps chiefly responsible for the financial reorganization of Brittany after 1365, was frequently with the Duke in his exile, acting as his personal treasurer, and was quite prepared to return to Brittany in 1379.[4] Perhaps the most surprising thing about this group is that they do not seem to have received any ecclesiastical preferments for their services to the Duke. John possessed two advowsons in the archdeaconry of Richmond,[5] two belonged to the manor of Castle Rising, and several of his other manors possessed advowsons. It may be that no suitable preferments fell vacant when John was in England. It seems probable that, when occasions to exercise privileges of presentation occurred, they were used, although there is no exploitation of these seigneurial ecclesiastical rights comparable to John's liberality with regard to annuities.

Before John became Earl of Richmond, Englishmen in his service were rewarded by lands and annuities in Brittany. In many cases this was almost inevitably a recognition of positions they already held when he came to power. A second generation of ducal servants continuing in his employment after 1364 received smaller grants, *fief-rentes*, and other favours.[6] It is interesting and important to note that when John's fortunes were reversed and he fled the duchy

---

[1] Issue Roll 462 m. 15; A.L.A. E 117, *passim*; C.F.R. 1377–83, 274; John le Neve, *Fasti* . . ., N.S., vii, *Chichester*, p. 17.

[2] A.L.A. E 118; *Preuves*, ii. 446–8.

[3] John le Neve, loc. cit., and above, p. 40, n. 4 (Wells); A.L.A. E 117, 5 Feb. 1378 (le Briz).

[4] B.M. Add. Ch. 7909 (1374), Melbourne acting as witness for Duke to an obligation to the Bishop of London; Treaty Roll 59 m. 25 (23 Feb. 1376), protection as clerk going to Brittany; C.P.P. 1342–1419, 531, for readiness to return; A.L.A. E 117, *passim*, with Duke in exile.

[5] A. H. Thompson, 'The Registers of the Archdeaconry of Richmond 1361–1442', *Yorks. Arch. Journal*, xxv (1919), 145.　　　　[6] Above, pp. 50–1.

in 1372, there was little attempt to compensate Breton servants from Richmond revenues. A study of the lists of annuitants and of those who, although of the same class as the annuitants, appear to have received no settled pension but to have enjoyed other forms of ducal largess, of the clerical staff of the household, and of the local officers who administered Richmond and the 1378 acquisitions shows that the number of Bretons benefiting from John's tenure of Richmond was negligible. There is nothing to suggest that in the fourteenth century there were administrative practices common to the Breton and Richmond estates, as there had been in the twelfth century. Witness lists in Richmond charters issued in the duchy during the twelfth century show English tenants of Richmond moving abroad with the Count-Earl.[1] Other tenants held lands in both England and Brittany, whilst the constable of Richmond might act with the Count in Brittany and a chancellor of the honour seems to have held his post by right of his office in Brittany. Guillaume le Briz, one of John IV's chaplains, was a Breton, but the only other Bretons to receive sustenance in England were a small group of soldiers and Joan Bazvalen. She was the only Breton annuitant on the honour of Richmond when John settled £50 p.a. on her and her husband Richard Fotheringhay on the occasion of their marriage in 1378.[2]

The main reason for the absence of Bretons as pensioners or administrators in England is probably political. Between July 1372, when John received the earldom, and May 1373, when he arrived in England to begin his exile, John had been in no position to make suitable arrangements for the administration of his honour in his absence. From May 1373

---

[1] Clay, *Early Yorkshire Charters*, iv, pp. ix–x, 105–7.

[2] A.L.A. E 117, no. 24, 23 May 1378, John IV to Wodeward to pay Laurence Coupegorge, Youn Trief, John Dorrey, and other Breton soldiers from Cheshunt receipts; ibid. E 116, fol. 20ʳ, 6 Aug. 1378, grant to Joan and Richard Fotheringhay. Joan's father Jean was a very important ducal councillor, cf. *Foedera*, iii. 508, *Preuves*, i. 1537–8, ii. 231–2, 379, 380, etc. The abbey of Bégard, founded by Count Stephen of Brittany in 1130 (*Preuves*, i. 562), and in possession of rights on Richmond from 1172 (Clay, *Early Yorkshire Charters*, iv (1935), 108, 113–15), tried to obtain payments in 1350 (*C.Inq.M. 1348–77*, 22). In 1383–4 and 1393–5 it was alleged that the annuity of £20 had been paid to the monks (Accts. For. 18 m. 62ʳ; Receipt Rolls 593 (15 Oct. 1393), 600 (29 Nov. 1395)).

to July 1379, apart from various military expeditions, John could study the problems of his honour at first hand. Since he was largely dependent on English aid, either from the King or from his English advisers, it was only natural that he should reward his supporters from his English revenues. Few Bretons deserved his gratitude, and he was not in a position to foresee the Breton volte-face of 1379. Once back in his duchy in 1379, he had to leave the administration of Richmond to his Duchess and his officials; whilst the confiscation of the honour in 1381 and the breakdown of the Anglo-Breton *entente* removed Richmond as a source of immediate patronage from his grasp. Until the English recognized John's claim to the honour unreservedly, there was little point in trying to reward Breton servants with annuities they could not enjoy. That the Duke spent so much energy and time pressing for the recognition of his rights is an indication not only of the honorific value of the earldom but also of its practical and financial utility to John IV.

The confiscation of 1381 was thus a severe blow to the Duke; whilst the part played by some of the Richmond annuitants in procuring the confiscation appears particularly gratuitous. On 5 November John Devereux had his 100-marks annuity on the Rape of Hastings confirmed by Richard II. A week later, on 12 November, the annuity was reassigned on the manor of Frampton, Lincolnshire, since Devereux had suggested to the King that the Duke's lands in England ought to be in his hand because of John's adherence to the French, and because the King had granted the Sussex manors to the Duchess for her sustenance in England.[1] By 16 November the whole honour was put to farm because of the Duke's current debts at the Exchequer and 'for other causes', the chief of which was John's homage to Charles VI on 27 September at Compiègne. By the main-prize of Devereux and Lord Neville the honour was committed to the care of Thomas Morwell and William Windsor.[2] It was normal procedure when a large estate was not passing to the direct heir to entrust it to servants of its

---

[1] *C.P.R. 1381–5*, 51, 53.
[2] *C.F.R. 1377–83*, 274.

former owner.[1] Morwell and Windsor farmed the honour until September 1383. During this period the Duchess was to receive £1,000 p.a. The farmers were to pay £280 p.a. in other fees and to account for £516. 4s. 10¼d. at the Exchequer.[2] At the same time John's receiver-general in England was still held responsible by the Exchequer for various Richmond revenues and for those from the 1378 acquisitions. In 1383 the receiver-general collected outstanding debts amounting to £349 in eighteen bailiwicks in Yorkshire and Cumberland, which he accounted for at the Exchequer.[3] John IV equally held the receiver-general responsible for his revenues. In 1384 he ordered him to make various payments, and some years after 1391 he was still trying to get satisfaction from the executors of John Fitz-Nicol, a former receiver-general, who had died in that year.[4]

During the interim period of 1381–3 the Duchess, although not receiving full payment of her allowance, was able to make one or two appointments, which the King confirmed.[5] As in 1372, when John IV took over from Gaunt, there appears to have been no wholesale expulsion of Richmond officials. Replacements by royal command were usually made only on the death of the previous officer. In this period also, Neville, a leading landholder in Yorkshire and an important royal creditor who already had a personal interest in Richmond affairs, seems to have been entrusted with some of the Yorkshire lands of Richmond. He is found making small grants of land from the honour and receiving quite substantial sums from the farmers for money owed him at the Exchequer. At one stage he is referred to as 'governor of the county of Richmond'. His hold on the lordship may have been a royal guarantee for the repayment of some of his loans.[6]

---

[1] Cf. Denholm-Young, *Seignorial Administration*, pp. 162–3, and Holmes, *The Estates of the Higher Nobility*, pp. 58, 75–8.　　　　[2] *C.F.R. 1377–83*, 274.

[3] *C.P.R. 1381–5*, 66; Min. Accts. 1086/1, G. Frithebank's accounts.

[4] Above, p. 185, n. 8; Nicolas, i. 49; Principal Probate Registry, Prerogative Court of Canterbury, Register of Wills, 7 Rous, fol. 53ᵛ, FitzNicol's will, 1391.

[5] *C.P.R. 1381–5*, 306; Chancery Warrants, file 482, no. 2907, 24 Aug. 1383.

[6] Min. Accts. 1086/2 m. 2, Darrell's accounts; Receipt Rolls 544 (25 Mar. 1382), 553 (10, 28 Nov. 1383), 559 (9 Dec. 1384); *C.P.R. 1381–5*, 492; Inq. ad quod damnum, file 400/29, nos. 1, 2; A. Steel, 'English Government Finance 1377–1413', *E.H.R.* li (1936), 588.

As for John's other lands at this time, in 1382 Richard II ordered the royal receivers of the lands exchanged for Brest to be intendant for their accounts since September 1378, but no accounts appear to have been presented.[1] In December 1384 the King confirmed a grant of £20 p.a. on the manor of Castle Rising, which the Duke had issued in the previous July for services to the Duchess.[2] There is also some slight evidence that the living at Rising was presented by John or his deputy in 1385; whilst none of his officers appears to have been dispossessed deliberately after 1381.[3]

After Michaelmas 1383 both the northern lordships of Richmond and Boston were accounted for directly at the Exchequer by a receiver appointed by the King.[4] The Duchess of Brittany, it will be remembered, had returned home in August. An auditor was also appointed for Richmond lands in the King's hand, and the southern manors were let at farm, frequently to those who already had an interest in collecting their annuities from individual manors.[5] Next, Parliament declared the honour forfeit in November 1384.[6] Soon afterwards, with the death of the Duchess of Brittany, her brother John Holland, in concert with Fitz-Nicol and Thomas Talbot, sought an injunction against the former farmers Morwell and Windsor. They alleged that various debts and portions had not been paid, and in February 1385, reciting the terms of the 1381 grant at farm, asked permission to pursue the farmers. They were granted a licence to do so.[7] Obviously experiencing difficulty in getting payment from some of the new farmers, they later petitioned again. But they had not proceeded very far when Holland was disgraced in July 1385 for his attack on the son of the

---

[1] *Foedera*, iv. 149.   [2] *C.P.R. 1381–5*, 491.

[3] F. Blomefield, *An Essay towards a Topographical History of . . . Norfolk*, ix. 58; Fotheringhay had his annuities confirmed at Rising and Sevenhampton on several occasions in the 1380s when the English Government was discussing Breton matters, cf. *C.P.R. 1381–5*, 402, ibid. *1389–92*, 106; Chancery Warrants, file 481, no. 2882, 3 Aug. 1383.

[4] *C.F.R. 1383–91*, 50; Min. Accts. 1280/10, nos. 1–10, quittances to Morwell, Windsor, and Darrell, 1383–4.

[5] C. Dawson, *History of Hastings Castle*, i. 220 n.; for farmers, see above, pp. 189–90.

[6] *Rot. Parl.* iii. 279.

[7] *C.P.R. 1381–5*, 540, and Anc. Pet., file 184, no. 9200.

Earl of Stafford during the King's expedition to Scotland.[1] Talbot's personal interest in the pursuit of the farmers is obvious. He had been present in Nantes when the Duchess had drawn up her will, leaving all rights she might have had in the honour to John IV, as well as her moveables.[2] Talbot had then come to England, presumably to implement the will, but also to collect £120 arrears of a pension that John IV had granted him on the lands that had been exchanged for Brest and that were now held by the Earl of Northumberland.[3] The interests of both Holland and Talbot had been prejudiced by the handing over of Richmond honour to Queen Anne.

She had received some honour lands in November 1384.[4] In March 1385 she granted Richard II the right to present to a living in the gift of the honour.[5] But once again there was no major change of officials. John Dent, who had been seneschal of Richmond in 1383–4, was acting as bailiff for Queen Anne's liberties in the lordship in 1386–8.[6] Bell, the King's receiver in Lincoln, who had served the Duchess of Brittany in the same capacity in 1381, was bailiff of the Queen's liberties in Lincolnshire throughout the 1380s.[7] Darrell, receiver of Richmond in 1383–4, and Thomas Salman, auditor of the honour in 1383–4, both continued in office for some time after 1384.[8] Anne does not appear to have enjoyed all the lands of the honour, but in the successive regrants to John IV in 1387, 1388, and 1391 her officers were not disturbed. In March 1391 the King ordered a view of certain letters of the Queen to Henry FitzHugh. She had leased to him the castle and lordship of Richmond for twelve years at an annual rent of £433. 6s. 8d., an amount

---

[1] Anc. Pet., file 183, no. 9145; Chancery Warrants, file 1343, no. 30; ibid., file 1346, no. 51, 14 Sept. 1385, order to seize Holland's lands 'pur evidente contempt et rebellion'; cf. *Polychronicon*, ix. 61–2.   [2] A.L.A. E 24, Joan's will.

[3] *C.P.R. 1381–5*, 540.

[4] Gale, no. xliv; cf. *C.P.R. 1381–5*, 511, and *C.C.R. 1385–9*, 12.

[5] Dawson, op. cit., i. 221 n.

[6] Min. Accts. 10862/2 m. 2; ibid. 1280/10, no. 6; Receipt Rolls 565 (28 July 1386), 572 (10 Nov. 1388).

[7] Receipt Rolls 544 (14 Dec. 1381), 572 (1 Dec. 1388), 574 (22 Nov. 1389), etc.; cf. J. S. Roskell, 'Parliamentary Representation of Lincolnshire', *Nottingham Mediaeval Studies*, iii (1959), 72–3.

[8] Receipt Roll 559, 4 Mar. 1385 (Darrell); ibid., 20 Dec. 1384, 4 Mar. 1385 (Salman).

which accords with the profits of the estate in 1383–4.[1] At
the end of 1391, orders were once more issued to put John
in possession of the honour. Anne, it was said, had received
other lands in compensation.[2] But there is little evidence to
show that the mandate was implemented. In 1392 Bell
accounted for Richmond lands in Lincolnshire as the Queen's
bailiff.[3] In 1395 a grant of the office of constable of Richmond was made for the term of one year after the Queen's
death, which had occurred in June 1394.[4]

All the evidence seems to indicate that the Queen held
some Richmond lands until her death. In 1394 Ralph, Lord
Neville, received a grant of Wensleydale Forest, and in 1395
he received Richmond lordship on the same terms as Fitz-
Hugh.[5] The previous holder of Wensleydale, Thomas
Etton, who had received his post from John IV in 1379,
had it confirmed by Richard II in 1380 and by Queen Anne
during her tenure of the honour.[6] The Queen's feoffees made
grants from Richmond lands after her death which were
later confirmed.[7] But, despite a few minor alienations, the
integrity of the honour was maintained much as it had been
since 1381. Some manors continued at farm.[8]

The fate of John's other lands is more problematic. In
May 1386 Thomas, Duke of Gloucester, was granted Castle
Rising 'to hold when it comes into the King's hand'. It was
acknowledged that John IV held it at that time 'in some
form'. In 1391 the grant to Gloucester was confirmed in
rebate of £110 p.a. of his pension at the Exchequer.[9] On
both these occasions the English Government seems to have
acted precipitately, making the grants before the political
negotiations that would allow them to grant Rising freely
had been successfully concluded. In 1393, besides an

---

[1] *C.P.R. 1388–92*, 393; Chancery Warrants, file 523, no. 7066; Gale, Addita-
menta, p. 281.   [2] *C.Ch.R. 1341–1417*, 327; *C.P.R. 1391–6*, 13.

[3] Receipt Roll 586 (10 Sept. 1392).

[4] Chancery Warrants, file 551, no. 9877, 5 Apr. 1395.

[5] *C.P.R. 1391–6*, 470; ibid. *1396–9*, 13; B.M. Add. Ch. 20582, 1 Oct. 1395,
indenture between FitzHugh and Neville.

[6] *C.P.R. 1377–81*, 436; ibid. *1391–6*, 470; Aston, *Thomas Arundel*, p. 281.

[7] *C.P.R. 1396–9*, 286, 290, 317, 319.

[8] *C.P.R. 1391–6*, 68, 101, 105, 217; Accts. For. 33 m. 49ᵛ, accounts of J. Bell for
Skirbeck soke, 1399, and above, p. 182, n. 4.

[9] *C.P.R. 1385–9*, 147; *C.Ch.R. 1341–1417*, 323.

apparent exercise of the right of presentation by John IV's deputies at Rising, there was an order to the Duke's bailiffs there not to disafforest without the King's permission.[1] This suggests that John had at least temporary possession of the manor. An inquisition of 1397 suggests the same conclusion,[2] whilst in the previous year the toll-booth revenues were collected in John's name.[3] But the effectiveness of John's lordship may be doubted. The manor was found by the inquisition to be impoverished and lacking tenants, and the jurors were ignorant of the Duke's name. In October 1397 the castle and manor of Rising were granted to the Duke of York.[4]

There is no evidence to show that John had enjoyed the revenues of his Cumberland manors, which were farmed in the 1380s and 1390s by the Earl of Northumberland and Ralph, Lord Neville.[5] The Wiltshire lands may have passed to Queen Anne. But in 1391, when Edmund, Duke of York, petitioned for lands on which to take his £1,000 annuity, Sevenhampton manor, amongst others, was granted to him for that purpose.[6] In the 1380s Richard Fotheringhay received one of his pensions from the Wiltshire revenues, but this lapsed when he died on crusade in 1390.[7] Once again this would suggest that during the period of the confiscation, whereas the Duke himself was rarely able to make use of his lands in England, those who had been associated with him in the 1370s were able to maintain their individual interests in the honour of Richmond and the lands acquired by the Duke in 1378. In the absence of effective ducal supervision or sanctions they were free to exploit the ducal lands for their own purposes.

In the spring of 1398 the English Government, who had adamantly refused to give effect to the previous regrants of

[1] Blomefield, *Essay*, ix. 58; *C.C.R. 1392–6*, 155.

[2] *C.Inq.M. 1392–9*, 130.

[3] Hist. MSS. Comm., *Eleventh Report, Appendix, part iii*, Corporation of King's Lynn, p. 245.

[4] *C.C.R. 1395–9*, 141; *C.P.R. 1396–9*, 213, 400, 404.

[5] Ibid. 39, 267; *C.C.R. 1396–9*, 141.

[6] *C.P.R. 1389–92*, 377.

[7] Ibid. 368–9, where his wife is referred to as Welsh; Principal Probate Registry, Prerogative Court of Canterbury, Registers of Wills, 7 Rous, fol. 53^r, Fotheringhay's will, proved 22 Nov. 1390.

Richmond to John IV, relented. It has been shown in a previous chapter that this decision rested heavily on the *rapprochement* of England and France in international affairs. Richard II's personal policy towards Brittany had been nearly always unsympathetic, until, in 1396, he decided on the return of Brest. In 1398 John IV visited England. His old debts were pardoned and he was reinvested with the earldom of Richmond.[1] Honour was satisfied when he took up his Garter stall. Yet it is difficult to avoid the conclusion that Richard II's surge of generosity was carefully calculated. On 20 April 1398 the lands of the honour of Richmond were granted to Joan, Lady Basset (John IV's sister), Nicholas Aldrewych, Antony Rys, and their heirs.[2] The editors of the *Complete Peerage* comment that 'the grant was not deemed to be superseded by the restoration of the Earldom to Joan's brother'.[3] Lady Basset and her companions certainly claimed in Henry's IV's reign that the grant had been to them and their heirs.[4] Confirmation of an appointment to an office at Richmond made by Lady Basset suggests that, with her co-grantees, she had exercised some prerogatives at Richmond at least temporarily.[5]

John IV's view, as that of Henry IV, was different. Between 26 May and 17 August 1398 Aldrewych and Rys were employed by the Duke to make an extent of the honour.[6] In another hand from that in which the main details of the extent are written, the Duke is warned: 'cerchez bien ceste libre entour et regardez pour vostre homageres par cause quil est grande prejudice a vous Mons. et a voz heires ce quils ne ount fait lour homage.'[7] Such advice would seem to come from the extent's compilers, who took considerable pains to establish the Duke's rights as Earl of Richmond. Certainly he assumed that the honour was his. On 27 August 1398 he ordered Aldrewych to pay the arrears of a £50 pension to the ducal butler

---

[1] *Foedera*, viii. 38; Chancery Miscellanea, file 28/6, no. 27, 1 May 1398, Richard pardons debts.   [2] Gale, no. clix; *Preuves*, ii. 681–2.

[3] *Complete Peerage*, x. 824, n. *h*; C.P.R. *1396–9*, 350, 28 Apr., order to put them in possession.   [4] Anc. Pet., file 93, nos. 4617, 4626.

[5] C.P.R. *1399–1401*, 546.

[6] A.L.A. E 116. They began at Cheshunt on 26 May (fol. 9ʳ) and ended at Richmond castle on 17 Aug. (fols. 4ᵛ–5ʳ).   [7] A.L.A. E 116, fol. 18ᵛ.

Geoffrey Horne from the receipts of Bassingbourn manor.[1] Robert Norman, a ducal chaplain, also seems to have had a grant on the revenues of Swaffham Market authorized by John IV.[2] Evidently John assumed that he was picking up the threads of administration as they had been left when he was last in possession of the honour. But the documentation of his enjoyment of Richmond until October 1399 is very slight. Rys and Aldrewych remained in England in 1399, and it may be assumed that they were employed on John's business rather than Lady Basset's, since Henry IV gave them permission to go to Brittany almost immediately after his succession.[3] Until more evidence is discovered it may be safer to conclude that John enjoyed the prestige of his title Earl of Richmond, but that the substance of the honour escaped him in the last two years of his life.

The final impression of the Brittany–Richmond link in the fourteenth century, therefore, must be that it did not mean a great deal to the actual tenants of the honorial lands, who were often oblivious of an absentee, or frequently changing, landlord. Nor did Richmond estate practices owe much to the Breton link. During this period John II, John III, and John IV all held the earldom of Richmond jointly with their dukedom of Brittany. But the intervals in which they held both territories in peacetime conditions are too short to allow us to see how the link would have worked normally.[4] There is some evidence that in the local estate organization there was a tradition of service, that office holders from father to son served the Earl of Richmond, and that soldiers could be recruited for service in Brittany in the Civil War and in the 1370s from Richmond estates.[5]

---

[1] A.L.A. E 116, fol. 20ʳ. Horne received 40 marks p.a. from John in 1379 (Chancery Warrants, file 473, no. 2082), was drawing payments in 1383 (Min. Accts. 1280/10, no. 1), and remained in John's service as butler in the 1390s (*C.C.R.* *1389–92*, 142).

[2] A.L.A. E 116, fol. 19ᵛ. He was drawing 12*d.* a day from 1381 to 1383 (Min. Accts. 1280/10, no. 2) and was to be provided with a suitable benefice by the Duke in 1398, until which time he would continue to draw his pension on receipts of Swaffham.   [3] Above, p. 141.

[4] A.L.A. E 20, accounts of James de Saint-Aubin, receiver for John II in England, 1305, show very little profit being transferred from Richmond to Brittany.

[5] Cf. Sherborne, *E.H.R.* lxxix (1964), 729. Warin de Bassingbourn, Kt., served in Brittany in the 1350s (Treaty Roll 31 m. 8, protection, 1353), and John de Bassingbourn served with John IV in 1364 and with FitzNicol in 1372 (Treaty

Continuity in estate management, secured by families with hereditary interests and by the continuation of important officials in their posts during the rapidly changing titular lordship of the honour, helped to alleviate some of the uncertainties in absentee direction. But apart from the years of John IV's exile, which were atypical in that the Duke of Brittany was resident on his English estates, political conditions prevented the Duke from enjoying these lands to the full.

John's hopes for Richmond, hopes that had been sustained through nearly twenty years of arduous political negotiation, in the end proved illusory for the most part. That the Duke had not been wasting his energies, however, seems evident from his experiences in the 1370s. An income of about £2,000 was no mean sum, even if most of it was swallowed up in running costs of the ducal household and estates. There had still been a proportion available for distribution as largess and for the attachment of English supporters to the ducal cause.

John's experiences before 1373, where Englishmen had served him loyally, if not disinterestedly, in Brittany, may have led him to expect similar loyalty from the companions of his exile in the 1370s. In this he was disappointed. Whereas service in the 1360s had been linked with the holding of estates in Brittany or with the expectation of quite considerable grants from the Duke in the form of *fief-rentes* and annuities, the opportunities for Englishmen in Brittany after 1379 were much less favourable. Few Englishmen returned with the Duke, and, of those who did, the majority soon came home.[1] There were safer ways of gaining medium rewards. Although one or two ducal annuitants in England held office at Brest, few returned to ducal service in the duchy after 1379. When it was discovered that these pensions could be drawn even when the Duke was out of favour with the English Government, the basis of the Duke's Breton lobby in England was seriously undermined. It is

Rolls 47 m. 7, 55 m. 33). The families of Aldrewych, Bassingbourn, Basset, Fitz-Nicol, Fotheringhay, and Neville all provided men who served John IV or his ancestors in Brittany and Richmond.

[1] See above, p. 185, n. 8; Adam Blakemore, who returned to Brittany in 1379, was back in England in the late 1380s (Receipt Roll 573, 29 May 1389).

evident that several of those on whom John depended in England were quick to protect their own interests but less ready to press ducal claims on an unsympathetic government. But John was not the man to renounce his rights lightly. In adverse conditions he had once enjoyed the revenues of Richmond. The English had beguiled him with frequent promises to return the honour after 1381. John's efforts to regain tenure suggest that he was lured by more than the illustrious title of his earldom of Richmond. He had seen its potentialities, and it was in his nature to seek that which he had lost.

VIII

CONCLUSION

At the beginning of this work emphasis was laid on the influence which the work of Arthur de la Borderie has had in establishing the pattern of John IV's reign as it appears to Breton historians. La Borderie's thesis may be generalized as follows: by maintaining the Montfortist cause when John was too young to fight his own battles and by placing him on the ducal throne, the English secured a client on French soil who showed his gratitude in 1372 by admitting English forces to his duchy. Only after the salutary lessons of his exile did John reassess his position and begin his rule afresh. This time the Duke acted more in concert with the ambitions of his seigneurs, thus preserving his rule and establishing traditions of ducal government which were important to his successors' exercise of quasi-independence from Valois France in the fifteenth century. This is the pattern which still holds favour.

In the present work this over-all picture has been challenged, particularly in the field of ducal foreign policy. In the first place, by showing that ducal policy, before Brittany was dragged into the Anglo-French war in 1372, was not quite so accommodating to English interests as has been maintained. Secondly, by showing that after the exile and the return to 'normal' legal relations with France in 1381, John did not cease to communicate with England in the kind of terms that so shocked La Borderie's fine patriotic sensibilities. It has been demonstrated that the 'duplicity' which marks the events leading to the 1372 alliance with England was the daily coinage of ducal dealings with the great powers. Calmette and Déprez's account of Anglo-Breton relations after 1378 thus deserves little credence.

On the other hand it might be objected that John's pursuit of an independent policy before 1372 was hardly of sufficient duration and conviction to invalidate the view that he was bound to side with Edward III in the Anglo-French war and that he was merely waiting for the most opportune moment to declare his allegiance. It is at this point that an appreciation of the importance of ducal domestic rule between 1365 and 1373 impinges on an interpretation of John's over-all policy. It has been suggested in this work that the traditional account of an administration run by English advisers for the Duke after 1364 needs amendment. It cannot be denied that there were important English advisers in ducal service, nor that considerable sums of money flowed out of Brittany into English pockets in the first years of John's rule. But the reconstructed administration was not based on precedents drawn from a Westminster model. Although there were English and Breton clerks who had served Edward III in the duchy, his administration had preserved Breton practices wherever possible. The reconstruction after 1364 proceeded by rediscovering these traditional Breton forms. The young Duke wished to free himself from the English incubus, so far as it was practical and expedient to do so. He associated Bretons with himself in government, handing to them the safeguard of castles and giving them advisory and administrative tasks. This domestic policy, in its endeavour to build up ducal authority, naturally led to an attack on the privileges of the greater seigneurs, among whom Clisson was outstanding. This, besides the more immediate rewards of French royal service, was a potent factor leading to discontent among ducal subjects. When disagreement over foreign policy was added, discontent turned to revolt.

When John allied with England, he was lured by the promise of military aid, legal concessions, and territorial gains. Almost invariably the use of English arms in Brittany did the Duke more harm than good. Brest was held and victualled from England during the Duke's exile, but English expeditionary forces to the duchy achieved no lasting or notable success. It was not English arms which restored John in 1379. The English garrison at Brest was a continual thorn in John's flesh thereafter. It is difficult to avoid the conclusion that English armed aid was, on several occasions, forced upon the Duke whether he wanted it or not. If it was not already obvious, the events of 1387–8 demonstrated that John's interest in English forces was mainly concerned with ensuring the continuance of his rule in Brittany. He often considered the use of English troops against his own subjects, but was not so eager to co-operate in English schemes against France.

The legal concessions offered by the English were inviting, promising as they did the possibility of freeing Brittany from homage obligations to the holder of the French crown. But, as the chances of Edward III or Richard II succeeding to that crown were remote, it was an easy concession to make.

Of greater importance were the immediate and projected territorial advantages of the 1372 Anglo-Breton alliance. Yet here again John revealed his concern to establish a firm footing in Brittany. Although Edward eventually offered the Duke as much as he could capture in France, the basis of the alliance was the concession of Richmond and of those Marcher lordships to which the Duke felt entitled, on the grounds of earlier possession by his predecessors, or which he considered necessary additions to strengthen Brittany against France. At all periods of John's reign there were negotiations with England, but almost without exception the Duke was concerned first and foremost with protecting what he already possessed. The Duke continually sought to escape fulfilling the clauses in any Anglo-Breton treaty which demanded material aid, thereby denying England the expected advantages of the alliance.

It is possible to argue, as some have done, that John had no need to interest himself in an English alliance. If he could not see his way to helping his sovereign he should have withdrawn from the Anglo-French struggle. This does indeed appear to have been his aim, especially after 1381; but the difficulties of neutrality have been demonstrated for a small state caught up in the conflict of two greater ones. Granted that John was, willingly or not, drawn into the fatal alliance with England, it cannot be argued that he passively accepted English exploitation of his duchy. The Anglo-Breton alliance, despite the disparity of the allies' respective strengths, was not one-sided in the advantages it conferred.

It is John's policy towards France that makes it clear that his attitude towards England was governed by political calculations which owed little to sentiment, despite the memory of favours received from Edward III. Here the same mixture of hard-headed bargaining, apparent concession, and renewed defiance is found. Here John pursued, with the same relentless diplomatic pressure that he employed in his attempts to regain Brest and Richmond, his claims in France, both as Duke of Brittany and as a private individual, to lands and rents in Rethel, Nevers, and elsewhere. John could not openly deny French sovereignty. But, by his lawyers' attempts to redefine his homage in 1366 and 1381 and by his prevarication in doing homage and fulfilling any of the services it entailed, he was able to diminish royal prestige in Brittany. He backed this up by increasing the competence of his own government to deal with duchy affairs and by excluding royal officers and royal influence. Not even warnings by the French King to the Breton seigneurs about the danger to themselves of the Duke's increasing powers could break the community of interest which John established with his subjects after 1381. On occasion, especially with regard to Clisson, the Duke was forced to climb down. But there is no division to be found in the two halves of John's reign as far as domestic policy or that towards France is concerned. In both periods John was anxious to exalt ducal power at the expense of his legal sovereign and of his seigneurs and bishops. The development of a *chambre des comptes* before 1373 is seen as a logical development of ducal institutions following the devising of new taxing powers during the Civil War. Likewise the emergence of the receiver-general, paralleled elsewhere in France, as a supervisor of revenue collection improved the Duke's control of his resources, while consultation with his seigneurs helped to broaden the basis of John's government.

The legacy of the 1372 alliance with England was John's renewed interest in Richmond and in the eventual lease of Brest in return for military support. John's prime endeavour in his policy towards England after 1381 was to obtain repossession of both these properties. Perhaps this was not a very ambitious policy, but it posed considerable problems for the Duke, which have been described in detail. English policy in this period may be characterized as one of promising future rewards for present services. It is doubtful whether the holding of Brest by the English contributed greatly to their war effort in the 1380s. In the 1390s the castle became less of a financial burden on England, but the consequent increase of ransoming and piracy, practised by the garrison, only made the Duke more determined to repossess it. The English government was caught between two stools: it wanted to maintain the advantages of a barbican policy, but it could not really afford the luxury of this scheme. If the cost of maintaining Brest could be transferred to Breton shoulders, even at the expense of alienating the Duke, the English were prepared to risk throwing Brittany into French arms. But they paid the price when they desired ducal co-operation. Likewise the Duke was disenchanted by English policy over Richmond. John lived in constant expectation of success, but with the Anglo-French war becoming a stalemate after 1388, the English had little need to woo him. His English friends and advisers drew their pensions from Richmond revenues after 1381, but their influence in government circles was exercised either too weakly or too selfishly to obtain for John a meaningful repossession of the earldom and honour. English policy from 1381 had been to satisfy a constant stream of envoys with small concessions. Naturally the Duke became lukewarm in his support of the English in their war and had every reason to seek his own ends.

It could be argued that John's obsession with the English alliance as revealed by the events of 1387–8 and 1392–3 (which so closely mirror those of 1372–3) brands him as an Anglophile. But the way in which he slipped out of his obligations once the domestic crises in Brittany were brought under control indicates that the alliance was an insurance policy. Safety clauses for retirement to England and the protection of his heir's rights in Brittany were prudent steps for a man who had previously experienced exile. John was pursuing his ends with the only methods available to the ruler of a small and vulnerable state that was in danger of becoming the client of a greater one. His success in attempting to steer a course between England and France in the 1380s and 1390s was precarious. Events like the madness of Charles VI and the seesawing of fortunes at Paris were beyond his control, even if they frequently worked out to his advantage. But not a little of his success was due to the flexibility of his statecraft.

John IV thus emerged as a ruler with distinctive policies, capable of using his position as Duke of Brittany to play an important, if not decisive, role in Anglo-French affairs. The present study has emphasized that it is necessary to consider domestic and foreign policies together in order to obtain a true understanding of John's rule. Since he was trying to create in Brittany as strong a ducal government as possible, it seems illogical to imply that when it came to foreign affairs he sought only to please his allies. John entertained no such altruistic fancies. His primary concern was ducal power exercised on behalf of what he considered Brittany's interests.

APPENDIX A

DOCUMENTS

1. Indenture between John de Montfort and Matthew Gournay for the farm of ducal *brefs* at Bordeaux and La Rochelle, dated at Vannes 26 March 1364 (A.L.A. E 201).

E N D E T N E D N E

Ceste endenture faite entre noble et puissant Seigneur Mons. Jehan duc de Bretaigne, conte de Montfort et viconte de Limoges dune part et Mons. Mahe de Gornay, chivaler, dautre part tesmoigne que le dit Mons. le duc a ottroie a ferme audit Mons. Mahe prennant et accep-tant jusques a cinq anz entiers commencanz le primier jour du mois davril prouchain venant touz les prouffiz des briefs qe le dit Mons. le duc doit et devra pranre lever et avoir par les diz cinq anz es villes de Bourdeaux et de la Rochelle pour quatre vinz tonneaux de vin de Gascoigne bon et souffisant par chascun an des diz cinq anz, les quielz vinz le dit Mons. Mahe est tenu rendre et paier en ses propres coulz, perils et despenz au dit duc ou sa cause aiant en la ville de Vannes ou en la ville de Guerrande. Cest asavoir quarante tonneaux de vin a chascune feste de la Saint Michiel en Monte Gargane[1] et quarante autres tonneaux ou derrain jour de chascun mois de Mars et en oultre les dictes choses en un an des dictes cinq annees paiera et rendra audit duc dix tonneaux de vin de Gascoigne bon et souffisant. Et si durant le dit temps en aucun an tonneau de vin vaille a Bourdeaux vint et cinq escuz ou moins le dit Mons. Mahe paiera et rendra celui an yceulz diz tonneaux de vin en une des dictes villes audit duc ou sa cause ou povoir de lui aiant. Et oultre ce faire satisffacion par chascun an a Mons. Symon Beureley, chivaler, de deux cenz marcs dargent ou la value et a Mons. Guillaume de Seris,[2] chivaler, de cinquante escuz dor qui leur sont donnez ou assignez par le dit duc sur les diz briefs. Et deliverra le dit duc et les siens dicelles sommes dor et dargent envers les diz Mons. Symon et Mons. Guillaume selon la teneur de leurs lettres. Et en cas que durant le dit temps de la dicte ferme les diz Mons. Simon et Mons. Guillaume trespasseroient de vie a mort ou aucun deulz, ou

---

[1] 16 Oct.

[2] 'Some Documents regarding the Fulfilment . . . of the Treaty of Brétigny, 1361–9', ed. P. Chaplais, *Camden Miscellany*, xix (1952), 52–3, for Seriz.

autrement par juste cause les donaisons ou assignacions faites au diz chivalers sur les diz briefs serroient rappellees ou aucune delles, les dictes sommes dor et dargent et chascune delles tourneront et revendront au prouffit du dit duc et sa cause aiant et les li rendra et paiera par chascun an le dit Mons. Mahe au dit duc ou a sa cause ou povoir a ce de lui aiant aus termes qe devent estre paiez aus diz chivalers par leurs dictes lettres sanz que le dit Mons. Mahe y puisse rien reclamer ou demander. Et mettra le dit Mons. Mahe en ses despenz tiels officers comme il vouldra a livrer pour lui les diz briefs et a en recevoir les emolumenz es dictes villes excepte le clerc que le duc a establi a Bourdeaux qui aura pour sa clergie les feages duez. Et pranra le dit Mons. Mahe par endentures les briefs du duc qui sont es dictes villes et aussi du duc autres briefs qui li seront necessaires pour cause de sa dicte ferme. Et a la fin du dit temps le dit Mons. Mahe rendra et deliverra franchement au duc ou sa cause aiant ou leur deputez le ramenant des briefs qui nauront este livrez deuement aus marcheanz et en rendra bon compte et loyal au duc ou sa cause aiant sanz nuls retenir ou faire retenir par fraude, malice ou mal engin ou prejudice du dit duc. Et faire jurer touz les gienz et officers qui sentremettront pour lui qe ainsit bien et loyaument les rendront au duc ou sa cause ou povoir de lui aiant sanz rien en receler ou faire celer ou retenir en aucune maniere et sanz nul empeschement ou debat sur ce faire ou procurer au duc ou aus siens. Et si aucuns debat ou empeschement estoit mis, fait ou procure en aucune maniere par le dit Mons. Mahe ou ses officers parquoi le dit duc ou sa cause ou povoir de lui aiant ne purroit joir franchement du dit ramenant de ses diz briefs qui nauroient este livrez loyaument aus marcheanz durant le dit temps, le dit Mons. Mahe est tenu en ses despenz a oster et faire oster le dit debat et a en desdomagier le duc si domage en avoit. Et si avant la fin des diz cinq anz paix seroit faite entre le duc et son adversaire sur leur debat du duchie de Bretaigne, le dit Mons. Mahe est tenu de rendre et delivrer franchement le ramenant des diz briefs qui nauront este livrez deuement sanz plus sentremettre des diz briefs ou cas quil plairoit au duc ou sa cause ou povoir de li aiant et a sa requeste. Et recevra le dit Mons. Mahe par lui ou autres compte et satisfacion pour le duc et en nom de lui de ses officers es dictes villes des diz briefs et des emolumenz du temps passe et jusques audit primier jour davril et en faire satisfacion deue auduc ou a sa cause aiant a sa requeste et donra quittance aus diz officers de ce quil recevra deulz pour le duc. Et les dictes choses et chascune delles tenir, fournir, faire et acomplir a promis et jure le dit Mons. Mahe sur les Sainz Evangelies de Dieu sanz venir encontre et soubz lobligacion de li et de ses hoirs et assignez et de leurs biens.

Donn' a Vannes soubz les seaux des dictes parties mis a ces lettres entrechangeablement le xxvi^e jour de Mars lan mil iii^c sexante et quatre.[1] Cest assavoir soubz le signet dudit Mons. Mahe[2] et le seel du Sire de Latimer pour le dit Mons. Mahe a sa reque[ste], donn' lan et le jour dessus diz.

Par Mons. le duc presentz le sire de Latimer, le chanceller et Mons.
Guillaume Soude.   Bediez.

Constat 'cest assavoir soubz le signet et le seel du Sire de Latimer pour le dit Mons. Mahe et a sa requeste'.[3]

Dorse: L'endenture de Mons. Mahe de Gornay pour les breffs de la mer a Bourd. et a la Rochelle.

2. Composition between John IV and William, Lord Latimer, for various debts incurred between 1360 and 1367, dated at Nantes 20 May 1367 (A.L.A. E 119, no. 8).

Sur ce que monsieur Guillaume Sire de Latimer demandoit avoir de monsieur Jehan duc de Bretaigne, conte de Montfort, certaines sommes dor dont mancion est faicte plus a plain en un rolle contenant ses demandes doudit monseignour le duc dont la tenour sensuit: Ce sont les choses que le Sire de Latimier demande allouance pour plusours choses et mises quil a fait pour monseignour le duc de Bretagne dont ledit Sire na eu nulle allouance au derrain acompt fait a Vannes le xv^e jour de Novembre lan mil troiscenz saixante et cinq.

Premierement, il demande allouance dune obligacion quil a mis a monsieur Rogier David pour les restaz de Tromgof davant quil peurent avoir deliverance dou fort dont il paia seix cenz escuz a la deliverance doudit fort, trois mille seix cenz et quinze escuz.

Item, paia le dit Sire de Latimer pour le duc a Hamptoun aux mariners et pour vesseaux dont il demande allouance, quatre cenz escuz.

Item, paia pour la mote de Saint Gille que monsieur Hue de Cavallay prent en destreignant les rampczons de Becherel et de Plermel par quoy ledit Sire de Latimier li commit achater a grant domage de lui, deiz mille escuz de laquelle somme il li est alloe a la prise de Redon seix mille escuz dequoy ledit Sire pardona a monseigneur le duc trois mille escuz et les autres trois mille le duc li a alloue par acquit et autrement labbe neust randu la dicte ville a celle foiz et ainssin le dit Sire demande quatre mille escuz.

---

[1] Easter fell on 24 Mar. in 1364.
[2] *Mahe* interlined.
[3] Original parchment, approximately 16 in. × 11 in., sealed on two tongues, one of which is missing. The other has a small brown armorial seal, a cross patonce.

Item, ledit Sire de Latimier fist venir monsour Thomas Moreaux hors de France au seige de Becherel a tant de gienz comme il pouroit par le commandement dou duc comme il fust commande a touz les autres cappitaines de Bretaigne dont ledit monsour Thomas amena oict vignz et oict combatanz, cest asavoir premierement ledit monsour Thomas Moreaux, monsour Robert Depert a sept hommes darmes en leurs compaignie et saize archiers venanz audit seige qui prendrent pour la journee mil escuz pour ce quils demouraient o lui le quartier enseuant. Et furent paiez par le quartier.

Item, Guillaume Morville a vignt hommes darmes et vignt archiers venanz audit seige et prenant la journee doux mille frans.

Item, Hugue de Suriton et Robinet de Twyfort a douze hommes darmes et quatorze archiers prananz la journee mil frans.

Item, Hankyn de Tildsley a vignt hommes darmes et vignt et deux archiers prannantz la journee sept cenz frans.

Item, Jehan Lovetoft a deiz hommes darmes et saize archiers qui prinstrent pour la journee sept cenz cinquante moutons.

Item, Robert filz Rouf, Guy filz Rouf, Thomelin Symon o quatre archiers qui prinstrent la journee trois cenz saixante et quinze escuz.

Item, pour camocas a Dynam pour monseur Spenc' quatre vignz escuz les queux furent allouez es derrains acompz et ne furent pas mis en sa descharge dou temps dont il fust Gardian fait a Poitiers et dont il demande allouance. Premierement il demande allouance par couvenant fait davant le duc a Callais pour monsour Gaultier Huet et cinquante hommes darmes et seix vignz sept archiers chascun homme darmes prannant le quartier saixante moutons et chascun archier trante moutons qui montent deiz mille deux cenz quinze escuz.

Item, il demande allouance que ledit monsour Gautier prent pour son corps pour ledit quartier doux mille escuz.

Item, il demande allouance pour vignt hommes darmes et cinquante archiers plus quil ne devoit tenir par couvenant le temps quil estoit Gardian par un quartier et oict sepmaines chascun homme darmes cent escuz et chascun archier cinquante escuz, value sept mille oict cenz quinze escuz.

Item, il demande allouance et paiement des despanz et mises quil a faiz par plusours faiz en Bretaigne et a Poitiers et au trette de la Paiz en Bretaigne et autrement quil a grossement despandu le sien en service dou duc dont il est grandement enpovre et le paiement dou duc et au roy tarde a cause de si gros despans par plusours foiz en son service qui montent vignt mille frans.

Item, ledit Sire de Latimier demande allouance de son aller a Paris en la compaignie dou Sire de Cliczon dont fust ordene davant le duc que chascun deux devoit prandre par chascun jour tant comme ils furent hors deiz frans, levesque de Saint Briouc presant, et feussent par de la en allant et venant saixante diz et oict jours qui montent sept cenz quatre vignz frans des quieux il a receu quatre cenz frans, demeure trois cenz quatre vignz frans.

Item, il demande allouance de la reparacion dou chastel de Saint Aulbin que le dit Sire a mis entour ledit chastel leaument doux mille escuz dont il grea auduc moittie cinq cenz dou sien senz avoir allouance si que la somme monte quil a plus mis a mille et cinq cenz escuz.

Item, il demande allouance de trois mil escuz que monseigneur le duc eust de monsour Hue de Carvellay de la ferme de Plormel du temps quil feust gardian fait a Poitiers.

Item, de monseur Thomas Fouk de la ferme de Henbont, mill escuz.

Item, de monseur Symon Burellay et Dageworth de la ferme de Saint Grimollay, trois mille escuz.

Item, de monsour Jehan de Guilgham et Grenagres de la ferme de Conk, mil escuz.

Item, de Jakes Ros de la ferme de Kemperille doudit temps, seix cenz escuz.

Item, de mons. Tanguy de Kermovan de la ferme de Kermoan[1]

Item, manbrance des rampczons de Pestivian les quelles furent livrees a monsour Gaultier Huet par commandement douduc[1]

Item, manbrance des souldaiers de Vannes et de Guerande qui furent rabatuz par ordennance faicte par le duc[1]

Item, manbrance des rampczons de Bleign[1]

Item, des rampczons de Fougere[1]

Item, demande la moitie de ses despens dou temps quil feust Gardian et demoura es bonnes villes fermees. Ledit monseigneur le duc disant au contraire que rien ne li en devoit, finablement apres plusours treitiez euz et faiz sur ce entreux oves leurs raisons dun coste et dautre fut acorde et compouse amiablement et de commun assante-ment entreux que pour touttes les demandes et peticions que ledit Sire de Latimer fesoit et povoit ou devoit faire auduc par raison des faiz et parcelles contenuz oudit rolle ledit monseignour le duc est tenu paier audit Sire de Latimier doze mille escuz dor Johannes ou leurs vallue en autre or ou autre monnoye[2] dont ledit Sire de Latimier est assigne et en quite ledit monseignour le duc par ces lettres. Et par ce se sont entrequitez lun lautre deulz de tout ce quils sentrepeussent demander par cause ou occasion des parcelles poinz et articles contenuz et

---

[1] No sum mentioned, but space left for insertion.

[2] *ou autre monnoye* interlined.

declerez oudit rolle dessus escript et des despans dicelles. Et ou cas
que le duc voudra faire aucunes demandes[1] et peticions audit Sire de
Latimer par cause et du temps quil fut Gardian pour lui durant les
guerres et depuis de quelconque chose que ce soit faire les poura, non
obstant ceste composicion et les raisons et deffansses doudit Sire de
Latimer seront sauves et oyes au conttraire et poura en oultre poursuyvre sus le laige toutes les demandes contenues ou dit rolle et autres,
reservees les deffansses douduc aussi au conttrairie. Et sil estoit trouve
que le duc devroit audit Sire de Latimier ladicte somme de doze mil
escuz, li vaudra en descharge de ce quil devra. Et ou cas que ledit Sire
de Latimier devra auduc par les raisons qui seront proposes et monstrees,
ledit Sire de Latimier li fera paesment et satisfacion de ce quil sera
trouve quil devra auduc pour tout le temps passe sanz fraude ne mal
engin. Et poura le duc poursuyvre et avoir les fermes de touz les
cappitaines et autres pour lanee que ledit Sire de Latimier fut fait
gardian de Bretaigne davant monseigneur le Prince a Poitiers. Et en
cest acord nest de rien comprise la debte que le dit Sire de Latimier
doit paier audit monseigneur le duc selon les endanteures faictes
entreux pour sey delivrer devers le Roy Dengleterre et demourent les
dictes endanteures et leurs dependences[2] en lours force et lours vertu
non obstant la composicion dessus dicte. Et ces choses ont les dictes
parties promis et jure tenir et accomplir sanz venir encontre. En
tesmoign des quelles choses les diz monseigneur le duc et le Sire de
Latimier ont mis lours seaux a ces lettres entrechangeablement.

Donne a Nantes le xxe jour de May lan mil troiscenz saixante et
sept. Et demandoit le dit Sire de Latimier allouance des ranczons de
Karahais et de la Roche es Asnes dou temps quil fut Gardian dont li
est fait reservacion comme des autres ci dessus escriptes. Donne comme
dessus. Constat 'ou autre monnaye' en enterlineaire mis de lassente-
ment des dites parties et constat 'et leurs dependences'. Donne comme
dessus.

Par le commandement des dites parties, presenz le Chanceller de
Bretaigne, Jehan le Barbu et le Receveur General.   Geffroy.[3]

3. Fealty of Thomas Melbourne, receiver-general of
Brittany, to John IV, 20 November 1368 (A.L.A. E 142).

Je Thomas de Melburne, prestre de la nation dangleterre, promet et
sui tenu et oblige que tout le temps que je vivre, je servire, aidere et
confortere bien et loialment mon tres redoubte seignour Monsieur

---

[1] Last four words repeated in MS.   [2] *et leurs dependences* interlined.
[3] Parchment, original. Sealed on two tongues with traces of John IV's and
Latimer's seals of red wax remaining.

Jehan, duc de Bretaigne, conte de Montfort, et comme son vray et loial vassal, officer, familier, servant et obeissant envers touz et contre touz sanz nul excepter et prochain a lui que a autres quiexconques. Et gardere et pourchacere sanz empescher ses droiz, profiz, nobleces et honors tant en prive que en appert envers touz et chacun deulx sanz aucune fiction ou dissimulacion et sanz les receler aucunement a son domage. Et eschever et empescher ses domages, mauls, vilaenies, grevances, difficultez, perils, diffamacions, injures et deshoneurs, ses conseils et secrez garder, lealment et secretement sanz les reveler aucunement en son prejudice. Et tout ce que je sentire tourner, panser ou machiner a sa grevance, mauls, diffamacions et domages de son corps ou de son duchie commant que ce soit ou puisse estre je le li revelere et fere savoir lealment et les empescher de tout mon povoir, tout le bon conseil et laide que je pourre le [li fere] de bon cuer de fait et de dit et les dites choses et chacune delles tendre et fere leaument et entierement sanz fiction, fraude ou mal engin, et sanz jamais faire ne venir encontre par moy ne par autre. Et me tiens a content de la donaison de rente quil ma faite pour ce et pour mes autres services faiz pour lui dont li ai fait foy et homage comme son homme lige et plus presme a lui qe a nul autre. Et ai jure sur les sainz evangiles de Dieu et sur sa vroye croiz et lespine de sa sainte corrone les dites choses faire et tenir entierement a mon povoir.

Donne souz mon propre seel,[1] tesmoign des dites choses, le xxe jour de moys de Novembre lan mil troiscenz soixante et huit.

Passe par Melburne de sa meyn propre, T.[2]

4. Quittance issued by Latimer's lieutenants at Bécherel to John IV, 23 April 1370 (B.N. MS. Nouv. acq. fr. 5216, no. 14).

Nous Jehan de Pert, connestable de Becherel, et Huchon de Milton, recepvour doudit lieu pour nostre tres cher et redoubte seignour Mons. Guillaume Sire de Latimier, en nom et comme ses procureurs et propres lieutenans avons eu et receu de tres puissant et nostre tres cher et redoubte seignour le duc de Bretaigne par la main Sire Thomas de Melburne, general recepvour de Bretaigne, la somme de troys mille ecuz dor Jahannes bons et de poys a valoir et porter aquit et descharge a nostre dit seignour le duc de Bretaigne sur les obligacions et penssions en quoy nostre dit seignour le duc de Bretaigne est tenu et oblige a nostre dit seignour le Sire de Latimier, de la quelle somme de troys

---

[1] No trace of this seal remains, but see *Preuves*, ii, plate 7, no. CXLV, and Douët d'Arcq, *Collection des sceaux*, no. 10,168.

[2] Parchment, original, approximately 13 in. × 5 in.

mille escuz nous tenons es noms que dit est pour conmptanz et bien paiez et en quitons et prometons faire quite nostre dit seignour le duc de Bretaigne, le dit Sire Thomas et touz autres a qui quitance en pouriet et doit apartenir et les en garder sanz domage vers nostre dit seignour le Sire de Latimier.

Donne soubz noz seaux le xxiiime jour davrill lan mil iii^c saexante et deiz.[1]

5. The articles of the Duke of Brittany, *c.* August 1388 (B.M. MS. Cott. Julius B. vi, fols. 55–6).

Les articles de la volente monseignour le duc de Bretaigne

Premer, pour lamour et la bonne volente quil a toudis vers le roy et son pais et pour lamour et la grande soustenance quil a eu par ses predecessours es quelx il se tient tant tenu come nul plus et ausi le desir quil a du grant proffit du roy et de son reaume et a ce faire estre aidant, le duc est en ferme porpos et volente de tenir toute laliance du roy et de ses biens veillanz come nagueres il a envoie devers le roy et son conseill par lettre sellee de son seel et passee de sa main par telle manere qe le roy et ses aliez puessent estre aseur de ly desorenavant et le duc sembablement du roy et de son aide a toutes ses afaires come son alie et bien veillant.

Cest asavoir, le duc de son corps toute sa puissance estre de la partie du roy vers touz et contre touz tenir les champs o ly ou o ses lieutenanz, les conseiller et aider en touz cas a son povoir et lour faire delivrance de ses villes et chateux et les loger par tout ou il poura par ainsin qe le roy et son reaume ly soint aidanz et a loir de son corps si auchun en avoit a son droit maintenir et garder vers touz et contre touz ses anemis sanz james ly faillir ne aler encontre par li ne par autre de par ly ne par nuls de ses aliez, ansois seront tenuz de garder et defendre le duc et son hoir vers touz et contre touz touz lour droiz, soverainetes et noblesses gardez et defenduz en touz cas et en touz endroiz sanz fraude ne mal engin.

Item, considere bien le duc la grant amour qe le roy a vers ly et par especial come monstre li a ceste foiz et plusours et les grans despens et coustages quil a fet de ceste daraine flote quil a envoiee en son aide les quelx il na osse loger pour ce quil nestoint montez quar ce neust este qe perdicion deulx et de son pais. Supliant au roy quil ne li desplesse et a touz les autres seignours qui venuz estoint en lour prometant leaument qe a toutes les fois quil vendront ou li envoieront gens montez et fors pour tenir les champs a li aider a conquerre son droit quelque part qe il soit et en avancement de la quarelle du roy il sera trove tout prest dacomplir toutes ses promesses et voudroit le duc qe la venue fut le plus

---

[1] Parchment, original, sealed on a tag. Pert's seal remains.

tost qe len pouroit et le plus secretement. Et en oultre que ceulx qui
a ly vendront ne le lessent point pour nul mandement qe len leur puesse
faire sanz le bon asentement du duc, ansois veult quil demorent o li et
conseille par eux et par nuls autres en touz ses fez et eux par ly come
vrais amis sanz fraude ne mal engin.

Item, si ainsin est quil soit avis au roy et a son conseil qe j fort
povoir ne pouroit mie venir si toste et qe il ne pouroint mie estre mis
en saisine des forteresses si bien come j petit povoir comme mons.
Edward Dalingrige la monstre audit duc, est le duc asentant qe j petit
povoir vienge tout primer de x^c ou xii^c et auront la sesine des forteresses
mes qe lautre povoir soit prest a descendre u pais tantost apres qe les
premers seront saisis des forteresses ou autrement il ne pouroint estre
logez ne receuz, et de cest darain povoir envoier voult le duc qe le
roy li soit tenu et son conseil et li envoie lettre scellee de son seal et
du sel auduc de Gloucestre, du conte Darondell, de Derbi, de Warwic,
du chanceler, du tresorer et de larcesveque de Canterb' et de son autre
conseil.

Item, veult le duc qe ceulx qui en son aide vendront soint o ly come
ses soudouairs jurez a li garder, maintenir et defendre come dit est
toutes ses noblesses en touz cas come duc de Bretaigne. Et qe touz les
conquestes faites en son pais, soint tenuz de li come de soverain en la
manere quil ont este avant ses houres, touz ses heritages a li et a son
hoir reservez o toutes lour noblesses en quelque lieu quil soient en
France ou aillours et qe les ransons qui seront fet en son pais et en
sa seignourie soint a ly en paiant les soudoiers resonablement qui a ce
auront travaille.

Item, qe nulle paiz ne treves courtes ne longues par trete ne autrement ne se puesse faire entre les deux rois ne lour aliez sanz le bon
asentement dudit duc et sil avient que trete de paiz ou de treves ce
face par nulle voie, veult le duc quil soit esleu pour j des commissaires
du roy dengletere et qe autrement ne se puesse nullement faire. Et sil
avient qe finalle paiz ou longues treves soit fet et que la guerre cesse du
tout, veult le duc qe len li rende ses forteresses o toutes lour aparte-
nances ou a son hoir de son corps ou qui cause aura deux a toute les foiz
quelles seront requisses par li ou par son hoir ou lour lieutenant comme
dit est sanz nul debat y mestre ne autre quelconques cause a prejudice
de li, de son hoir en paiant les gages au soudoiers resonablement de ce
quil auront servi; et si Dieu fet sa volente du duc sanz hoir de son
corps, face le Roy du pais ce qe bon li semblera et en oultre li donne le
duc tout son droit ausi avant comme faire le puet. Sauve le douaire sa
famme qe il veult quele soit lessee en jouir en la manere qe elle est
asinee et son droit maintenu et garde come cely du duc et ausi le
partage de la terre pour la suer audit duc comme reson est, la quelle na

pas este asignee, encore veult quele ayt enterement son droit comme il apartient par lordenance du roy et de son conseil.

Item, sil avenoit qe le duc par age ou par non povoir de son corps ne peust plus travailler es armes ou quil y pleust a vivre en repos en Engleterre, veult durant sa vie si hoir navoit qe en son non[1] et pour ly soit son droit maintenu, garde et porseu par guerre ou par paiz ou par quelque autre voie qe porsuette ou deffense ce pouroit faire ausi enterement comme sil y estoit de son propre corps. Et si hoir de son corps avoit, quil soit maintenu et garde come vrai duc de Bretaigne et tout son droit garde comme dit est et le droit de sa femme sanz rien amenusser de lour noblesses ne de lour terres pour nul trete de paiz ne de treves ne dautre acord qe faire se puesse entre les rois ne lour alies par voie de mariage ne nulle autre quelconques cause.

Item, veult le duc que len li rende presentement tout son heritage en Engleterre et toute son autre terre tant qe par eschange de Brest qe autrement o toutes les arerages dicelles pour le temps quil ont este hors de sa main. Et en oultre ordener de ly et de sa famme et de lour hoir de lour corps pour lour estat maintenir honourablement comme lour estat le requiert, cest asavoir diz mille libres desterlins de rante par chacun an en Engleterre. En considerant les grans pertes quil aura de son pais qui tournera le plus contre ly par cause de ceste aliance et en voie de le perdre a james et sa vie et son honour en aventure, quil plesse mie au roy et a son conseill quil soit si grandement deshonoure qe son estat soit apetisse pour ly obeir veu les grans perils ou il se mest pour lamour de ly.

A toutes ses choses tenir et acomplir veult le duc qe le roy et son conseil desus nommez li soint tenuz par lettre du roy sellee de son sel et de son conseill comme dit est sanz fraude ne mal engin et le duc dautre part soblige par ses presentes sellees de son sel et passees de sa main sembablement de fermement tenir et garder et acomplir toutes ses chosses a tout son povoir sans james aler encontre par ainsin qe le roy et son conseill le facent ausi de lour partie et envoier auduc lour lettre sellee de lour seaux comme dit est par les premers entrevenenz, en oultre veult le duc toutes ses chosses acordes qe le roy, ses hoirs apres li rois dengleterre[2] qui quil soint, barons de son pais, comptes, prelaz et autre seignours les plus grans du pais estre obliges en plain parlement par lettre selles de touz lour seaux jurez a toutes ses articles tenir sanz james aler encontre et veult le duc qe len li envoie toutes ses lettres desus nommez o les premers venenz come dit est.

Passe par moy le duc de ma main.[3]

---

[1] MS. *sic.* [2] *rois dengleterre* interlined.
[3] Parchment, original, sealed on a tongue; no trace of the seal remains.

APPENDIX B

PAYMENTS TO ENGLISH CREDITORS BY JOHN IV, 1365–1373

Section 1: Payments to Edward III

Date of quittance	Given by	Reason for quittance	Amount[1]
6 Apr. 1366	Helmyng Leget in King's Chamber	part of 30,000 marks owing from 1362 agreements	£2,868 15s. 0d.[2]
6 Dec. 1367	Edward III	'en partie de paiement de trente milles marcs' paid in by Latimer	£6,666 13s. 4d.[3]
4 Jan. 1369	Edward III	'in partem solutionis summarum in quibus dictus filius noster nobis tenetur'	£1,928 18s. 0d.[4]
6 Feb. 1369	Edward III	'in partem solutionis triginta milium marcarum'	£1,973 11s. 8d.[5]
			£13,437 18s. 0d.[6]

Section 2: Payments to former English captains in écus John

17 May 1366	T. Thweng	'for certain causes'	600[7]
7 Sept. 1366	Jack Ros	'en descharge a mon dit seignour sur les choses en quoy il mest tenu tant a cause de moy que a cause de Mons. Hues de Calviley'	500[8]
14 Nov. 1366	W. Huet kt.	'de tout le meuble quil me doit . . . a cause de moy et des souldaiers et gagiers, et mises et coustages faiz pour lui et en ses guerres . . .'	14,000[9]

[1] In the explanatory notes to this table the following exchange rates, which can only be approximations for many of the sums involved, are used:

£1 sterling = 6 *livres tournois* (Tout, *Chapters*, iii. 243).
1 *écu* John = 2s. 8d. sterling (Accts. Var. 176/9 m. 1, Wyngreworth's accounts 1361–2).
1 *écu* John = 15s. *tournois*, 1363 value (A. Cherest, *L'Archiprêtre*, p. 399).
1 *livre bretonne* = 1 *livre tournois*, 1374 value (Touchard, *Le Commerce maritime breton*, p. 99).

See P. Timbal, *La Guerre de Cent Ans vue à travers les registres du Parlement*, pp. 503–4, for other rates.   [2] B.N. MS. Nouv. acq. fr. 5216, no. 4.
[3] *Foedera*, iii. 837.   [4] Ibid. 855.   [5] Ibid. 858.
[6] 80,626*l.t.*   [7] A.L.A. E 119/7, no. 2.
[8] Ibid., no. 4; on 1 Nov. 1365 Hugh Calveley had agreed with John IV that the Duke owed him 11,000 *écus* John for past services and that the Duke would pay Calveley an annual fee of 1,500*l.br.*, B.N. MS. Nouv. acq. fr. 5216, no. 2.
[9] Ibid., no. 6.

Date of quittance	Given by	Reason for quittance	Amount
12 May 1367	T. Fouk (Fog) kt.	wages and fees for keeping of town of Hennebont	580[1]
8 Oct. 1367	T. Beauchamp kt.	'de toutes et chacune des debtes, lettres, obligacions queuxconques que jay euees pris et ma donnees . . .'	4,000[2]
12 Oct. 1367	T. Beauchamp kt.	as above	2,000[3]
9 Mar. 1370	T. Symond kt.	wages for service between 11 Nov. 1364 and 11 Feb. 1370	2,100[4]
			23,780[5]

Section 3: *Payments and quittances to and from the companies in écus John*

Date of quittance	Given by	Reason for quittance	Amount
1 Dec. 1368	J. Cresswell and D. Holograve	'for their company'	4,000[6]
1 Dec. 1368	J. Cresswell and D. Holograve	'for their company'	1,000[7]
30 Dec. 1368	W. Bardoulx, W. Sichier, H. Felton, and others	'la somme qui apartienne es Compaignons qui solent demorer o Mons. Robert Briket, que Dieu asoule, dou paement deu es granz Compaignes a cest terme de nouel . . . par lacordance faite entre Mons. de Bretaigne et les dictes Compaignes . . .'	no sum given[8]
30 Dec. 1368	R. Chaene, G. Worselay, R. Mittone kts., and others 'Cappitaines et chevataenns des routes des Englaes des Granz Compaignes . . .'	'laquelle somme ledit Monsour devoet a nous et autres compaignes et routes au terme de Nouel . . . par certaine acordance . . .'	27,500[9]
31 Dec. 1368	G. Worselay kt. 'Capitain de part des Rout' des Angloys . . .'	'de son obligacion pour le terme de novel . . .'	5,010[10]
22 Feb. 1369	Robert Chaene, etc.	as on 30 Dec. 1368	27,500[11]
			65,010[12]

---

[1] B.N. MS. Nouv. acq. fr. 5216, no. 7. [2] Ibid., no. 8.
[3] Ibid., no. 9, perhaps a quittance for half the above sum.
[4] A.L.A. E 210. [5] 17,835*l.t.*
[6] A.L.A. E 119/11, no. 2. [7] B.N. MS. Nouv. acq. fr. 5216, no. 10.
[8] Ibid., no. 11.
[9] A.L.A. E 119/12, printed in Borderie, iv. 113.
[10] B.N. MS. Nouv. acq. fr. 5216, no. 12.
[11] A.L.A. E 119/13, printed in Borderie, iv. 113. [12] 48,757*l.t.*/10*s.*

Section 4: Quittances from William, Lord Latimer, and his lieutenants in écus John

Date of quittance	Given by	Reason for quittance	Amount
22 Mar. 1366	sealed by Latimer and Valence at Bécherel	indenture witnessing that Latimer had delivered money to Valence to take to Edward III in rebate of John IV's debts. Of 25,000 écus which the Duke had delivered to Latimer, 3,000 écus were to cover his expenses	25,000[1]
10 Oct. 1367	Latimer	'de la somme que nous li devons pour les ranczons de Trougof et de Becherel et pour ... paesment a sa descharge de ce quil doit a mes lige Mons. le Roi Dengleterre . . . que nous portons audit Mons. le Roi . . .'	50,000[2]
10 Oct. 1367	Latimer	'quil me devoit audit terme pour cause de la donacion quil ma fait'	500l.br.[3]
5 Mar. 1370	Jacques de la Plaunche	'pour certaine acordaunce'	4,500[4]
23 Apr. 1370	John Pert and Huchon Milton	'sur les obligacions et pensions en quoy nostre dit Seignour le duc de Bretaigne est tenu et oblige a nostre dit Seignour le Sire de Latimier'	3,000[5]
			82,500 + 500l.br.[6]

Section 5: Miscellaneous quittances, probably from Englishmen

1 Feb. 1366	Adam Fraunceys, merchant of London	part repayment of 500-marks loan	431 'moutons,[7] 246 francs, and 46 écus
6 Sept. 1366	Hugh Arel	retained in household of John IV	300 écus[8]

[1] A.L.A. E 119, no. 1; see also payment under 6 Apr. 1366, Section 1. Although 22,000 × 2s. 8d. = £2,933. 6s. 8d., the difference is probably to be explained by depreciation in changing écus into sterling.

[2] Ibid., E 119/9, no. 1; see also payment under 6 Dec. 1367, Section 1. It is an exact sterling equivalent where the écu = 2s. 8d.

[3] Ibid., no. 2; approximately worth 500l.t.

[4] B.N. MS. Nouv. acq. fr. 5216, no. 13.

[5] Ibid., no. 14, cf. above, pp. 211–12.

[6] 62,375l.t.

[7] B.N. MS. Nouv. acq. fr. 5216, no. 3; no attempt is made here to translate this and the following miscellaneous payments into livres tournois.

[8] A.L.A. E 210.

Date of quittance	Given by	Reason for quittance	Amount
7 Sept. 1366	Guillaume Soude	'aveques le quel jay demore en son service tant son tresorier comme autrement ma bien et leaument paez entierement . . .'	no figure given[1]
? 1366	Robert Knolles	for Adam Fraunceys	1500 écus[2]
12 Apr. 1371	Guillaume Crespin	part of ransom money for Gilles d'Argenton kt., his prisoner	200 francs[3]
10 Jan. 1372	Guillaume Cok kt.	for ransom of prisoner	400 francs[4]
20 July 1372	Edward III	for anything owed for Bécherel	no figure given[5]

[1] B.N. MS. Nouv. acq. fr. 5216, no. 5.
[2] A.L.A. E 238 fol. 71ᵛ.
[3] Ibid. E 233.
[4] Ibid. E 209.
[5] *Foedera*, iii. 955.

APPENDIX C

CAPTAINS AT BREST, 1343–1397

Captain	Appointed	Acting	Annual wage
John Gatesdene	2 Dec. 1343[1]		
Richard Fangfosse		1350[2] as receiver for Eleanor, Countess of Ormond	
John Maynard	28 July 1352[3]		
Matthew Gournay	20 Nov. 1357	still in 1360–1[4]	
Geoffrey de Poulglou		1372[5]	
John, Lord Neville		Oct. 1372 until 4 Aug. 1373 at least[6]	
John Devereux		24 Dec. 1374 and still on 27 June 1375[7]	
John Austin and John Lakingheath		23 Aug. 1376[8]	
Robert Knolles	9 Jan. 1378	9 Jan.–10 June 1378[9]	
Richard Abberbury and John Golafre	18 Feb. 1378 and 10 Apr. 1378	10 June 1378– 20 May 1379	10,000 marks[10]
Hugh Calveley and Thomas Percy	4 Mar. 1379 and 18 May 1380	20 May 1378– 29 Aug. 1381	8,000 marks and 7,000 marks[11]
Thomas Percy	2 July 1381, 1 Sept. 1384, and 7 Dec. 1385	29 Aug. 1381– 18 Feb. 1386	4,250 marks, then 3,250 marks[12]
John Roches	18 Dec. 1385	18 Feb. 1386– 15 Mar. 1388	2,000 marks[13]
Richard, Earl of Arundel	25 Mar. 1388	24 June 1388– 25 July 1389	4,000 marks[14]
John Holland, Earl of Huntingdon	1 June 1389, 5 Dec. 1391, and 25 Oct. 1392	25 July 1389– 30 June 1397	3,000 marks[15]

[1] *Foedera*, ii. 1240. [2] Chancery Miscellanea, bundle 35/10, no. 60.
[3] *Foedera*, iii. 247. [4] Ibid. 383; Accts. Var. 174/4 and 5.
[5] *Preuves*, ii. 708 (A.L.A. E 134/2).
[6] *Rot. Parl.* ii. 328, iii. 53; *Anonimalle Chronicle*, ed. Galbraith, p. 71; Froissart, ed. Luce, viii, pp. lxx, lxxx; A.N. J 642/22.
[7] *Foedera*, iii. 1020; 'Anglo-French Negotiations', ed. Perroy, *Camden Miscellany*, xix (1952), 24. [8] *Foedera*, iii. 1062. [9] Accts. Var. 36/30.
[10] Ibid. 37/30, nos. 1, 2, 38/9, 37/27, no. 26, 68/7, no. 171, and Accts. For. 13 m. F[r].
[11] Accts. Var. 37/30, nos. 3, 4; *Foedera*, iv. 58; Accts. For. 16 m. 42[r].
[12] Accts. Var. 68/10, no. 238; *C.P.R. 1381–5*, 25, 492; Accts. Var. 68/10, no. 237; *Foedera*, iv. 133, vii. 452.
[13] Chancery Miscellanea, bundle 6/4, roll 1 m. 1[v]; Accts. For. 16 m. 42[r]; Treaty Rolls 70 m. 25, 72 m. 15; Issue Roll 510 m. 23. [14] Accts. Var. 41/8, 68/11, no. 258.
[15] Privy Seal Files 1/54a; Accts. Var. 68/11, no. 270, 69/1, no. 278; A.L.A. E 120/1; *Preuves*, ii. 708.

Q

APPENDIX D

KING'S AND CAPTAINS' RECEIVERS AT BREST
1378–1397

Receiver	Appointed	Acting
Cok Barbour		before 10 June 1378[1]
Thomas Norwych	1 Apr. 1378 7 Apr. 1379	10 June 1378–7 July 1381[2]
Philip Dernford	1 Mar. 1381	from 7 July 1381[3]
John Godard		4 May 1381[4]
Philip Dernford	18 Feb. 1386[5]	
John Draper		4 Aug. 1387–6 Mar. 1388[6]
John Hayward		24 Apr. 1388[7]
Robert Pobelowe		18 Nov. 1389[8]
John Raulyn		5 July 1393[9]
John Morley		20 Sept. 1396[10]
William Alyngton		possibly 1388–9 and 13 May 1395; definitely on 29 June 1397[11]

[1] Accts. Var. 38/8, no. 7.

[2] Ibid., no. 21; Chancery Warrants, file 456, no. 304; Accts. For. 18 m. 64^r; Chancery Warrants, file 459, no. 698.

[3] Accts. For. 18 m. 64^r; Accts. Var. 38/8, no. 20.

[4] Accts. Var. 38/8, no. 14, acting for Percy and Calveley.

[5] Accts. For. 20 m. 7^r.

[6] Treaty Roll 72 m. 23; Issue Roll 518 m. 24.

[7] Treaty Roll 72 m. 8, as a merchant and mariner of Taunton serving under Arundel at Brest 'in municione eorundem castri et ville moratur', protection for coming year.

[8] Memoranda Roll 166 (E. 159), Brev. dir. bar., Michaelmas 13 Ric. II, m. 32^v.

[9] Treaty Roll 78 m. 18 'super vitelagio eorundem castri et ville moratur'.

[10] Treaty Roll 81 m. 11.

[11] Privy Seal Files 1/31; A.L.A. E 201, E 120/2, no. 1. For his later career see J. S. Roskell, 'William Allington of Horseheath, Speaker in the Parliament of 1429–30', *Proc. Camb. Ant. Soc.*, lii (1959), 30–42.

APPENDIX E

SUMMARY ACCOUNT OF COST OF KEEPING BREST, 1378–1389

Period	Captain	Cost (in sterling)
Apr. 1378–20 May 1379	R. Abberbury and J. Golafre	£6,763 5s. 4d.[1]
20 May 1379–24 June 1381	Hugh Calveley and Thomas Percy	£11,158 13s. 4½d.[2]
24 June 1381–18 Feb. 1386	Thomas Percy	£13,118 18s. 8d.[3]
18 Feb. 1386–23 June 1388	John Roches	£4,329 19s. 9d.[4]
23 June 1388–25 July 1389	Richard, Earl of Arundel	£2,908 8s. 4d.[5]
		£38,279. 5s. 5½d.

[1] Accts. For. 13 m. F[r].

[2] Ibid. 16 m. 42[r].

[3] Ibid. 20 m. 7[r].

[4] Issue Roll 541 m. 20; cf. Issue Roll evidence for payment of £4,644. 5s. 10d. between Jan. 1386 and 17 July 1388 in cash, tallies, assignments, and victuals (Issue Rolls 510–19).

[5] Accts. For. 27 m. 4[v].

BIBLIOGRAPHY

THIS is not an exhaustive list of all sources consulted. In the case of secondary historical works which contain *pièces justificatives* an asterisk precedes the title of the work.

The Bibliography is divided into four main sections:

    A. Bibliographical aids

    B. Documents in manuscript
        i. England
       ii. France

    C. Documents in print
        i. Published and calendared documents
       ii. Chronicles

    D. Historical works
        i. Published works
       ii. Unpublished theses

A. BIBLIOGRAPHICAL AIDS

Archives de la France monastique, xix. *Abbayes et Prieurés de l'ancienne France, viii, Province ecclésiastique de Tours*, ed. Dom J. M. Besse, Ligugé and Paris 1920, pp. 193 ff.

Berranger, H., *Guide des archives de la Loire-Atlantique*, i. *Séries A à H*, Nantes 1962.

Halgouet, H. du, *Répertoire sommaire des documents et manuscrits de l'histoire de Bretagne antérieurs à 1789 conservés dans les dépôts publics de Paris*, vol. i, *Bibliothèque Nationale et Archives Nationales*, Saint-Brieuc 1914.

Sacher, F., *Bibliographie de la Bretagne*, Rennes 1881.

Touchard, H., 'Les Archives anglaises et l'histoire du commerce breton à la fin du Moyen Âge', *M.H.B.* xxxiii (1953), 129–43.

—— 'Les sources de l'étude quantitative du commerce médiéval breton', *Les Sources de l'histoire maritime en Europe, du Moyen Âge au XVIIIᵉ siècle*, ed. M. Mollat *et al.*, Paris 1962.

B. DOCUMENTS IN MANUSCRIPT

(i) *England*

(*a*) Public Record Office, London

C. 47	Chancery miscellanea
C. 49	Parliament and Council proceedings
C. 61	Gascon rolls
C. 76	Treaty rolls
C. 81	Chancery warrants
C. 135	Chancery inquisitions, *Post mortem*, Edward III

C. 143   Chancery inquisitions, *Ad quod damnum*
C. 145   Chancery inquisitions, miscellaneous
E. 28   Council and Privy Seal files
E. 30   Treasury of the Receipt, diplomatic documents
E. 36   Treasury of the Receipt, miscellaneous books
E. 101   King's Remembrancer, accounts, various
E. 159   King's Remembrancer, memoranda rolls
E. 358   Lord Treasurer's Remembrancer, miscellaneous accounts
E. 364   Lord Treasurer's Remembrancer, enrolled accounts
E. 372   Pipe rolls
E. 401   Receipt rolls
E. 403   Issue rolls
E. 404   Warrants for issues
S.C. 6   Ministers' accounts
S.C. 8   Ancient petitions

(*b*) British Museum, London
Cottonian MSS. Caligula D. iii, Julius B. vi
Additional MSS. 24062, 24512, 30749–52, 35115, 37494
Additional Charters 30–2, 39, 40, 3348–56, 5829, 7909, 7914, 20582, 40225

(*c*) Principal Probate Registry, London
Prerogative Court of Canterbury, Register of Wills, 7 Rous

(*d*) Bodleian Library, Oxford
Carte MS. 113
Oriel College MS. 46
Rawlinson MS. B. 152

(*e*) University Library, Cambridge
MS. Dd. iii. 53

(*f*) Edinburgh University Library
MS. 183 (formerly Laing MS. 351)

(*g*) Exeter City Library
Dartmouth Deed 60670

(ii) *France*

(*a*) Archives départementales de la Loire-Atlantique, Nantes
Série B
Série E (cf. M. Berranger's guide in A above, and the *Inventaire sommaire des Archives départementales antérieures à 1790, Loire-Inférieure,* ed. L. Maître, iii, Nantes 1879)

(*b*) Archives départementales d'Ille-et-Vilaine, Rennes
Série 1F. 587–627, 1111, 1650 (La Borderie papers)

(*c*) Archives Nationales, Paris
Séries J, K, JJ, KK

(*d*) Bibliothèque municipale, Nantes
Fonds Bizeul

(*e*) Bibliothèque Nationale, Paris
MSS. Clairambault, nos. 21, 22, 33, 77

MSS. Fonds français, nos. 4482, 20405, 20590, 20616, 20885, 22319–31, 22339, 22354, 22362, 25765–6, 25999–6002, 26006, 26011–12, 26019, 26022, 26024, 32510
MS. Fonds latin, no. 6003
MSS. Nouvelles acquisitions françaises, nos. 3653, 5216, 7620–1
Pièces originales, dossiers 789, 1015, 2030

C. DOCUMENTS IN PRINT

(i) *Published and calendared documents*
'Anglo-French negotiations at Bruges 1374–7', ed. É. Perroy, Royal Hist. Society, *Camden Miscellany*, xix (1952), London.
Anglo-Norman letters and petitions from All Souls MS. 182, ed. M. D. Legge, Anglo-Norman Text Society, iii, Oxford 1941.
Antient kalendars and inventories of the Treasury of His Majesty's Exchequer, ed. Sir F. Palgrave, 3 vols., London 1836.
Calendar of charter rolls.
Calendar of close rolls.
Calendar of fine rolls.
Calendar of inquisitions, miscellaneous.
Calendar of inquisitions, Post mortem.
Calendar of papal letters.
Calendar of papal petitions.
Calendar of patent rolls.
Calendar of plea and memoranda rolls of the City of London, ii. *1364–81*, iii. *1381–1412*, ed. A. H. Thomas, Cambridge 1929–32.
Cartulaire de l'abbaye de Saint-Sulpice-la-Forêt, Ille-et-Vilaine, ed. Dom Anger, Rennes 1911.
'Cartulaire des Sires de Rays', ed. R. Blanchard, *Arch. hist. Poitou*, xxviii (1898), xxx (1900).
'Cartulaire du Morbihan', ed. P. Lacroix-Thomas, *Bulletin de la Société polymathique du Morbihan*, 1934–8, revised numeration edn., previously published as 'Cartulaire du Morbihan', ed. L. Rosenzweig, *Rev. historique de l'Ouest, Documents*, ix–xiii (1893–7).
Catalogue des rolles gascons, normans et françois, ed. T. Carte, 2 vols., London 1743.
Compte de William Gunthorp, trésorier de Calais 1371–2, ed. É. Perroy, Arras 1959.
Comptes du Trésor, ed. R. Fawtier, Paris 1930.
Delpit, J., *Collection générale des documents français qui se trouvent en Angleterre*, Paris 1847.
'Diplomatic correspondence of Richard II', ed. É. Perroy, Royal Hist. Society, Camden 3rd ser., xlviii (1933), London.
Du Tillet, Jean, *Recueil des guerres et traictez d'entre les roys de France et d'Angleterre*, Paris 1588.
Early Yorkshire charters: the honour of Richmond, ed. Sir Charles Clay, 2 vols., Wakefield 1935–6.

Foedera, conventiones, litterae, etc., ed. T. Rymer *et al.*, vols. vi–viii (1708–9), London, and ed. A. Clarke *et al.* for the Record Commission, 4 vols., London 1816–69.

Inventaire analytique des archives anciennes de la mairie d'Angers, ed. C. Port, Angers and Paris 1861.

Inventaires mobiliers et extraits des comptes des ducs de Bourgogne de la maison de Valois 1363–1477, i. *1363–77*, ii. *1378–90*, ed. B. Prost, Paris 1902–13.

Inventaire sommaire des archives départementales du Pas-de-Calais, série A, ed. J. M. Richard, 2 vols., Arras 1878–87.

Izarn, E., *Le Compte des recettes et dépenses du roi de Navarre en France et en Normandie de 1367 à 1370*, Paris 1895.

'John of Gaunt's register 1372–6', ed. S. Armitage-Smith, Royal Hist. Society, Camden 3rd ser., xx, xxi (1911), London.

'John of Gaunt's register 1379–83', ed. E. C. Lodge and R. Somerville, Royal Hist. Society, Camden 3rd ser., lvi, lvii (1937), London.

Journal de Jean le Fèvre, évêque de Chartres, chancelier des rois de Sicile, Louis I et Louis II d'Anjou, ed. H. Moranvillé, Paris 1887.

La Très Ancienne Coutume de Bretagne, ed. M. Planiol, Rennes 1896.

Lettres des rois, reines et autres personnages des cours de France et d'Angleterre depuis Louis VII jusqu'à Henri IV, ed. J. J. Champollion-Figeac, ii. *1301–1515, C.D.I.*, Paris 1847.

Lettres et mandements de Jean V, duc de Bretagne, ed. R. Blanchard, Société des bibliophiles bretons, vols. iv–viii, Nantes 1889–95.

Lettres secrètes et curiales du pape Grégoire XI 1370–8, relatives à la France, ed. L. Mirot and H. Jassemin, Bibliothèque des Écoles françaises d'Athènes et de Rome, Paris 1935–7.

Mandements et actes divers de Charles V, ed. L. Delisle, *C.D.I.*, Paris 1874.

Morice, Dom P. H., *Mémoires pour servir de preuves à l'histoire ecclésiastique et civile de Bretagne*, 3 vols., Paris 1742–6.

Nouveau recueil d'actes inédits des ducs et princes de Bretagne, ed. A. de la Borderie, Rennes 1902.

Ordonnances des rois de France de la troisième race, ed. D. Secousse, vols. iv–viii, Paris 1734–50.

Plaine, Dom F., *Monuments du procès de canonisation du bienheureux Charles de Blois, duc de Bretagne, 1320–64*, Saint-Brieuc 1921.

Privilèges accordés par les ducs de Bretagne et les rois de France aux bourgeois habitants, maires et échevins de la ville de Nantes, ed. S. de la Nicollière-Teijeiro, Société des bibliophiles bretons, i, Nantes 1883.

Proceedings and ordinances of the Privy Council of England, ed. Sir N. Harris Nicolas, i, London 1834.

Recueil des documents concernant le Poitou, contenus dans les registres de la chancellerie de France, ed. P. Guérin, vols. iii–v (1348–90), being vols. xvii (1886), xix (1888), and xxi (1891) of the main series of *Arch. hist. Poitou*.

Registrum honoris de Richmond, ed. R. Gale, London 1722.

Reports, brought from the Lords, on the dignity of a peer of the realm, viii (1826), London.

Rotuli parliamentorum 1273–1503, 6 vols., Record Commission, 1783.

Secousse, D., *Mémoire pour servir à l'histoire de Charles II, roi de Navarre et comte d'Évreux*, 2 vols., Paris 1755–8.

'Some documents regarding the fulfilment and interpretation of the treaty of Brétigny 1361–9', ed. P. Chaplais, Royal Hist. Society, *Camden Miscellany*, xix (1952), London.

Songe du vergier, Paris 1492.

'Songe du verger qui parle de la disputacion du clerc et du chevalier', in *Traitez des droits et libertez de l'église gallicane*, ed. J. L. Brunet, Paris 1731.

Timbal, P. C., *La Guerre de Cent Ans vue à travers les registres du Parlement 1337–69*, Paris 1961.

'Voyage de Nicolas de Bosc, évêque de Bayeux, pour négocier la paix entre les couronnes de France et d'Angleterre', *Voyage littéraire de deux religieux Bénédictins de la Congrégation de Saint-Maur*, ed. E. Martène and U. Durand, Paris 1724.

(ii) *Chronicles*

Anonimalle chronicle 1333–81, ed. V. H. Galbraith, Manchester 1927.

Chronica Johannis de Reading et anonymi Cantuariensis, ed. J. Tait, Manchester 1914.

Chronicon Angliae 1328–88, ed. E. M. Thompson, R.S., 1874.

Chronicon Briocense, ed. in Lobineau, ii (1707) and *Preuves*, ii (1744).

Chronicon Henrici Knighton, ed. J. R. Lumby, 2 vols., R.S., 1889–95.

Chronicque de la Traison et Mort de Richart Deux Roy Dengleterre, ed. B. Williams, London 1846.

Chronique du bon duc Loys de Bourbon, ed. A. M. Chazaud, S.H.F., 1876.

Chronique du Religieux de Saint-Denys, ed. L. Bellaguet, 6 vols., C.D.I., 1839–52.

Chronique normande du quatorzième siècle, ed. A. and E. Molinier, S.H.F., 1887.

Chroniques des règnes de Jean II et de Charles V, ed. R. Delachenal, 4 vols., S.H.F., 1910–20.

Chronographia regum Francorum, ed. H. Moranvillé, 3 vols., S.H.F., 1891–7.

Cuvelier, Jean, *Chronique de Bertrand du Guesclin*, ed. E. Charrière, 2 vols., C.D.I., 1839.

Favent, Thomas, 'Historia mirabilis parliamenti', ed. M. McKisack, Royal Hist. Society, *Camden Miscellany*, xiv (1926), London.

Froissart, Jean, *Chroniques de Jean Froissart*, ed. S. Luce, G. Raynaud, L. and A. Mirot, 14 vols., S.H.F., 1869–1966 continuing.

—— *Œuvres de Jean Froissart*, ed. Baron Kervyn de Lettenhove, 25 vols., Brussels 1867–77.

Lescot, Richard, *Chronique de Richard Lescot, religieux de Saint-Denis 1328–44, suivie de la continuation de cette chronique 1344–64*, ed. J. Lemoine, S.H.F., 1896.

Polychronicon Ranulphi Higden, ed. J. R. Lumby, R.S., vol. ix (1886).

Saint-André, Guillaume de, *Le Libvre du bon Jehan, duc de Bretaigne*, printed as an appendix in Cuvelier, *Chronique de Bertrand du Guesclin*, ed. E. Charrière, ii, C.D.I., Paris 1839.

Saint-Paul, Jean de, *Chronique*, ed. A. de la Borderie, Nantes 1881.

Venette, Jean de, *Chronique*, ed. R. A. Newhall, New York 1953.
Walsingham, Thomas, *Historia Anglicana 1271–1422*, ed. H. T. Riley, 2 vols., R.S., 1863–4.

D. HISTORICAL WORKS

(i) Published works

Anselme, Père, *Histoire généalogique et chronologique de la maison royale de France*, 3rd edn., 9 vols., Paris 1726–33.
Anstis, E., *The register of the most noble Order of the Garter*, 2 vols., London 1724.
Argentré, Bertrand d', *Histoire de Bretagne*, 3rd edn., Paris 1618.
Armitage-Smith, S., *John of Gaunt, Duke of Lancaster*, London 1904.
Aston, M., 'The impeachment of Bishop Despenser', *B.I.H.R.* xxxviii (1965), 127–48.
—— *Thomas Arundel*, Oxford 1967.
Autume, M. Masson d', **Cherbourg pendant la guerre de Cent Ans de 1354 à 1450*, Saint-Lô 1948.
Baldwin, J. F., **The King's Council during the Middle Ages*, Oxford 1913.
Bayley, C. C., 'The campaign of 1375 and the Good Parliament', *E.H.R.* lv (1940), 370–83.
Beltz, G. F., *Memorials of the Order of the Garter*, London 1841.
Bigot, A., *Essai sur les monnaies de Bretagne*, Paris 1857.
Blomefield, F., *An essay towards a topographical history of the county of Norfolk*, 11 vols., London 1805–10.
Bock, F., **'Some new documents illustrating the early years of the Hundred Years War, 1353–6', *Bulletin of the John Rylands Library*, xv (1931), 60–99.
Bossuat, A., *Perrinet Gressart et François de Surienne*, Paris 1936.
Bougouin, E., **'La navigation commerciale sur la Basse-Loire au milieu du xive siècle', *Rev. Hist.* clxxv (1935), 482–96.
Bridbury, A. R., *England and the salt trade in the later Middle Ages*, Oxford 1955.
Broussillon, Bertrand de, **La Maison de Craon, 1050–1480*, 2 vols., Paris 1893.
Bruel, F., **'Inventaire de meubles et de titres trouvés au château du Josselin à la mort du connétable de Clisson, 1407', *B.E.C.* lxvi (1905), 193–245.
Burley, S. J., 'The victualling of Calais, 1347–1365', *B.I.H.R.* xxxi (1958), 49–57.
Caeneghem, R. van, 'Les appels flamands au parlement de Paris au moyen âge', *Études d'histoire du droit privé offertes à Pierre Petot*, Paris 1959, pp. 61–8.
Calmette, J., see Déprez, below.
Campbell, J., 'England, Scotland and the Hundred Years War in the fourteenth century', *Europe in the late Middle Ages*, ed. J. Hale, R. Highfield, and Beryl Smalley, London 1965, pp. 184–216.
Caron, E., *Monnaies féodales françaises*, Paris 1882.
Cazelles, R., *La Société politique et la crise de la royauté sous Philippe de Valois*, Paris 1958.

Chaplais, P., 'The chancery of Guyenne, 1289–1453', *Studies presented to Sir Hilary Jenkinson*, ed. J. Conway Davies, Oxford 1957, pp. 61–96.

—— 'La souveraineté du roi de France et le pouvoir législatif en Guyenne au début du xiv⁴ siècle', *Le Moyen Âge*, lxix (1963), 449–69.

Cherest, A., *L'Archiprêtre; épisodes de la guerre de Cent Ans au quatorzième siècle*, Paris 1879.

Cokayne, G. E., see *Complete peerage*.

Colvin, H. M., *et al.*, *The history of the King's works: the Middle Ages*, 2 vols., London 1963.

Complete peerage of England, Scotland, Ireland, Great Britain and the United Kingdom, extant, extinct or dormant, The, by G. E. C[okayne], new edn., ed. V. Gibbs, H. A. Doubleday, G. H. White, and Lord Howard de Walden, 13 vols., London 1910–59.

Congrès archéologique de France, lxxxi⁴ session tenue à Brest et Vannes en 1914, Paris and Caen 1919.

Contamine, P., **Azincourt*, Paris 1964.

—— 'Batailles, bannières, compagnies', *Les Cahiers vernonnais*, iv (1964), 19–32.

Courteault, H., ***'La fuite et les aventures de Pierre de Craon en Espagne', *B.E.C.* lii (1891), 431–48.

Dawson, C., **History of Hastings castle*, 2 vols., London 1909.

Delachenal, R., *Histoire de Charles V*, 5 vols., Paris 1909–31.

Delisle, L., **Histoire du château et des sires de Saint-Sauveur-le-Vicomte*, Paris 1867.

—— ***'Pièces soustraites au trésor des chartes des ducs de Bretagne', *B.E.C.* liv (1893), 413–17, lviii (1897), 379–80.

Denholm-Young, N., *Seignorial administration in England*, Oxford 1937.

Déprez, E., *Les Préliminaires de la guerre de Cent Ans*, Paris 1902.

—— 'La querelle de Bretagne', *M.H.B.* vii (1926), 25–60.

—— and Calmette, J., *La France et l'Angleterre en conflit, Histoire générale: Histoire du Moyen Âge*, ed. G. Glotz, vii (part i), Paris 1937.

Douët d'Arcq, L., *Collection des sceaux*, 3 vols., Paris 1863–8.

Du Chesne, A., **Histoire de la maison de Chastillon-sur-Marne*, Paris 1621.

Fillon, B., *Jean Chandos, connétable d'Aquitaine et sénéchal de Poitou*, London, Fontenay, and Nantes 1856.

Fino, J.-F., *Forteresses de la France médiévale*, Paris 1967.

Fourmont, H., **Histoire de la chambre des comptes de Bretagne*, Paris 1854.

Fowler, K. A., 'Les finances et la discipline dans les armées anglaises en France au xiv⁴ siècle', *Les Cahiers vernonnais*, iv (1964), 55–84.

—— *The age of Plantagenet and Valois*, London 1967.

Geslin de Bourgogne, J., and Barthélemy, A. de, **Anciens Évêchés de Bretagne*, 4 vols., Paris and Saint-Brieuc 1855–79.

Hamilton Thompson, A., ***'Registers of the archdeaconry of Richmond, 1361–1442', *Yorkshire Archaeological Journal*, xxv (1919), 129–268.

Hay, D., 'The division of spoils of war', *T.R.H.S.*, 5th ser., iv (1954), 91–109.

Hay du Chastelet, Paul, **Histoire de Bertrand du Guesclin*, Paris 1666.

Hewitt, H. J., *The organization of war under Edward III*, Manchester 1966.

Holmes, G. A., *The estates of the higher nobility in fourteenth-century England*, Cambridge 1957.

Jarry, E., 'La "voie de fait" et l'alliance franco-milanaise, 1386–1395', *B.E.C.* liii (1892), 213–53, 505–70.

Jassemin, H., 'Le contrôle financier en Bourgogne sous les derniers ducs capétiens, 1274–1353', *B.E.C.* lxxix (1918), 102–41.

Jeulin, P., *L'Évolution du port de Nantes*, Paris 1929.

—— 'L'hommage de la Bretagne', *Annales de Bretagne*, xli (1934), 380–473.

—— 'Aperçus sur le comté de Richmond', *Annales de Bretagne*, xlii (1935), 263–304.

Joubert, A., **Étude sur les comptes de Mace Darné, maître des œuvres de Louis Ier, duc d'Anjou, 1367–76*, Angers 1890.

Keen, M. H., *The laws of war in the late Middle Ages*, London and Toronto 1965.

Keeney, B. C., *Judgement by peers*, Harvard 1949.

Labande, E.-R., 'Une ambassade de Rinaldo Orsini et Pierre de Craon à Florence, Milan et Avignon, 1383', *Mélanges d'archéologie et d'histoire*, l (1933), 194–220.

Labande, L. H., *Les Doria de France*, Paris 1899.

La Borderie, Arthur de, *'La politique de Jean IV, 1364–73', *Revue de l'Ouest*, ii (1855), 545–68.

—— *Correspondance historique des bénédictins bretons, 1688–1730*, Paris 1880.

—— *'Le siège de Brest en 1387', *Revue de Bretagne, de Vendée et d'Anjou*, ii (1889), 198–203.

—— *Essai sur la géographie féodale de la Bretagne*, Rennes 1889.

—— *Le Règne de Jean IV, duc de Bretagne, 1364–99*, Rennes 1893.

—— *'L'architecture militaire en Bretagne du Moyen Âge: recueil de documents relatifs aux monuments de l'architecture militaire du Moyen Âge en Bretagne, 1222–1497', *Association Bretonne*, 1894.

—— *Les Neuf Barons de Bretagne*, Rennes 1895.

—— *Histoire de Bretagne*, 6 vols., Rennes 1896–1914, completed by B. Pocquet.

Lacour, R., *Le Gouvernement de l'apanage de Jean, duc de Berry, 1360–1416*, Paris 1934.

Lannou, M. le, *Géographie de la Bretagne*, 2 vols., Rennes 1950–2.

Lefranc, A., *Olivier de Clisson*, Paris 1898.

Leguai, A., 'Un aspect de la formation des États princiers en France à la fin du moyen âge: les réformes administratives de Louis II, duc de Bourbon', *Le Moyen Âge*, lxx (1964), 49–72.

Lehoux, F., *Jean de France, duc de Berri*, 4 vols., Paris 1966–8.

Le Patourel, J., *The medieval administration of the Channel Islands, 1199–1399*, Oxford 1937.

—— 'L'administration ducale dans la Bretagne montfortiste, 1345–62', *R.H.D.F.E.*, 4th ser., xxxii (1954), 144–7.

—— Review of A. H. Burne, *The Crécy War*, in *E.H.R.* lxxi (1956), 329–30.

—— 'Edward III and the kingdom of France', *History*, xliii (1958), 179–89.

—— 'The treaty of Brétigny 1360', *T.R.H.S.*, 5th ser., x (1960), 19–39.

Le Patourel, J., 'The king and the princes in fourteenth-century France', *Europe in the late Middle Ages*, ed. J. Hale *et al.*, London 1965, pp. 155–83.

Levot, P., *Histoire de la ville et du port de Brest*, i. *La ville et le port jusqu'en 1681*, Paris and Brest 1861.

Lewis, P. S., 'The failure of the French medieval estates', *Past and Present*, 23 (1962), 3–24.

Lobineau, Dom Gui-Alexis, **Histoire de Bretagne*, 2 vols., Paris 1707.

Lot, F., and Fawtier, R., *Histoire des institutions françaises au Moyen Âge*, 3 vols., Paris 1957–62.

Lubimenko, I., *Jean de Bretagne, comte de Richmond*, Paris 1908.

Luce, S., **Histoire de Bertrand du Guesclin; la jeunesse de Bertrand*, Paris 1876.

Lyon, B. D., *From fief to indenture*, Cambridge, Mass. 1957.

McKisack, M., *The fourteenth century*, Oxford History of England, vol. v, Oxford 1959.

Maître, L., 'Domaines de Bretagne dépendants de la couronne ducale', *Annales de Bretagne*, xxxviii (1928), 188–207.

Mirot, L., 'Isabelle de France, reine d'Angleterre, 1389–1409', *Revue d'histoire diplomatique*, xviii (1904), 545–73, xix (1905), 60–95, 161–91, 481–522.

Moisant, J., *Le Prince Noir en Aquitaine*, Paris 1894.

Moranvillé, H., **Étude sur la vie de Jean le Mercier*, Mémoires présentés par divers savants à l'Académie des Inscriptions et Belles-Lettres, 2ᵉ sér., vi, 2ᵉ partie, Paris 1883.

——— **'Conférences entre la France et l'Angleterre, 1388–1393'*, *B.E.C.* l (1889), 355–80.

Nordberg, M., *Les Ducs et la royauté. Étude sur la rivalité des ducs d'Orléans et de Bourgogne, 1392–1407*, Studia historica Upsaliensia xii, Uppsala 1964.

Oheix, A., *Étude sur les sénéchaux de Bretagne des origines au XIVᵉ siècle*, Paris 1913.

O'Neil, B. H. St. J., *Castles and cannon*, Oxford 1960.

Palmer, J. J. N., 'The Anglo-French peace negotiations, 1390–1396', *T.R.H.S.*, 5th ser., xvi (1966), 81–94.

——— 'Articles for a final peace between England and France, 16 June 1393', *B.I.H.R.* xxxix (1966), 180–5.

Perroy, É., *L'Angleterre et le Grand Schisme d'Occident*, Paris 1933.

——— 'Feudalism or principalities in fifteenth-century France', *B.I.H.R.* xx (1943–5), 181–5.

——— 'Gras profits et rançons pendant la guerre de Cent Ans; l'affaire du comte de Denia', *Mélanges Louis Halphen*, Paris 1951, pp. 573–80.

——— 'Louis de Male et les négociations de paix franco-anglaise', *Revue belge de philologie et d'histoire*, xxvii (1951), 138–50.

——— *The Hundred Years War*, London 1951, reprinted 1959.

——— 'L'État bourbonnais', Lot et Fawtier, i. 289–317.

Plaine, Dom F., 'La journée d'Auray', *Association Bretonne*, 1875, pp. 85–100.

Planiol, M., *Histoire des institutions de la Bretagne*, 3 vols., Rennes 1953–5.

Pocquet du Haut-Jussé, B.-A., *'Les faux États de Bretagne de 1315 et les premiers États de Bretagne', *B.E.C.* lxxxvi (1925), 388–406.

—— *Les Papes et les ducs de Bretagne,* 2 vols., Paris 1928.

—— 'François II, duc de Bretagne, et l'Angleterre, 1458–88', *M.H.B.* ix (1928), 171–511.

—— 'Les séjours de Philippe le Hardi, duc de Bourgogne, en Bretagne, 1372, 1394, 1402', *M.H.B.* xvi (1935), 1–61.

—— *'Le plus ancien rôle des comptes du duché, 1262', *M.H.B.* xxvi (1946), 49–68.

—— 'Le grand fief breton', Lot et Fawtier, i. 267–88.

—— 'La genèse du législatif dans le duché de Bretagne', *R.H.D.F.E.*, 4th ser., xl (1962), 351–72.

—— 'La dernière phase de la vie de Du Guesclin: l'affaire de Bretagne', *B.E.C.* cxxv (1967), 142–89.

Postan, M. M., 'The costs of the Hundred Years War', *Past and Present,* 27 (1964), 34–53.

Rey, M., *Les Finances royales sous Charles VI, les causes du déficit, 1388–1413,* Paris 1965.

Rhein, A., *La Seigneurie de Montfort-en-Iveline,* Versailles 1910.

Richard, J., 'Les institutions ducales dans le duché de Bourgogne', Lot et Fawtier, i. 209–47.

Roncière, C. de la, *Histoire de la marine française,* i–ii, Paris 1899–1900.

Russell, P. E., *The English intervention in Spain and Portugal in the time of Edward III and Richard II,* Oxford 1955.

Samaran, C., *'Pour l'histoire des Grandes Compagnies. Le "vuidement" de Château-Gontier par les Anglais, 1369', *Mélanges Louis Halphen,* Paris 1951, pp. 641–4.

Sautel-Boulet, M., 'Le rôle juridictionnel de la cour des Pairs aux xiiie et xive siècles', *Recueil de travaux offert à M. Clovis Brunel,* 2 vols., Paris 1955, ii. 507–20.

Sherborne, J. W., 'Indentured retinues and English expeditions to France, 1369–1380', *E.H.R.* lxxix (1964), 718–46.

—— 'The English navy: shipping and manpower, 1369–1389', *Past and Present,* 37 (1967), 163–75.

Somerville, R., *History of the duchy of Lancaster,* i. *1265–1603,* London 1953.

Steel, A., *Richard II,* Cambridge 1941, reprinted 1962.

Storey, R. L., 'The wardens of the marches of England towards Scotland, 1377–1489', *E.H.R.* lxxii (1957), 593–615.

Strayer, J., 'The laicization of French and English society in the thirteenth century', *Speculum,* xv (1940), 76–86.

Taylor, C. H., 'The composition of baronial assemblies in France 1315–1320', *Speculum,* xxix (1954), 437–59.

Texier, E., *Étude sur la cour ducale et les origines du Parlement de Bretagne,* Rennes 1905.

Thibault, M., *Isabeau de Bavière, reine de France; la jeunesse, 1370–1405,* Paris 1903.

Touchard, H., 'Les brefs de Bretagne', *Revue d'histoire économique et sociale,* xxxiv (1956), 116–40.

Touchard, H., *Le Commerce maritime breton*, Paris 1967.

Tout, T. F., 'Some neglected fights between Crécy and Poitiers', *E.H.R.* xx (1905), 726–30.

—— *'Firearms in England in the fourteenth century', *E.H.R.* xxvi (1911), 666–702.

—— *Chapters in the administrative history of medieval England*, 6 vols., Manchester 1920–33.

Tucoo-Chala, P., *Gaston Fébus et la vicomté de Béarn, 1343–1391*, Bordeaux 1960.

Vaughan, R., *Philip the Bold*, London 1962.

Whitaker, T. D., **History of Richmondshire*, 2 vols., London 1823.

Williams, T., 'The importance of the Channel Isles in British relation [*sic*] with the Continent during the thirteenth and fourteenth centuries: a study in historical geography', *Bulletin de la Société Jersiaise*, xi (1928), 1–89.

Zeiller, Martin, *Topographia Galliae*, 3 vols., Frankfurt-am-Mayn 1655–7.

(ii) *Unpublished theses*

Alexander, A. F. O'D., 'The war with France in 1377', London Ph.D. thesis 1934, summarized in *B.I.H.R.* xii (1934–5), 190–2.

Fowler, K. A., 'Henry of Grosmont, first duke of Lancaster, 1310–61', Leeds Ph.D. thesis 1961, some of the material of which is now more readily accessible in *The King's Lieutenant. Henry of Grosmont, First Duke of Lancaster 1310–1361*, London, 1969.

Martin, Carola, 'The enforcement of the rights of the kings of France in the duchy and county of Burgundy, 1285–1363', Oxford B.Litt. thesis 1965.

Palmer, J. J. N., 'The Anglo-French peace negotiations, 1386–99', London Ph.D. thesis 1967.

Renaudin, Y., 'Les domaines des ducs de Bretagne. Leur administration du XIIIᵉ au XVᵉ siècle', École des Chartes, summarized in *Positions des thèses de l'École des Chartes*, 1957. Copy at Arch. dép., Nantes.

Vale, M. G. A., 'War, government, and politics in English Gascony 1399–1453', Oxford D.Phil. thesis 1967, published now as *English Gascony 1399–1453. A Study of War, Government and Politics during the later stages of the Hundred Years' War*, Oxford 1970.

INDEX